THE MAKING OF A PUBLISHER

Photo by Werner Wolff, Black Star

VICTOR WEYBRIGHT

THE MAKING
OF A PUBLISHER

———————————— ❀ ————————————

A Life in the 20th Century
Book Revolution
by

VICTOR WEYBRIGHT

Weidenfeld and Nicolson
5 Winsley Street London W1

Printed in Great Britain by
Lowe & Brydone (Printers) Ltd., London

TO TRUMAN MACDONALD TALLEY

PREFACE

As a country boy in Maryland, watching for the rural route mailman to arrive with his bundle of letters, newspapers and periodicals, I dreamed of the day when I would help make it possible for everyone to have the best of everything to read. My dream came true.

There was a long apprenticeship. There were many other pioneers—notably Penguin Books in England, and Pocket Books in the United States and Canada. There were imaginative printers, such as W. F. Hall; and magazine wholesalers in a thousand towns and cities. A century ago, of course, most American books were cheap paperbacks, ranging from pirated British titles, before the American copyright act, to synthetic dime novels. But they were never distributed on the scale of my own Signet and Mentor series in the mid-twentieth century.

World War II brought Armed Forces Editions and the G. I. Bill of Rights, and gave me my chance to publish successfully, with taste and purpose, and to make an early and genuine contribution to the Book Revolution. I was asked by Sir Allen Lane to do in America what he had done in England. The timing was right. I did, multiplied by many powers.

This book is my story—of youthful yearning; of gaining a

grasp of life and letters; of hitching my wagon to a star with a grand goal and a fierce sense of purpose.

The reader will discover that I sometimes misgauged the dynamics of the Book Revolution, like a farmer who loses his hand in a harvesting machine, by not always realizing that the machine of itself is not benign, not human, necessarily, in its relentless momentum.

Thousands of readers and teachers and members of the literary profession and publishing industry have hailed my valiant efforts to help bring about the Book Revolution. This narrative reveals why and how it came about. Above all, it attempts to give some insight into the background, the groping, and—I hope—the dedication to an ideal, which have shaped my life, my career and my modest contribution to culture and communication.

V. W.
March, 1967

Chapter I

A CARROLL COUNTY CHILDHOOD

————————◦◦◦◦————————

Let the Wealthy & Great,
Roll in Splendor & State,
I envy them not I declare it;
I eat my own Lamb,
My chickens and Ham,
I shear my own Fleece & I wear it,
I have Lawns, I have Bow'rs
I have Fruits, I have Flowers,
The Lark is my morning alarmer:
So jolly Boys now,
Here's God speed the Plough,
Long Life & succefs to the Farmer.
                    —Old Country Toast

THE WORLD I KNEW in my childhood was astonishingly close to that of the eighteenth century. Our language was graceful but hearty English, cadenced to convey feeling without mawkishness, and with echoes of the poetry of Old England as well as the grave prose of the Founding Fathers. We believed in Man, the Almighty, Maryland and the United States of America, in that order. We respected ladies and our elders, and we were kind to domestic animals. But we were ruthlessly cruel to predatory varmints and intolerant of liars and cheats and of persons or creatures that were slovenly or lazy. We regarded Virginians and Pennsylvanians, twenty-five miles to south and north, respectively, with uninformed suspicion as show-offs of aristocratic airs or as rude examples of mean frugality.

Except for the railway, the telegraph, the camera, the reaping machine and other nineteenth-century inventions, life in Carroll County was very little different actually from that of the late seventeenth century, when most of my ancestors had settled in Maryland. My rubicund great-grandfather, on my father's side, had been a friend, neighbor and occasional legal client of Francis Scott Key, who lived a mile away at Terra Rubra, and who had written "The Star-Spangled Banner" in Baltimore Harbor during the British invasion of 1814. Great-grandfather's grandfather had known Key's father, who had served as an officer in the Continental Army from Boston to Yorktown with various local units of the Maryland Line.

My grandmother on my mother's side recalled many a girlhood encounter with John Greenleaf Whittier's aged and crotchety heroine, Barbara Fritchie, who as a girl of sixteen had been presented by President Washington with a china bowl after she served him his coffee when he passed through Frederick on his way from Mount Vernon to Philadelphia.

The domestic architecture of the big house had grown from an earlier log house whose foot-square hewn oak ribs, concealed beneath clapboard, provided snug protection from the north winds in winter and cool insulation, when curtains were drawn, in the summer. There was an outdoor summer kitchen, a brick smokehouse, ovens for baking, a washhouse and a woodshed spacious enough for indoor splitting of firewood in bad weather. The cellar was a fragrant multi-room store of a year's supply of preserved meats and vegetables, fruits and jams, apples, potatoes, vinegar in barrels, huge cans of lard for cooking and stone jars of old fat for soapmaking.

There was a complete basement kitchen with a dumbwaiter to the dining room above. It looked and smelled as ancient as the storage shed by the kitchen garden and truck patch where the old hand implements were kept for occasional use—sickles, scythes, cradle scythes for grain; flails; flax and wool cards; spinning wheels; all the paraphernalia that had been collected during several hundred years of the slow encroachment of invention and convenience.

Nearly all of my ancestors—from England, France, Holland, Germany and Scotland—had lived obscurely and comfortably in the Monocacy River Valley east of the Blue Ridge from their earliest days in the New World. I remember my grandfather stating on several occasions, with no intention of boasting, that none of his family had ever worked for hire except in the army or on the jury. This was not intended to belittle others perhaps less fortunately situated, but to establish an attitude he hoped that all his progeny would adopt as their own. In today's complex of vast institutions, managed by salaried organization men, this may sound naively archaic. But a fierce desire to be one's own master was shared in the main by all of my youthful friends.

Simple youngsters who were not intellectually inclined, if they chose to leave the farms, learned a trade that would enable them to set up shop along the road or in a nearby village. Others, with greater ambition or opportunity, studied for a profession—law, medicine, engineering, teaching or the clergy. In this local hierarchy of occupations the farmer remained solidly supreme as a man of recognized independence.

The atmosphere of the times in Maryland, in the early 1900's, was different from that which prevailed in many places only because it reflected a fixed mode of life through eight or ten generations. Those few who left the farms and county seats to seek greater opportunities and make their way elsewhere did not necessarily do better than those who re-

mained. They achieved an unenvied visibility as sophisticated veterans of competitive city life when they came home
to visit.

To dwell too much on the past, without a genuine effort
to understand the nature of one's times, produces antiquar-
ians, not historians. Our situation was that the past and
present were not marked by dramatic differences, so we all
felt that the men of old were with us in the same fashion as
our neighbors who slept beneath the stars in the local grave-
yard.

Today, many of my successful contemporaries, in their
latter-day affluence, sometimes crow like spent chanticleers
on the midden of their private pasts, apprehensive of men
and institutions that are new and different. Perhaps because
of the blind acceptance of our cheerful lot, we did not face
any such disturbing challenge in the days of my youth.

It is not my intent to create a paradise, never to be re-
gained, out of my bucolic memories. I have to confess, however, that my childhood was carefree and happy. Even now
when I revisit the Red Lands of western Maryland, I am
overcome by a peculiarly poignant nostalgia for some of the
poetic aspects which have now vanished without a trace
except in memory. Most vividly persistent are my recurring
reveries of youthful admiration for the heavy draft horses,
matched Percherons or Clydesdales, that used to ornament
the local roads, drawing wagon loads of wheat, corn and rye
to the grist mills, the distilleries and the local grain ele-
vators. No modern motor truck can match the majesty of
those stately teams in brass-studded harness, with a proud
teamster driving six-in-hand.

Nor, for pure poetry in motion, as every visitor to a horse
show knows, can any procession of automobiles match the
grandeur of spanking pairs of well-trained and graceful
horses harnessed to traps, gigs, coaches, surreys, band-

wagons, buggies or carts. The proud, gaited animals always seemed conscious of the gleaming equipages that they drew behind them, carrying passengers who did not take travel for granted, but who instead seemed to feel that even the slightest journey was an occasion.

We and our neighbors lived very close to nature, familiar with the husbandry of domestic creatures—horses, cattle, swine, sheep, chickens, turkeys, ducks, geese and guineas; and as knowledgeable as foxes about the wild animals and birds and their magic life and habits in wood and field. Except when entertaining company at home, every event meant saddling or harnessing a horse. The rolling hills and dirt roads eliminated bicycles as a habitual mode of transport. In the winter there were sleigh bells—now so obsolete that they bring a premium at country auctions—to warn other travelers of one's approach in the narrow passages hewn through the drifts.

During the spring thaw there was a fortnight of nearly bottomless mud. But in the spring, too, there was a special flavor and bouquet in the country air—blossoms, woodsmoke from the cleanup and the sharp hartshorn from the open stable doors. On the way to farm sales, to horse races or to divine service we passed newly plowed and cultivated fields prepared for corn.

The icehouse was full of great squares of frozen Monocacy water harvested from the old dam and kept beneath a cover of sawdust from the timber sawing on the farm during the winter. If one was lucky, one could find where the farmhands had slyly hidden their beer to chill beneath the most casually untracked spot beyond the place where the first cakes of ice had been taken for the wooden bucket of iced drinking water that went with the farm workers everywhere from May until September.

It used to be a guessing game among the boys of the countryside to name the man who had stacked the straw in the farmyards, which survived upright through the winter despite the antic rubbing of the cattle at the base of the carefully constructed stacks. I remember the discovery of my own early capacity for observation when, before the age of six, I had learned to distinguish George Frocks's square stacks, Tom Nelson's round stacks and the long peaked stacks, resembling fancy cottages from the story books, favored by Davy Winters.

These minor pastimes, discussing and admiring the ephemeral monuments of the farmyards, may sound trivial. However, before the day of mechanization and contour tillage to avoid soil erosion, there was a sort of Pythagorian grid recurring constantly over every aspect of the landscape—neatly aligned piles of lime lying in the open air to slake before being spread with a shovel by hand; symmetrically spaced shocks of wheat; haycocks in neat array; straight rows of autumn corn shocks; and later, fodder shocks punctuated with piles of yellow corn. All such patterns are now obliterated by the labor-saving devices of nearly instant harvesting with tractors and machines.

At twilight or during the dark of an afternoon storm the rows of shocks always seemed to me to resemble the tents of a vast and mysterious army of Indians, Crusaders or Redcoats in formal but glorious bivouac before a mighty battle.

The quilted beauty of the old-fashioned fields was a classic theme for art, or at least for calendar art. The achievement of it was the result of backbreaking labor by the farmers and their hired hands. But even the work around the seasons had its psychological compensations which transcended the meager pay. There was always cheerful company and companionship on every task of a sort which no modern farmer will ever know—harvesting grain or hay or ice; butchering pigs or lambs or beef.

The round of activities brought people into close proximity with an opportunity to observe strength, personality and character. We learned from our father and uncles, in an unspoken ritual like that of primitive tribesmen, to identify the manifestations of generations of family breeding and training, and also to take an opportunity to predict the capabilities of boys and young men by their approach to the job at hand. Pride, gentility, generosity, truthfulness, politeness, cleanliness and a gracious relaxed deportment, were part of our upbringing. We never questioned the goodness of ladies or the literal truth of the Apostles' Creed. We reflected the essence of Herder's philosophy of society, of belonging consciously and inescapably to our community culture, though none of us was aware of the extent to which our romantic patriotism and devotion to classical heroes collided with Herder's faith in the unity of man in a world which he himself creates, and speaks for, as an individual product of his formative associations.

Perhaps the most notable local institution was the little two-room school, which has long ago given way to a consolidated county school system. The land on which it stood, a mile away, was donated to the hamlet of Keysville by Francis Scott Key, who is still remembered for his generous devotion to the affairs of the district.

Through a maneuver of my grandfather and his friends when a local private school had closed after the death of the master, the library of nearly two thousand books was transferred to the little Keysville school, uncensored and unlocked, all easily available. Many of us read them all, including Darwin, Herbert Spencer, Gibbon, Voltaire, Herder, Luther, Locke, Mill, Macaulay and Burke, Surtees, George Eliot, Mark Twain, Dickens, Thackeray, Emerson, Thoreau, Whitman, Defoe, Cooper, Scott, translations of the Greeks and the Romans, Foxe's *Martyrs* and many books that would now be

taboo as too gamey for the young. A series of copiously illustrated and annotated medical volumes were all dog-eared
by eagerly curious boys who enjoyed the vicarious erotic
shock of anatomical discovery.

We raced through *Les Miserables* and *The Count of
Monte Cristo,* as enraptured as by later movie serials, before
we were nine years old. Encouraged by my grandfather, I had
learned to read simple adult books and newspapers at the
age of four. I soon introduced the wonder and joy of my own
fanatic addiction to literature to my schoolmates. I still remember the discovery of lyric poetry at the age of six when
Shelley and Keats were encountered alongside Wordsworth,
Longfellow and Poe.

My lyric streak was followed by a fervor of interest in history, undoubtedly inspired by the muckraking and political
reporting of the day which reflected what we considered
naughty disrespect for established men and institutions during the political campaigns of Theodore Roosevelt and
Woodrow Wilson. I have never in all my life forgotten the
iconoclastic highlight of the period which reached us daily
through the early skeptical writing of H. L. Mencken in the
Baltimore Sunpapers, then the daily gospel of upland Maryland. By good chance the wife of the local storekeeper in the
village of Detour had known Mencken when she was a young
nurse in Baltimore and he had been her patient, so we all
felt as if we had known first hand at a tender age the most
stimulating sage since the days of Dr. Johnson.

Mencken influenced the realism of a later age through his
audacious editorship of *The Smart Set* and of *The American
Mercury.* Once, just before the advent of Prohibition, when
I told him during a chance encounter in Baltimore that he
had been responsible for the precociousness of some twenty-
five Carroll County boys long before they had reached the
age of high school or even of puberty, he archly pretended

to shed a tear into his beer at the old Rennert Hotel. He said he had written his best and bitterest pieces for the edification of professors at The Johns Hopkins. Soon after, he published a devastating item which referred to the rustic boobs of Carroll County. I always assumed he had done so to see if his adolescent admirers could take it. We gleefully passed it around as an indictment of our smug elders.

All of my family except myself were musically endowed. When I discovered that I was obviously tone deaf and incapable even of playing the bass in duets at the piano with my twin sister, I strove to assert my elementary superiority in other directions. I memorized and recited poetry to anyone who would listen. At about the age of ten when I had mastered, as I thought, the Greek Classics from Bulfinch to the point where I could fault Hawthorne's *Tanglewood Tales,* I enjoyed a terrifying example of applied romanticism at its worst.

Still as real to me as the day it occurred is the August afternoon when I was allowed to ride the lazyboard—a plank swung under the wagon bed to give footing—and operate the brakes on an eight-horse expedition to LeGore lime kiln some six hilly miles down the Frederick turnpike. The farm teamster, George Winters, who rode the rear wheelhorse and managed two pairs of horses and a pair of mules in front of him, warned me not to release the rubber bar if he latched it in position at the top of a descent on the road.

As we headed home, the unslaked cargo bulged the sideboards with its weight. Soon after we pulled away from the kiln, it became apparent that a thunderstorm was heading our way over the Blue Ridge and would probably overtake us before we reached home. It is a quality of newly burnt but unslaked lime to explode like the crater of a volcano when combined with water, to heat and smoke, to crackle and boil, before subsiding into flakey lime; or, if more water is added, to turn into the paste used for whitewash. The storm struck us. As soon as the rain began, the lime began to crackle and steam. The teamster could not draw the panicked team to a halt to help me lock the brakes. I had to do my best to hold the rubber bar down with my scant weight, and I almost succeeded in stalling the wheels down the first long grade. There was no way, amid the smoke and steam, for me to communicate with the driver.

Weakened by acrid and suffocating fumes, I held to the rubber bar for four careening miles until George Winters ran the team into a roadside ditch that stalled them. He pacified the horses and mules. I helped him unloose the traces and harness so we could abandon the erupting wagon. We succeeded without losing an animal. When we got the horses and mules homeward bound in the gusty rain, with me mounted on the lead mule to confine their pace, he shouted:

"You are braver than old man Frost who was decorated under fire at Gettysburg."

I did not confess to him that I had been unaware of the present danger because, in a classical trance induced by the excitement, I had been imagining myself as Prometheus all the time the furor was at its peak. Only when we returned next day to salvage the running gear of the vehicle which had been saved from destruction by the heavy wagon bed did it occur to me that whatever courage I had displayed came not from religious faith but from romantic identification with Greek mythology.

I had unwittingly exalted myself as all heroes must by assuming a role out of a heritage of the past from which neither reason nor fear could have swerved me at the time. In active fancy, I had been, for a tumultuous twenty minutes, Prometheus triumphant upon a chariot of fire.

Today's educators tend to discourage what they consider the sterile classicism of memorizing endless gems of literature. For all I know they may be right in doing so. What is learned by rote does not sink in at once. But the reservoir of remembered poetry in my head as a child not only nourished ultimate wisdom and grace, which affected my entire relationship to the world, but sometimes served as an immediate device to attract attention. Even an audience who did not understand was likely to be awed by a burst of Shakespeare. Once, when a band of gypsies camped in our woods and resorted to the mystery of their Romany tongue to exclude me from admittance into their strange but fascinating group, I launched a recitation, as if it were coming naturally from my own creative imagination, of William Cullen Bryant's "Thanatopsis." They marveled at the very first sentence,

> To him who in the love of Nature holds
> Communion with her visible forms, she speaks
> A various language . . .

They were as spellbound by my declamatory performance as I was by their unfathomable chatter. Before long, we were teaching one another words and manners.

In those days many of these nomads spent their winters in Baltimore, having their wagons made or repaired by the Leon Hardt Wagon Company, which specialized in vehicles for gypsies and hucksters. The wagons were built with a short wheel base and low front wheels that enabled them to make a neat turn if it appeared desirable to reverse direction hastily in a narrow road. As time ran on, I became affectionately acquainted with gypsies, their lore and their language, in many countries and in many parts of the United States. I learned that gypsy-lovers constituted a warmhearted freemasonry of scholars, anthropologists, musicologists, poets and philologists. The Paris Exposition of 1900 had introduced red-coated gypsy musicians from eastern Europe to the sophisticated hotels and restaurants of the Edwardian Age in Europe and America.

While I was *en rapport* with the ordinary nomads along the Monocacy, the *nouveau riche* of New York and Newport were introducing flashy gypsy bands at their gala debutante parties and balls. Some fifteen years later I met Augustus John in London, and he delighted me by speaking Romany in accents which I could understand. Later he served as president of the Gypsy Lore Society and upon his death was succeeded by Professor Walter Starkie—a remarkable scholar in music, gypsy lore, Celtic and Hispanic literature, and translator of my eventual edition of *Don Quixote*—now at the University of California in Los Angeles but for many years director of the Abbey Theater in Dublin. I didn't meet Professor Starkie until the late 1920's when he came to tea in New York with Elizabeth Robins Pennell, the widow of the famous etcher Joseph Pennell and a niece of Charles Godfrey Leland who had founded the Folklore Congress at Paris in 1889 and the Gypsy Lore Society in the 1890's. I had learned from them that I had been a member of the society five years earlier than Walter Starkie, which is worth mentioning only because it evidenced a genuinely early interest in the natural rebel, the non-conformist, the tempter and the picturesque from far away.

I was equally enchanted by the colorful tramps who called at the back door of our farmhouse for a handout from time to time. In those days they were not derelicts, but hardy misfits who apparently enjoyed their alienation from organized society and were prepared to pay for it with extreme discomfort and by becoming proficient in some novel way of making a living. Some of the wanderers performed most useful functions—mending clocks and umbrellas, making baskets to order, or concocting eternal calendars that correctly placed the days of the week for centuries backward and ahead, regardless of leap year. The untalented hoboes stuck pretty close to the railway line.

In addition to gypsies and tramps, there were other itinerant visitors, peddlers, tinsmiths and exterminators. The most exciting exterminator of varmints was an old Civil War veteran named Daddy Hollanbar, who turned up annually with several ferrets and eight or nine couples of rat terriers. For a small price he would guarantee to get rid of every wild creature except swallows and pigeons from all of the barns, sheds, stables, corn cribs and outbuildings. His noisy massacre of undesirable rats, mice, even skunks, precipitated a general holiday among all of the farmhands who could not miss the spectacle and wild commotion, no matter what chore remained undone.

There was a constant throng of regular or seasonal workers addressing themselves to special tasks. Immediately after Christmas the first cold wave was a signal for harvesting ice from the dam. The road horses were shod with sharp calks to keep them from slipping on the ice and on the uphill road from the river. There were usually half a dozen men sawing the ice and loading it on wagons while the team shuttled back and forth to the icehouse. When that chore was finished all of the heavy harnesses were inspected, cleaned, repaired, oiled and prepared for the year ahead.

The hauling of manure from the stables seems, in retrospect, to have been an endless winter assignment for two or three men, and was a chore which I artfully dodged, even on Saturdays when I was home from school. I was no Hercules with a dung fork. I much preferred to help Will Share make brooms in the loft above the carpenter and blacksmith shop, which was the only farm outbuilding in which a stove was permitted. It was a snug and pleasant job, and I soon became very proficient at rolling the brooms with taut wire which held the broom corn to the broomsticks, then pressing them into shape, sewing them and trimming them. They were locked into a cupboard and rationed to house and barn by my father who regarded them as more precious than many other implements which were easily accessible, often carried off and lost on the job and which could not be replaced without making purchases at the store.

During the winter at Hollow Rock every piece of machinery was carefully inspected and repaired for use in the heavy sowing and harvesting in the seasons ahead. Blades on all cutting tools were sharpened. In fine weather two or three men split and tipped chestnut rails, bored and shaped posts for spring fence-making as soon as the ground thawed sufficiently to plant a post and hang a gate.

I can't recall that we had a strand of barbed wire until the coming of World War I forced the necessity to improvise fencing hastily, no matter how untidy or dangerous to men and animals.

From spring plowing for corn and oats until autumn cultivating for winter wheat and rye, there was scarcely a lull in communal activity. Haying was fragrant and pleasant, amid a galaxy of bees and butterflies. The shocking and subsequent pitching of wheat sheaves into the barn or onto outdoor stacks was hard labor from beginning to end. Then followed the pleasant road journeys with the wagons, taking wheat and corn to market, fetching lime and fertilizer back.

My great-grandfather was credited with bringing to Carroll County the first guano, bird droppings from Peru, which was shipped to Baltimore. Nitrate became a subject on which conversation recurred throughout the later talk of Muscle Shoals after World War I. This was nearly a generation before we learned to give the soil its basic balance of nitrate by scientific rotation of legumes.

It was not until the beginning of World War I in Europe, when I was eleven years old, that it ever occurred to me that life would not go on as it had been lived in Maryland, with little change, forever and a day. The fantastically sudden development of the automobile and paved roads seemed to be related to the distant war, and along with the rise in farm prices—until price fixing went into effect after America entered the conflict—gave a surge of uneasy and unaccustomed pocket money that enabled us for the first time to spend impulsively on luxuries as well as necessities when we went to Taneytown, Westminster, Frederick and, more frequently, to Baltimore City. Steel cleated gasoline tractors appeared on nearly every farm. Harness horses began to disappear, along with heavy draft animals.

Each phase of progress seemed to make it possible for one man to do three or four times as much with less effort. The departure of the horses meant more feed and pasture for the dairy herd, more cows to supply the fluid milk market of Baltimore. We never seemed to miss as part of the labor force the young men who went off and worked in the cantonment construction and the war industries or joined the armed forces. Within two or three years the farm became lonely by comparison with the countryside of only a decade earlier. The towns and the cities seemed to attract the best and the worst of the country population, leaving behind prosperous farmers who had entered a money economy with a determined and often expressed intention to make the best of it. Marginal village houses soon fell to vacant disrepair and ruin.

Within a few years a dozen nearby tenant houses became empty, deserted, unattended ghost dwellings, collapsing into melancholy abandonment. There was something ominous about the creeping decay of community life, so quickly a prey to the attitudes of ambition and stark efficiency. I and many of my young friends, even before we completed high school, hoped we could explore further opportunities before committing ourselves to cast our lot as countrymen. We were aware of the accelerated tide of progress that was bound to affect us all.

I can recall one episode while I attended the high school at Westminster, the county seat, that disheartened me with my earlier resolve to engage in farming as a total career. When the special train for World War I draftees was scheduled to pick up the young men from Carroll County, the conscripts were advised to wear old clothes that they could throw away when they were issued their uniforms upon arrival at Camp Meade. As I waited with the throng at the Westminster station, I suddenly realized that the town draftees were so arrogant and showy that they were actually the best-dressed men present, most of them in the standard spring uniform of the time—white flannel trousers, white shoes, blue coats and stiff straw hats.

I wondered about the one man from near my own village of Keysville who had not been reserved for farm employment—Jimmie, who was something of a character in the neighborhood because he had twice been to France as a representative of a local stallion company to purchase and bring home a Percheron for the Horse Breeding Cooperative. Half a dozen farmers took turns stabling his mammoth equine protégé, until he stood for service in the spring at Jimmie's permanent headquarters on his family's nearby farm.

Somehow, I had always imagined that Jimmie had spent a riotous time in France drinking wine and enjoying the finest foods in the company of wicked mademoiselles, although there were a few nasty wiseacres who whispered that he had traveled to and from France in his overalls on a filthy, animal-carrying freighter—nothing like the *Titanic!*— and did not even enjoy the amenities of a cabin. I innocently thought that Jimmie, who at any rate had picked up what passed for facile erotic French among us, would be a dazzling figure when he reached France in uniform.

To my ineffable sorrow and dismay I discovered Jimmie among the gala crowd of conscripted dandies who were taking their war lightly in full gala party array. He was slouched in the day coach half drunk wearing patched and faded denims and a cheap, frayed straw hat, having relied upon the instructions to wear discardable clothing on the one-way trip to join the Army. He stood out in strange contrast to the town lads as the pathetic yokel that he was, and had been, his status deflated beyond repair. My pride in our village hero was dashed.

I recall that I shed a tear and at first pretended that there was no connection between us. Then as the band began to play, and the familiar Western Maryland Railway whistle sounded the note of departure, my better nature triumphed, and I gave him a proud salute of fond farewell and ignored the disdain of the crowd. I shook his hand through the open train window.

It was for me an unforgettable moment of sad disenchantment with the sweet life which I had cherished in the country up to then. It induced a brooding, puzzled awareness of my limitations as a provincial. Like my family and my neighbors, perhaps at first I hardened my attitudes toward the less fortunate who were distant or departing or not to remain in sight nearby. Unlike my neighbors I resolved then and there that if I were to go out in the world to seek my fortune, I would probably do so in the spring, in white trousers, a blue coat and a new stiff straw hat. It was a silly and self-centered thought, but one which made me determine not to proceed with higher education in Western Maryland College at Westminster but to face the challenge of the great white cities far away.

Jimmie never returned. He was buried in France where

he died during the influenza epidemic of 1918. When I remember him now, I still sense his importance as a curious milestone in my own life, nebulous though our acquaintance was, because of the fashion in which he dramatized what was happening to the countryside.

If there had been no World War I, our halcyon days might have lasted just a little bit longer. But the urbanization of industrial and mercantile America, coinciding with the swift mechanization of agriculture, had gained too much momentum ever to stand still again.

Many of my generation who were culturally isolated in the towns and villages and who went up to the city for education and recreation and ultimately for careers and professions, were too shrewd to remain. Some of us discussed and dreamed of reaping a fortune and then returning to the scenes of our youth. A few ultimately did so. One of the extraordinary consequences of the cultural desolation of the countryside was the fact that ten years later, and throughout the great depression of the 1930's, we could, and some of us did, redress the situation which we left when we departed. The radio and ultimately television, cheap books and good roads, improved the amenities of the countryside and artificially eliminated loneliness; but these factors did not contribute much to the rebirth of a splendid rural culture.

In my part of Maryland the renaissance came about by the return of native sons who sought to lead a sort of double life—a city man by profession and a countryman by preference. My own return to my birthplace, as a farmer, did not occur until the early days of the New Deal. By that time I had lived in New York and Chicago, traveled widely abroad, and made many friends in Washington, New York, California and elsewhere who added greatly through their many visits to Hollow Rock Farm to the part I was ultimately to play in a new concept of local country life.

None of this would be of great consequence if it were personal and subjective. But like Owen D. Young at Van Hornsville, New York, and Louis Bromfield at Malabar Farm in Ohio after World War II, I was part of a trend. By good chance, my early life and training and genuine hope for the highest standards of local fulfillment remained alive even though dormant during my predominantly city years in college and while engaged in publishing and journalism and getting a foothold in related pursuits. It was possible, therefore, for some of us to bring to city life something of the benign idealism of a country squire and later to bring back to country life a bit of the learning, the sophistication, the tolerance, the commitments and the often violent articulations of the city. How this came about, or rather why it came about, and what it revealed of my times is really the purpose of this book.

When several years ago Morton and Lucia White published their challenging volume, *The Intellectual Versus the City,* they proved to be prophetic as well as historical critics of traditional American attitudes toward American cities. It would be only a slight oversimplification to summarize their findings so sweepingly as to say that they could find no important and influential American, except Benjamin Franklin, in our entire history up to the middle of the twentieth century who was a genuinely appreciative and constructive urban citizen.

They made it clear that the pioneers, the Founding Fathers, the New England villagers, the restless settlers of the West all were anti-city, and that even the men of wealth and culture in the early industrial age, although living sumptuously in New York, Chicago or San Francisco, actually made their isolated mansions or country estates the center of their true existence.

Some tried to improve the city, but none dared try to

make it a comprehensively good place for all its population to live, work and play. Intellectuals, likewise, including the radicals and early welfare workers, are described as curiously antagonistic to American cities even when paradoxically attracted by the color, majesty and esthetic charm of the magnificently conceived and planned cities of Europe and Great Britain. John Dewey, according to the Whites, was nostalgically thinking of homely chores in' New England farmhouses rather than working in modern cities in his development of the pragmatic educational theory of learning by doing things together.

It is little wonder that my generation, possibly the last to be preponderantly rural, was not oriented to the ineluctable destiny of the American city as the major center and concern of American civilization.

On our schoolboy excursions to Baltimore, Annapolis, Philadelphia and Washington to see the famous landmarks we avoided contact with the dilapidated parts of town—the slums that existed in the alleys and on the edge of the downtown areas. It was well known that the heavy industry of Baltimore was attracting unskilled workers from the South and from the hinterland of Maryland, poor whites and Negroes who soon lost the natural politeness and grace of their lives on the farms and in the villages. At that time we were scarcely aware of the grimly isolated mining camps in the bituminous and anthracite areas of West Virginia and Pennsylvania.

We tended, without being told, to think of the industrial workers and distant miners as foreigners. No one that I knew had ever been inside a mine, a steel mill or a really big factory. The Whites have documented this typically myopic American aversion not only to mingling with rough factory hands but also to any direct participation in making the city a fit home for heroes of the bench and counter of industry and trade.

Labor unions and radicalism were, to most of us, derived from the ghettos and slums of Europe, from city squatters who didn't have the gumption to endure life on a farm. The only sympathetic agitators that I encountered as a youth were those who favored farm reforms and the Populist movement symbolized by William Jennings Bryan. Our simple logic could not move us at that time to perceive that the human problem of a whole world affected by the scientific and industrial revolution reflected discontents that were related, and interrelated, on the farms and in the towns and cities.

The brain-drain of the truly ambitious from the countryside could easily have been noted without any tutelage; but in my own case it was magazines such as the *New Republic* and the writings by Lincoln Steffens, Upton Sinclair, Jane Addams, Theodore Dreiser and others which shocked me into realization that the world in which I lived was not static anywhere from our own doorsteps to the farthest reaches of the world.

Until then, most books had seemed as removed from my own actual practical experience as if they had been archaeological and remote—of a time and place as distinct from the present as the lessons of the arrowheads and Red Indian artifacts which I had collected by the thousands on Hollow Rock Farm. It was a long overdue awareness to come to an omnivorous adolescent reader.

Thinking back, I can almost remember the day when it was obvious that winning the war in Europe was not the final solution of mankind's woes. In 1917 I had befriended a strange wiry Quaker, a conscientious objector, who had been assigned to a neighboring farm when his status as a pacifist was certified by the army authorities at Camp Meade. He had come to help the threshing crew at Hollow Rock and had obviously not been in physcial training for such strenuous work. I swapped jobs with him for a few hours, and let him drive the water cart from the pond to the big steam traction engine while I pitched sheaves from the stack to which he had been assigned.

This man, by no means a radical, was simply a pacifist with a Quaker conviction against violence. Nevertheless, as a college graduate interested in the comparatively new science of sociology, he did bring to my attention many provocative aspects of understanding his point of view about nonviolence as a social and religious doctrine. His heroes and friends were nearly all professors and writers in New York and Chicago, notable among them, Randolph Bourne. Although I never came to accept his total aversion to taking life even in a war, I did come to appreciate the drive, the Christian morality and the courage which had led him to become a conscientious objector.

When the war ended, he suddenly disappeared into errands of mercy, first as a medical volunteer in the influenza epidemic, and later as a member of the American Friends' Service Committee in Europe. We corresponded occasionally and, by coincidence, it was eventually this man, Professor William F. Byron, of the University of Chicago, who stimulated my interest in social studies and in making an effort to join the group of residents at Hull House and to matriculate at the University of Chicago. This did not come about suddenly. It was to a considerable degree a matter of pure chance. But if anyone could claim to have diverted my attention from smug self-satisfaction to larger concerns, it would be, in the first instance, Byron.

The odd thing about Byron was that although he was widely read in history, economics and psychology, and was a serious scholar, he was not a seminal intellectual or philosopher. His attitudes had been shaped more by Quaker discipline than by reason. But, like many Quakers, he was so gently stubborn and considerate that later he had a profound humane effect upon his students at Chicago and subsequently at Northwestern. To me the obvious weakness in his retreat from a positive position to one of nonparticipation was a kind of last-ditch defense of his own convictions, an unexpressed willingness to shun real problems, and a tendency to stand serenely on his own faith in his own rightness. I remember my annoyance at his expressed hostility to blood sport and, above all, his horror that in the middle of the war we country boys hunted racoons at night for the pure joy of atavistic pursuit, bringing the trembling quarry to their deaths amid the mad music of hounds. He considered fox hunting and all blood sport an invention of a barbaric devil. He did concede, however, that boys and men who chased and killed animals for pleasure could take up arms against the foe of the country without being absolute savages. His main concern was with the sacredness of all living things. This was the mainspring of his interest in social problems. Intolerant though he was, I learned from him many lessons in tolerance.

I recall on one occasion how he became, for an uncontrolled moment, livid with rage when trapped by an inconsistency that I pointed out to him during a colloquy one day when the silo filling machinery broke down. I mentioned that I had never met a poor Quaker even though there were a number of Quaker farmers in our part of Maryland and, further, that I had never heard of a Negro Quaker. I suggested that he was a member of a smug club that was too exclusive and too self-serving, and that he had set himself up as rather a privileged character out of uniform. It was only years later, around 1950, over a very un-Quakerish New York lunch accompanied by cocktails and wine that he confessed that he had never quite forgiven me that attack.

"Because it had too much truth in it," he said. He had smarted for more than thirty years before admitting that during World War I he had indeed become a privileged martyr by stressing the conventional religious pacifist values rather than by an all-out acknowledgment of a larger social philosophy.

"I think 'thee' was justified," he said.

"The spirit moves me to keep silent now," I replied, raising my glass as a token of greater appreciation than he possibly could have surmised.

Chapter II

TWO YEARS AT HULL HOUSE

And did those feet in ancient time
  Walk upon England's mountains green?
And was the holy Lamb of God
  On England's pleasant pastures seen?

And did the Countenance Divine
  Shine forth upon our clouded hills?
And was Jerusalem builded here
  Among these dark Satanic mills?

Bring me my bow of burning gold!
  Bring me my arrows of desire!
Bring me my spear! O clouds, unfold!
  Bring me my chariot of fire!

I will not cease from mental fight,
  Nor shall my sword sleep in my hand,
Till we have built Jerusalem
  In England's green and pleasant land.
      —"Jerusalem" by William Blake

IF THIS WERE an intimate autobiography rather than a selective panorama of my times and of the men and institutions I have observed, it would be hopeless for me to recall all of the salient circumstances of being catapulted into the twentieth century upon graduation from Westminster High School at the age of seventeen. The story would have to portray so many friends, including graceful, fragrant, preponderantly innocent young ladies of Maryland, that it would be embarrassing, as well as difficult, to proceed.

The year 1920 gave me my first chance to demonstrate my ability to make money. Working with a local drover, I engaged in three or four substantial cattle deals, actually selling bred heifers short in anticipation of falling prices. I bought a Model "T" Ford roadster with self-starter and detachable tire rims, a town wardrobe complete with a dinner jacket and a tail coat, and a new riding habit with marvelously flared breeches and champagne topped hunting boots. I then set out to explore the nearby world and what I might do to achieve a place in it. By pleasantly unhurried touring I inspected a number of educational centers within several hundred miles, from Charlottesville to Princeton. I took a few courses at New Windsor, mainly mathematics and philosophy, and eventually settled upon the Wharton School of Finance and Business Administration at the University of Pennsylvania in Philadelphia as the quickest avenue to business competence and material success. I had never been away from Hollow Rock Farm for more than a month at a time. My family, room, books, saddles, guns and half-bred mare, Nellie, were, I was certain, as permanent a part of my life as the paraphernalia in Ulysses's home establishment at Ithaca.

In Philadelphia I drew a comfortable room in Morris House overlooking the Quadrangle. Then I registered for courses. I soon realized that it was naive to assume that a ready aptitude for shrewd country trading was related to courses in corporate administration, accounting and management. I derived a great deal of immediate practical knowledge from the courses in commercial law; agency, contracts, torts and so on. I was tempted even before midterm to try several elective courses in history, psychology, literature and art. Perhaps the most useful learning of all was Professor

Child's course on Shakespeare and Professor Weygandt's course on Contemporary American Literature. I avidly attended all of the special guest lectures which were arranged for all students who could secure tickets, among them an extraordinary appearance by Stephen Butler Leacock, whom I had regarded as a humorist but who dazzled me by his rugged exposition of economic theory, pre-Keynes, from a most conservative point of view. There was only a small radical group on the campus, with which I was not involved, but for whose courage if not ideas I soon came to have great admiration. They wanted a lecture by Scott Nearing who had been ousted from the University as a leftist. The Wharton School seemed to attract two widely different sorts of student: the sons of established business proprietors who aspired to carry on their family businesses, and a great many others who wanted to get a foothold in the managerial bureaucracy of big business.

Many nights, when our studying was over, we would elect one of the group in our dormitory to sneak up Locust Street to the bootlegger so that we could drink whiskey, smoke our pipes and conduct a clubby discussion of our aspirations in life.

Determined to get better acquainted with Philadelphia, I volunteered for one evening's work a week in a boy's club linked to a social settlement. I was assigned the supervision and instruction of a group of teen-agers who were learning the printing trade. All I knew of printing was what I had observed at the job press of the *Carroll Record* in Taneytown, but by much application and practice and the assistance of local job printers enlisted by others, I managed to keep up with the class. Half of them at least, and by all odds the brightest half, were Jewish boys whose parents had come from Russia and Poland. They were all of high-school age. How they managed to do their homework after they took up nighttime printing, I shall never know. Sometimes they insisted on remaining at their printing activities until the light and power of the building were turned off at half past eleven.

When I reported to my classmates what a remarkable graphic arts program I was engaged in at the boy's club, a few of them came around to visit. The Wharton School had taught us well. We soon organized a scheme to sell advertising on blotters which we would distribute free. We netted several thousand dollars after paying the boys nonunion rates for their typesetting and printing. It was not easy to get a sharp and clear impression on blotting paper. The inking had to be handled with precision. I managed the enterprise. Other students solicited the ads. The boys' club apprentices enjoyed seeing a practical result of their activities. It was a great joke among us that, like Tom Sawyer with the white-wash, we had induced others to do our work.

The Wharton School was really a sort of orphan of the University, not quite an accepted part of the larger liberal arts and graduate pattern of life which dominated the faculty and most student activities. For one reason, many of the Wharton School professors were serving part time, being also engaged in business downtown, in banks, insurance companies, railroad offices and law firms from which they apparently earned the largest part of their incomes. The Wharton faculty conducted a certain amount of scouting for business personnel, even among the freshmen, suggesting that if all went well, they could assist on placement upon, or even summer jobs before, graduation.

I am certain that I would have benefited enormously if I had continued at the Wharton School. But after a little more than a year, I began to feel trapped in a too narrow setting. I might have been wiser to have swung directly and wholeheartedly over to the liberal arts college, but I felt a deep-seated apprehension about committing myself into any direction until I knew more of the world beyond Pennsylvania and the university.

I decided to consult two of my uncles, one an officer of the B & O Railroad, and the other a banker-farmer in Westminster. We sat by the fire at Meadowbrook, my uncle's farm, and talked for several hours about the future. I had confided brashly to both of them that I had a double objective—fame and fortune. My Uncle Ray, a widely read and cultivated man although he had never gone beyond high school, sympathized with my desire to keep one foot in the country and the other foot in town. He suggested that instead of returning to college, I take time out to investigate what I really could do, really wanted to do, and if it turned out well, keep on going; otherwise, back to college. My other uncle, Walter, who was living in affluent style in Baltimore, greatly relieved that he was no longer tied to country life and its never-ending chores, deplored the idea of a double life. He said that the only way to achieve what one wanted was to start at the bottom, as he had done, and twenty-five years later be a respected, well-paid officer of a large corporation, with an inside knowledge of investments. "Go for commerce," he said.

Looking back, I now wonder what these kindly relatives, confronted by my problems, really thought of me in my moment of uncertainty.

I chose to leave the Wharton School and have a go at a career which would keep me close to the farm which I loved. I had no difficulty whatever getting a job as an aide to the head of the local plant of the Western Maryland Dairy, where milk was pasteurized for dispatch to the city, the surplus being processed into cheese, ice-cream mix and dried skim milk for animal feeding at a time before dried milk was widely used for human consumption.

I don't think I have ever regretted the decision. For nearly a year I was in constant touch with the city and with some four hundred local farmers in the heart of the Baltimore milkshed. I learned a great deal not only about food production and processing but about the detailed annual planning of supply and marketing. The hours at the plant were from seven until three. I had long afternoons for reading, fishing, visiting, going to Baltimore to chat with the newspapermen I had come to know and also with local friends who were undergraduates at The Johns Hopkins.

Years later I found these pleasant early-start and early-away hours were almost universal in Africa south of the Sahara, where the natives imposed their desire for family life in the afternoons upon the Europeans. Also, on the West Coast in California, where the three-hour time difference with Wall Street meant that financial personnel started work at seven and had the entire afternoon for sport or hobbies, the pattern was similar. I've never since the dairy days really had a free afternoon on a work day until now in 1966. Daylight saving is really a niggardly compromise, cheerfully accepted as ideal by urban and suburban dwellers who have never known the joy of greeting the dawn or the excruciating paradise of winning the fight against the seductive challenge of empty and listless idleness afternoon upon afternoon around the calendar of the year.

When the manager of the local plant approached me with the suggestion that I was now ready to be assigned to headquarters in Baltimore, I felt uneasy. I had reached a firm conclusion that if I were really to go to the city, I did not want to be identified with a manufacturing concern, but with an articulate profession—not necessarily the life of a reporter, but involvement with publishing or writing.

To me, in those callow days, the greatest attraction about publishing and the graphic arts was that one could become a useful and influential impresario without, as I thought, doing all of the work. I had almost subconsciously become aware of the fact that the great newspaper publishers, Hearst, Pulitzer and Van Lear Black of The *Sunpapers,* gave the word on how and what they wanted to publish; then, while others ran the business, they traveled about the world and the country getting a firsthand look in order to check up on their objectives. I was a good observer, a good traveler, a good negotiator; but I was a general without an army. I had seen my name in print in the local weekly newspapers and on several space-rate pieces in the Baltimore newspapers and was not egotistically impressed by direct and visible performance as a writer. It was perhaps a happy estimate of my own nature, which then and now was gregarious as well as reflective, to realize that I could never endure the long apprenticeship of solitary effort involved in writing as an all-out profession.

Through my Uncle Walter I had met some of his Baltimore friends who were authors, usually rather shabby and disgruntled men whom he had encouraged because, deep down, even though he was a railroad official, he had an affinity for scholars and dreamers. I visited him in the city, at his insistence, remaining several months, going to the Enoch Pratt Library nearly every day, frequently visiting the fabulous book department of the Hoschild Kohn Department Store and becoming acquainted with most of the booksellers along Charles Street and in the cross streets of downtown Baltimore.

One day, on a briefer sojourn several years before, as I was carrying an armload of books up the street, I had halted to watch Cardinal Gibbons who was benignly admiring the tulip bed next to his residence adjacent to the Cathedral. I bade him good morning, and we fell into conversation. He told me that he had a special affection for Carroll County because of his good friends of the Shriver family at Union Mills near Westminster. Many of the large Shriver clan were my friends, too. They were part of a prominent Catholic group that included the Boyles, the Carrolls and the Shaws. For ten minutes the Cardinal abandoned his inspection of the flower bed and discussed the future of young men in an age of tremendous change.

I did not realize until then that this extraordinary prelate had for decades taken an interest in social and economic affairs. He recommended that I read the Encyclicals of Pope Leo XIII. I did not even know what an encyclical was and asked him to explain. He did so.

"But I am a Protestant, sir," I remember saying defensively.

"I am not trying to convert you to my religion," he replied, "but to contribute something to your education and knowledge of world history."

The brief colloquy made a deep impression. I did read the Encyclicals and some of James Cardinal Gibbons' own writings and was struck by the boldness and candor of his utterances on social conditions, labor and the obligations of business to do more than merely make money. I was not really interested in his religion so much as in the startling discovery that beneath his Medieval garb he was a Modern.

On the basis of a few inquiries among my Catholic friends, I found that some of them considered him rather advanced in his views. On one occasion not long before his final illness, I went to the Cathedral to hear him preach. His homely Irish face, earnest brogue and common sense without pretense were unforgettable and dispelled whatever small prejudice I had against the Roman Catholic Church as an institution blindly devoted to the enforcement of dogma handed down from Rome.

In my generation I do not believe that the parochial schools or Jesuit colleges such as Mount Saint Mary's, four miles from Hollow Rock Farm, were greatly influenced by Cardinal Gibbons. In retrospect it seems that his great role was to demonstrate that a Catholic churchman could be, as part of his religion, a most active exponent of social justice. He was emancipated from the narrow qualities characteristic of many parish priests and Protestant parsons.

When I spoke with my uncle, a thorough Baltimorean with a Catholic wife, he told me that Cardinal Gibbons had won the heart of the Protestant sector of the city years earlier when a large dinner had been given by a civic group to honor him upon his return from Rome with his Red Hat. The story goes that one of the speakers, after a series of toasts, had inquired of the Cardinal whether he still believed in the infallibility of the Pope. Cardinal Gibbons was reported as replying with a twinkle, "He called me Cardinal Gibbone!"

The extraordinary quality of Baltimore in those days is that it was adorned, if not really ruled, by an aristocratic oligarchy which did not actually include the Cathedral—but the group at *The Sunpapers,* The Johns Hopkins and the Green Spring and Worthington Valley squirearchy, who were engaged in business, law, shipping, insurance and manufacturing in Baltimore.

The city would have given me, I am certain, a tremendous opportunity simply because of a Maryland heritage and fondness for the things which seemed to matter most; tolerance, politeness, a love of good conversation and local patriotism with the least possible display. Baltimore was already becoming known as a community in which Northern money was more frequently married than earned by those determined to live the life of a fox-hunting man in the Valley, sometimes roguishly called the Valley of Kept Men.

I decided against remaining in Baltimore. The life seemed

too diversionary from my ultimate hopes. I wasn't ready for the plunge. I welcomed an invitation from a cousin to come with him to the wilds of West Virginia for a season. Raymond Colton, a decorated veteran of World War I and a trained engineer, was put in charge of a number of operations in planning the highways in the Kanawha River Valley in the Charleston area.

I spent some six months with him on survey parties, enjoying every moment of the temporary job. I learned to use the transit and the level, to lay out future highways, using complicated logarithmic and slide rule calculations of curves, of cut and fill, to insure the greatest economy and beauty in grading and building the roads. Some of the time we were billeted in the better hotels in Charleston, but very often we lived a safari-like life in tents in the mountains with an excellent ex-army cook who seemed to have access to the most reliable moonshiners within reach.

Charleston had been a wartime boom city and was then a rich community surrounded by the comparative poverty of the Appalachian coal miners, some of whom had just gone through bloody union strife in Harlan and Logan Counties in what was locally described as a kind of final act of the old Hatfield-McCoy feud. I had taken with me to the wilderness some two hundred books, a second-hand typewriter and enough paper to have written the history of mankind. I confined my writing, however, to a number of theoretical papers for my own orientation. I have long since lost these notes, but the gist of my thoughts at the time remains clear even today.

My hypothesis was that if city life and even the life of isolated industrial areas could reflect some of the warm-hearted consideration of others that had been characteristic of life on a prosperous farm, American progress would soon create the finest civilization on earth and at the same time generate great fortunes and positions for those who brought the ideal conditions into being.

At that time Henry Ford was the American hero who had got rich by putting a world stuck in the mud on wheels and paying high wages to his own employees in Dearborn. There was something missing in Henry Ford, and indeed in most of the industry of the period—particularly the heavy industry—and that, it seemed to me, was almost total ignorance of the magnitude of the overall job that had to be done. Roads were obvious, and the public investment was tremendous; but schools, rural electric power, medical care and common economic decency toward the unemployed and underpaid were largely ignored. The true capitalist, as I saw it, would be the man who related in his objectives, first of all, the greater distribution at a profit of his product without demolishing the environment and welfare of his suppliers, his workers and his customers.

The automobile and the movies seemed to be creating only an illusion of happiness, tempting people to false escapism in film palaces and destroying pride in home, work, school or the care of children. The perspective of the wilderness (with infrequent access to newspapers and before the development of radio) gave me almost Olympian detachment as I discussed and wrote my notes far into the night. Our bivouac seminar was especially stimulating because, although I was the youngest of the crew, all of us were really on temporary duty while making up our minds what to do next.

We read about the Jazz Age, but we were not of it except for an occasional dance in Charleston. We read about Sacco and Vanzetti and unanimously agreed that although they might be guilty, it had not been proven by their trial. Nearly all of our general assumptions and conclusions were through the years borne out by events, but at the time we were wholly without influence as we educated one another by commentary

on our reading of books, magazines and occasional newspapers.

When I received a letter, addressed to me at Hollow Rock
Farm and forwarded, from Professor William F. Byron of
the University of Chicago inquiring what I was doing, I
sent him a sheaf of my papers composed in the mountain
forest and said that I was about ready to make my next move,
probably back to college. After a considerable period he
replied saying that if I forwarded my academic résumé, he
would endeavor to get me matriculated at the University of
Chicago. I decided to go to Chicago, and took the C & O
from Charleston.

My luggage got lost, not to be recovered for weeks, but I
arrived at the Twelfth Street Station, took a taxi to Hull
House and into a new and congenial incarnation. I was
twenty. The first thing that Byron did was to introduce me to
his Swedish wife, Evelyn, and then to Miss Addams.

We climbed the wide mahogany-banistered stairway of
the old mansion to Miss Addams' apartment—into which
she had moved when she and Ellen Gates Starr founded the
settlement house in 1889. On first beholding the greatest
woman that America had yet produced, at the zenith of her
career, I had expected something wholly different from the
calm, gracious, humorous and still handsome woman who
greeted me.

She turned around from her desk, where she had been
writing letters in longhand, and asked that we sit down and
take tea with her. She wanted to know at once whether Mr.
Byron had found accommodations for me, whether I had
been shown the buildings of Hull House and whether I was
a fast and accurate reader and typist. I said that I couldn't
qualify as a stenographer, but that I had learned to type
moderately fast through a great deal of practice over several
years.

While my glance absorbed the Dürer prints and auto-graphed photographs on the wall opposite me, she and Byron then conducted a brief and gossipy conversation from which I was not excluded even though I was not acquainted with the names—obviously all residents—who were mentioned as returning from vacation or travel to establish themselves for another year at Hull House. There was a "back-to-school" rhythm to the account. It appeared that I was to supplement the assignment of a part-time secretary and at the same time, under the direction of Byron, to assume some of the marginal responsibilities of an enterprise which included thirteen buildings, seventy-odd residents in rooms and apart-ments, a little theater, craftsmanship facilities (ceramics, weaving, printing, etc.), an auditorium, a boys' club, a day nursery, apart from the activities of several tenants in the buildings, such as the Juvenile Protective Association and the Immigrants Protective League, not to mention a branch of the post office which housed the McManus sisters who also served as bookkeepers and accountants.

There was a coffee house modeled after an English pub except that it was without a bar, and a residents' dining room served from the same kitchen, both presently running far behind in their budget. In addition to all of these activi-ties, plus a music school and an art school, the settlement owned a Wisconsin summer camp for mothers and children that was grandly styled the Bowen Country Club after Mrs. Joseph T. Bowen, the prominent Chicago citizen who had founded it and who was one of Miss Addams' closest friends.

I wondered for a moment how this congeries of activities allowed Miss Addams time for her lectures, her writing and her many civic activities. I was so struck dumb with amaze-ment that I asked no questions. In due course I would learn the secret of the poise and tranquility of this obviously dy-namic woman. It was, of course, revealed in *Twenty Years at Hull House* and some of the other books which she had written. She set a goal and delegated responsibility to people in whom she had complete confidence.

She had apparently bestowed upon Byron more duties than he could possibly undertake on top of his academic work, and he had nominated me to help carry part of the burden. Unfortunately, he had not fully informed me of the wide range of my job as a special assistant and acting secretary both to Miss Addams and himself. She asked me a number of searching questions—age, hobbies, family, favorite literature. Then the tea arrived and she simply said,

"I hope you will find yourself happy and useful."

Whereupon the conversation turned to talk of conditions in Germany, Soviet Russia and Great Britain, with many references to the various activities of her friends abroad, in the United States and in Chicago.

I arose upon a cue from Byron, thanked Miss Addams for tea and excused myself so that the "new boy" could be discussed in private.

For a few weeks I was just a Hull House employee, not quite a full-fledged resident, comfortably installed in a little plywood penthouse shack that had been built on the roof of one of the buildings of the Hull House complex during the war as emergency accommodations for the staff. It was equipped with plumbing, a kitchenette and a fireplace and had a small porch commanding a splendid view of the buildings in the Loop a mile and a half away.

Hull House was situated at Polk and Halsted streets in an area long blighted by neglect as waves of European immigrants during many decades had moved in upon arrival. To the north on Halsted Street and the diagonally intersecting Blue Island Avenue there was a Greek section with hundreds of native coffeehouses. Next to that was a typical "Little Italy" of restaurants and Italian grocery stores. Southward toward Maxwell Street there was a predominantly Jewish neighborhood, with nearby enclaves of Irish and the beginnings of the first Mexican and Negro invasion of the West Side of Chicago.

The beautiful old mansion which had been acquired in 1889 was graciously furnished. As Dr. Alice Hamilton wrote in 1943:

> Life at Hull House was very simple so far as luxuries went, but it was full of beauty. The two founders had brought with them many charming furnishings, and whatever they bought later had the two qualities of durability and beauty. Our food was inexpensive, but dinner was served to us in a long, paneled dining room, lighted with chandeliers of Spanish wrought iron; breakfast, in a charming little coffeehouse built in imitation of an English inn. To me, the life there satisfied every longing—for companionship, for the excitement of new experiences, for constant intellectual stimulation, and for the sense of being caught up in a big movement which enlisted my enthusiastic loyalty.

Miss Addams had been born in a year that was "Chicago-conscious." Lincoln had been nominated in a city which in thirty years had grown from 100 to more than 100,000. That sounds tame nowadays, when one expects new cities to grow like mushrooms, but in 1860 Chicago was a unique and awe-inspiring phenomenon on the Western Plain. Four short years before, Charles J. Hull had built a stately country seat on the outskirts of the town. By 1889, when Jane Addams was twenty-nine years old, this red-brick mansion stood in the heart of one of the longest and meanest thoroughfares in the world—Halsted Street.

As a small girl in Cedarville, Illinois, Miss Addams had dreamed of having a large house in the middle of horrid little streets and inviting the neighbors in. In *Twenty Years at Hull House* she reveals that the first exciting suggestion "of the great world of moral enterprise and serious undertakings" came when she was twelve. She discovered her father gazing moodily at his newspaper and asked what troubled him. "Joseph Mazzini is dead," he replied. She had never heard of Mazzini; she was certain her father had no close friend by that name. It sounded very foreign. Then her father told her of Mazzini, who in faraway Italy had striven all his life for the freedom of his country.

When her father had finished, Miss Addams says, "I obtained a sense of the genuine relationship which may exist between men who share large hopes and like desires, even though they differ in nationality, language and creed; that those things count for absolutely nothing between groups of men who are trying to abolish slavery in America or to throw off Hapsburg oppression in Italy."

From the very beginnings of Hull House, which was more or less patterned after the first metropolitan settlement house, Toynbee Hall in London, Miss Addams and Miss Starr had no difficulty in attracting brilliant and dedicated young people who wanted to feel and observe firsthand the life of a poor neighborhood in the city, and to help by a two-way osmosis to adjust the poor to higher aspirations, materially and culturally, and at the same time learn firsthand the realities of life in a way not otherwise possible for the educated classes, predominantly Anglo-Saxon, in the jungles of the growing city. In its first twenty years Hull House grew to the institutional size which existed upon my arrival in a vast smelly district between mills and railroad stations, an area already mainly zoned for factories.

No scientist in a laboratory could have had a more ideal opportunity for observations than I had in the swarming bottleneck of slum, skid row and quasi-slum between the railroad depots and Halsted Street. At Hull House foresight kept pace with curiosity. Observations and maps were made in the earliest days, and Hull House began to function as bathroom, parlor, garden, library, gymnasium and community meeting place until these adjuncts of living developed elsewhere through the efforts of those who had come in contact with the vision of New World progress brought to them by their neighbors in the settlement house.

When I first met her, Miss Addams was in her early sixties. Within a day or two I also met most of the residents and discovered Miss Addams thoroughly enjoyed their civilized and articulate company. She was proud of her erstwhile residents, Gerard Swope, Francis Hackett, Walter S. Gifford, Mackenzie King, Julia Lathrop, Edith Abbott as well as a score of neighborhood boys including Sidney Hillman and Benny Goodman (who had already made their marks in business, labor, art, music, scholarship and literature).

I managed to find time during my first week in Chicago to go to the University on the South Side and register for several courses—sociology, English and history. By good chance, Robert Morss Lovett, one of the influential members of the English faculty, was a resident of Hull House. Lovett and his wife Ida, were not reluctant to adopt me as a member of their sparkling literary circle.

A young professor at Chicago who also lived at Hull House was Howard Mumford Jones, who had arrived by way of Texas and the University of Wisconsin. He, too, from our first meeting, and later while at Chapel Hill and at Harvard, tended to regard me as more than simply one of his students; as something of a special protégé.

Hull House was a catalyst. I reveled in all of the banter and serious discussion, the humor and the hard work, in this sophisticated sort of coeducational lay monastery hidden away on the West Side of Chicago. Every resident was required to put in two evenings a week—or afternoons if free—at volunteer work in one of the settlement's activities. One of my first volunteer experiences was to teach a mixed adult

c

immigrant class simple English. My textbook, as was the custom, was an out-of-date Sears Roebuck Catalogue donated for the purpose from leftover copies by Julius Rosenwald, founder and head of Sears Roebuck, who was on the board of Hull House.

I sometimes helped in the printing shop where I had an elementary competence gained earlier in Philadelphia. We printed nearly all of the material needed in the settlement as well as appeals for funds to support the educational work and the summer camp. Dr. Alice Hamilton was frequently in residence when visiting her sister, Norah Hamilton, the artist and etcher. Dr. Hamilton was a pioneer in occupational medicine and a crusader against health hazards in industry. She had been the first woman on the Harvard faculty. They were sisters of Miss Edith Hamilton, the classicist and teacher, who eventually became the finest writer of our time on Greek classics and mythology. Miss Edith would usually join her two sisters in Chicago before they went off for the summer together.

Residents and previous residents of Hull House were always welcome in the residents' dining room. Scarcely a day passed without an eminent guest—Vachel Lindsay reciting his poetry; Carl Sandburg with his guitar; Charles Beard, the historian; John Dewey; Clarence Darrow; and from time to time Gerard Swope whose daughter, Henrietta, was a temporary resident. The Swopes had met each other at Hull House when both were residents and had been married there. There was scarcely a banker or businessman in the city who did not call on Miss Addams from time to time, undisturbed by the Bohemian and even radical reputation ascribed to the settlement because of the indubitable presence of some politically very controversial persons as frequent guests.

The effect of this life upon me was more exhilarating than that of the University. It constantly tested my capacity for observation and for social, political and literary judgment. It was a continuous seminar on life in the large.

My routine was, for two years, a long day with never a dull moment. I came to enjoy the trips to the South Side to the campus, the excursions into the countryside and, above all, weekend visits to the Indiana Dunes. A group of us chipped together to rent a cottage on a small estate on the Dunes and went out nearly every Saturday afternoon that we could manage to get away. This was then one of the most magnificent, unspoiled natural sanctuaries in the Middle West, miles of clean white beach along the clear water of Lake Michigan, with a verge of shifting sand, swamps, forests, abounding in rare flora and fauna.

Miss Addams was a voluminous correspondent with all sorts of people all over the world. Sometimes she scratched a rough draft of a letter which I was supposed to interpret and complete and make ready for her signature. When she went on trips for more than a few days she left blank letters signed for me to answer, after she became certain of my ability more or less to approximate her simple and direct style.

One of Miss Addams' in-law relatives, Marcia, was married to Haldeman-Julius, who published the Little Blue Books in Girard, Kansas. I ultimately became well acquainted with that curious publishing enterprise. In its fashion it was a precursor of the inexpensive paperbound books of today except that the sales were done by mail-order advertising in big city newspapers. The books themselves were not really books but excerpts, condensations, specially written essays, often given a sensational title but otherwise not deceptive in content. One couldn't expect more for five cents.

Another occasional Kansas visitor whom I came to know and love and later to see occasionally in New York was William Allen White, editor of the *Emporia Gazette*. He liked to pick the brains of Miss Addams and her associates and in turn let us pick his brains for facts, epigrams and political observations. He was not as homespun as he pretended and was perfectly at home on the Gold Coast of Chicago, in the mansions of the near North Side, as well as among such New York friends as Thomas Lamont, the Morgan partner, and Paul Cravath, the lawyer. He was a swift and graceful writer, anything but a man of his vaunted small-town limitations.

While at Hull House I wrote and published many articles, book reviews and even a few poems; but nothing pleased me more than my work on a revision of the so-called Hull House catalogue, a brief history and account of activities which was sold to visitors who came in great numbers to visit the institution. The previous edition had been prewar. It was my hope that the post-World War I edition could be rewritten in better expository style without offending anyone whose activity was portrayed.

I labored on this opus for months in all of my spare time and, to my amazement, there was not a quibble by anyone down the line when I put the draft on Miss Addams' desk. For several days I heard nothing about it. I endured agonizing suspense lest I had muddled a sacred institutional project. Then suddenly I was simply asked by Professor Byron how soon we could get them printed and what would be the cost and the profit in quantities of five thousand, seventy-five hundred and ten thousand. I had four bids on just these quantities in hand and fortunately the low bid was from the old friend who had always printed the lavishly illustrated catalogue in the past.

The University of Chicago was acknowledged throughout the world as the cradle of the new science of sociology. Books, reflecting intensive inductive research, or social theory, written by members of the faculty, set the tone for graduate social studies elsewhere. Professor Frederick M. Thrasher wrote the first substantial book on juvenile gangs, based upon observations of the formation into some thirteen hundred groups of adolescent boys more dedicated to mischief, because it was conspicuous, than to constructive purposes. Hull House and other agencies in Chicago attempted to canalize the energy of these groups of young people into activities—educational, athletic, musical, vocational—that would enable them to demonstrate their status even among the wilder gangs that could not be lured into any kind of supervision.

The University had established, under the direction of Miss Sophonisba Breckinridge, a school of social service administration. She and her faculty associates frequently met with us at Hull House, where she had once lived, and we all had from them a dim vision of what was ultimately to be described as the Welfare State.

One process at the University was to use inductive research findings to illuminate and dramatize the problems of people in the city and thus help to formulate and pilot the first programs for such developments as psychiatric social work, family case work and even the beginning of such commonplace institutions as day nurseries for the children of working mothers. Chicago had become famous, while a young university, for its Oriental Studies, particularly in the field of Egyptology under the direction of Professor James Henry Breasted. What the sociologists in alliance with the lawyers, historians, economists and psychologists were endeavoring to do was to reconstruct, just as definitely as the archaeologists were doing for dead societies, an understandable picture of a living and changing modern industrial and urban society.

Many of these academic enterprises had their modest beginnings in the Hull House of an earlier day. Those engaged in these fields came to Hull House for interchange of opinion in the same manner, I later discovered, as scholars in England at All Souls, the only Oxford college without a student body.

Though Hull House had no monopoly of talent in the social sciences, in league with the University and by virtue of its articulate group of residents, it was influential beyond any other center of the period. It was no accident that Sidney Hillman, who had gone to night class at Hull House and achieved the leadership of the Amalgamated Clothing Workers, was disposed to avoid strife in bargaining with manufacturers in the region by accepting an impartial arbitrator, who was a Hull House resident, Professor Arthur J. Todd.

Professor Todd and his wife, Nancy, were the only Christian Science residents at Hull House while I was there, and from them I learned what a compulsive religion could lead them to undertake in the amelioration of life and living conditions. They were practical do-gooders, not even reformers, interested in bringing people together to discuss differences before situations got out of hand in savage labor-management hostilities.

Another strange but lively pair of missionaries were the Yarros family. They were Russian Jews, dynamically intellectual, uninhibited, Slavic in appearance, Edwardian in dress and manners. Victor Yarros was a law partner of Clarence Darrow and a writer of editorials for the *Chicago Evening News* under Carroll Binder's editorship. Whenever possible he reviewed symphony concerts and opera for the paper. His wife, Rachel, was a medical doctor, a pioneer campaigner for birth control and social hygiene (as the effort to eliminate venereal disease was known in the twenties). From time to time when Dr. Yarros was invited to give illustrated lectures in cooperation with local industries, she recruited me to turn the crank on her primitive film projector which was not automatically run by an electric motor.

Her candid approach to the problems of venereal disease eventually became acceptable in the Chicago area not only by management but by selected groups of employees, from the stockyard firms and International Harvester to the big financial institutions downtown. The Yarros' campaign undoubtedly had a great deal of effect upon her *bête noir,* Colonel McCormick, whose *Chicago Tribune* was the only newspaper of the period that campaigned openly and dramatically against the spread of venereal disease and for prompt and proper medical handling of those unfortunate enough to be infected.

The interchange of ideas was frequently enlivened by paying guests who remained for several weeks at a time. S. K. Ratcliffe, then at the peak of his popularity as a British lecturer in America, always stayed with us at Hull House. On one occasion when he could not make a schedule of lectures, he sent his substitute, John Langdon-Davies, who was attempting to succeed Havelock Ellis as a student of sex and the dance. He also playfully claimed to be an advocate of nudism.

Another British visitor who created a unique intellectual impression was Sylvester Gates, who spent one summer after finishing at the Harvard Law School, and who was introduced to us by Professor Felix Frankfurter. Through the years ever since, we have been in frequent contact personally and professionally. He is now Deputy Chairman of the Westminster Bank and Chairman of the Bank of West Africa, but in those days he was inclined toward poetry and literary criticism before commencing his London career as a barrister. He was one of a comparatively small group of exceptional Oxford men who survived World War I to make a mark on their times—among them Anthony Eden, Sir Kenneth Clark, Lord David Cecil and Anthony Asquith.

Sylvester became an immediate member of our Dunes group, openly initiating the practice of reading poetry aloud in the evenings. Nearly twenty years later when, during World War II, he was Home Controller of the Ministry of Information and I was at our Embassy in London, we resumed our conversations as if we had seen one another only yesterday. J. F. Horrabin, who had done the maps and drawings for H. G. Wells' *Outline of History,* came to Chicago at the instance of Mr. Wells, and with him I visited artists and illustrators who, although little known in Chicago, seemed to have an international reputation.

A most charming elderly visitor, whom it was a special pleasure for me to escort in printing circles, was Mrs. Cobden Sanderson, a member of the pre-Raphaelite group in London, whose husband had founded the Kelmscott Press and produced a famous edition of Chaucer. From her I learned a great deal about type design and fine paper.

Often two remarkable men sojourned at Hull House for brief periods, Roger Baldwin and Paul U. Kellogg. Roger had founded the American Civil Liberties Union and was, although a pacifist, a fighting liberal, ever ready to defend the First Amendment to the Constitution no matter how unpopular the individual or cause that was censored or attacked. His activities were not generally admired during the Harding and Coolidge administrations, but probably as much as any other man in our history since the days of Thomas Jefferson, he understood the meaning of the Bill of Rights and its basic application to new issues as they arose in modern industrial society.

Paul Kellogg was editor of the *Survey* and eventually the *Survey Graphic,* a magazine of social interpretation which took its name from a civic study of Pittsburgh in the period between 1908 and 1912. The *Pittsburgh Inquiry,* one of the first major research projects in American social conditions, was dubbed the "Pittsburgh Survey" by Kellogg, who thus injected the word "survey" into its modern connotation rather than restricted to its old application to civil engineering. I remember his telling me how he came to use the word "survey," but I have never been able to substantiate it. It seems that he had been told that the *Domesday Book* in England after the Norman invasion was subtitled, "A Survey of Saxon Land and Folk." Why not apply the term to the Pittsburgh studies? They were published as the *Pittsburgh Survey* and ultimately the word became the imprint of two pioneering publications—*Survey* and *Survey Graphic.*

I began writing occasional reviews and brief items for the Survey publications in the middle 1920's, and in 1926 Clare McClure, then the wife of Howard Mumford Jones, and I edited a special issue of the *Survey Graphic* on the gypsies. This project, published in 1927, and entitled "New World Gypsy Trails," eventually led to my becoming an associate of Paul Kellogg as managing editor in 1935. In the decade prior to that time, I had come to know not only the research and editorial staffs, but their board of trustees and many of their principal outside authors.

The extraordinary relationships developed in Chicago were not based upon simple propinquity or logrolling but upon a sort of consensus of progressive, humane, courageous and courteous explorations and reportage of a more sophisticated sort than that of the earlier muckrakers.

Some years later, looking at the little frigate colophon designed by Hendrik Willem van Loon which appeared on our masthead at *Survey,* Felix Frankfurter said, "You were in the crow's nest viewing the uncharted seas of American Life," which later became the keynote of one of his speeches at an annual meeting of Survey Associates.

c*

Social and professional mobility in the Chicago of the 1920's was so incredible that in the course of a typical week, I might find myself visiting Harold Swift in the stockyards; chatting with gangsters such as Diamond Joe Esposito at the garage where I kept my little Ford; attending a poetry reading at Harriet Monroe's salon on the near North Side; taking half a dozen courses at the University; enjoying a glimpse of the wild set at the Dill Pickle Club; visiting the Black and Tan dance halls with Miguel Covarrubias; and playing a role in the Hull House Theater in a series of one-act plays which we wrote and produced to a full house immediately after dinner under the auspices of a voluntary repertory club which Howard Mumford Jones dubbed the DemiTasse Players.

There is no substitute for youthful curiosity and energy. The house painter, who worked under my direction, was a young Norwegian who, although he strikingly resembled the Prince of Wales, was an IWW who knew all the fiery ballads of the revolution which he was undoubtedly working to bring about. Every now and then after startling the staid McManus sisters in the accounting office with one of the house painter's "pie in the sky" radical songs, I would change my playful game and hold them spellbound with stories of Roger Brooke Taney going to Mass every day in Maryland from the age of sixteen until he died as Chief Justice after inducting seven Presidents into office. They were devout Catholics who were never completely persuaded of the morality of some of the Hull House residents who were known to be slow in payment of their monthly accounts even when they obviously had money to spend at Spino's Italian restaurant and speakeasy across Polk Street from their office windows.

Ellen Gates Starr, co-founder with Miss Addams of Hull House, was a Catholic convert. Forsaking all worldly or reform activities and devoting her time entirely to her book bindery, she taught an advanced class of students all that she had learned in Florence, Paris and London.

While I was at Hull House only one neighborhood family had moved into a residential apartment, Hector Toniatti and his wife, Julia. A Venetian by birth, he was an imaginative jewelry designer by profession. He was already, to the horror of the residents, an admirer of Mussolini, who was little known at the time. Only a year ago when I visited him in his office on Wacker Drive, he still had on display an autographed photograph of Il Duce. Miss Addams was very tolerant toward this romantic fixation on Mussolini, knowing well that it was only an extension of Hector's own ego at a time when few Italians had achieved a secure position in the upper reaches of Chicago society, and that, in a fashion, Hector was reflecting the same sort of exhibitionism as Mussolini but without the dictatorial urge.

Actually Hector was a virtuous man and a useful helper on every good cause in the local Italian community. The only time I ever saw him in a violent rage, fortified by wine, was when I reported to him that John Dill Robinson, medical officer of the city government, insisted that most Italians never bathed but covered their bodies with olive oil and scraped their skins with oyster shells, a custom handed down from the days of Romulus and Remus.

Hull House was not a congenial spot to men such as Big Bill Thompson, the mayor. But it did attract all of the eminent psychiatrists, psychologists and early psychoanalysts of the group which gave Clarence Darrow the basis for the historic summation in the Loeb-Leopold Case.

Although Hull House was often hated and attacked by politicians, most of them eventually came to admit that Hull House and its residents made Jane Addams Chicago's most useful citizen. I remember many of these hard-bitten and entrenched political bosses boasting that their objectives and campaign issues were derived from Hull House, which they had been watching ever since 1912 when Miss Addams seconded the nomination of Theodore Roosevelt at the Progressive Party Convention—the first woman so to do in any party convention—eight years before the Women's Suffrage Amendment was passed. The politicians used the reformers as straws in the wind of change.

The important quality of life at Hull House in the 1920's, as from the beginning, was the commitment of the residents to a cheerful and voluntary life of service, quite apart from their outside commercial and professional vocations. Even the most self-indulgent of us were punctilious in the performance of our volunteer tasks, not because Miss Addams or the rules willed it so, but because we believed that a few years of helping people would temper the harshness of city life for others and perhaps make better citizens of us as well.

It is undoubtedly true that altruism feeds upon a kind of selfishness, an unspoken awareness of a favored position—but how else can a philanthropist, a businessman, a politician, a country squire or a welfare worker, or any other leader otherwise account for his motivation? The accrued benefits, to me, at least, were equivalent to those of life in a university. I probably learned as much from the humble people in the neighborhood who used the settlement as an educational or welfare organization as I learned from the residents and their outside guests, but that was education of a different order from exposure to the leading thinkers, researchers, writers and reformers of the day.

Indeed, there was something very poignant in dealing with the striving of older immigrants to adjust themselves to American life in a raw and seemingly heartless city. Most of them had arrived in Chicago with a fixed language and established habits which could not be altered fast enough to suit the impatient younger members of their families. Many of the adolescents were ashamed of their parents and at the same time not self-assured enough to enjoy themselves as typical Americans. They were members of a minority in the general life of the city. It was not until the third generation that most members of these ethnic groups could feel at home in school, on the job and in the community.

Although they were not significantly different from the English-speaking people from the hinterland, who were flocking to the city, they themselves felt that they were different. Some sought self-expression in continuing the language of their parents and grandparents as a second language, even learning the folk songs and folk dances of the countries of their family origin; but, for the most part, they seemed to want to imitate the conformist folkways and mores of the entrenched Anglo-Saxon population, even to the point of changing their names and, in many cases, their religion.

The Irish and the Negroes had the obvious advantage of easy social mobility depending almost entirely upon their economic status. The Hull House Players, an amateur theater group which frequently performed in the Little Theater, were under the spell of the Abbey Theater in Dublin. The Negroes were just beginning to reflect the artistic renaissance of the new Harlem in New York and the new South Side of Chicago with a musical link to New Orleans, Memphis and St. Louis. But much as Irish and Negroes might flaunt their dramatic and musical heritage, they were, except when on the stage, indistinguishable from other Americans or Chicagoans of similar background.

Perhaps the least assimilable neighbors were the one hundred or so gypsies who wintered in vacant shops in the neighborhood and who came to Hull House to beg or tell fortunes. One winter I persuaded the gypsies to give an exhibition of their dances, which I had observed in their encampments in the stores where they lived with no furniture except great heaps of mattresses and quilts which they carried off with them in their ancient cars when they took to the road. It was something of a success and attracted a mixed crowd from the neighborhood as well as fashionable visitors from downtown Chicago.

At one of these unplanned and only vaguely announced performances, I was delighted to find a tall, lean, smiling young Russian who understood the gypsy coppersmith dialect and who was familiar with their music. He was Ilya Tolstoy, a grandson of Leo Tolstoy. We became fast friends. He was more devoted even than I to gypsy music and dances.

As a teen-ager in Russia he had worked with the American Friends' Service Committee during the Revolution and had been one of a group who during the crucial wintertime had brought several thousand horses from east of the Urals in time for the spring plowing in the Tula region. Permission had been secured for him to come to Iowa State University at Ames to train for an agrarian career in his homeland. Soon tiring of the austere life and rigid discipline at Ames and not intending to return to Russia, he decided to make a break for the city.

He joined a Russian riding school in Chicago. He had visited Hull House upon arrival and met Miss Addams, who had shown him the large mural paintings on the walls on either side of the Hull House Theater—one, a giant representation of Abraham Lincoln on a flatboat; the other, an extraordinary panorama of Leo Tolstoy wearing a smock and helping the peasants with their harvest in Russia.

Miss Addams had visited Leo Tolstoy at his Russian farm in the 1880's. He was one of the men who, like Lincoln, had profoundly influenced her thinking.

Ilya and I both did some minor writing about the gypsies for the local press. Eventually he made his way in the world as a photographer, explorer, scientist and producer of natural history films.

Several years after our first meeting I was in Chicago during the performance of the Miracle Play starring Lady Diana Manners and Iris Tree, and Ilya invited me to come along with them to spend an evening after the show visiting the gypsies. Together he and I organized a cleanup in the most attractive encampment and bought red wine for the occasion. Then, armed with some gold pieces, we escorted the ladies to our gypsy party. They were already friends of Augustus John, who in England had taught them some of the gypsy songs of his native Wales, so that the entertainment was not entirely unexpected.

Ilya not only joined in the dances with the gypsy men, but also gave an impromptu demonstration of an old Russian game which one of his relatives used to play. He left the room and then had himself borne in on a plank by several gypsies impersonating pallbearers. He was wrapped in a blanket, feigning death. As the troupe played their fiddles and sang their songs, he gradually stirred, then sat up; and finally he leaped to life in a startling and strenuous Russian gypsy dance. The effect was as dramatic as a genuine resurrection. Accompanying us on this evening was a shy, slight stranger in a tight overcoat and a bowler hat, who was never properly introduced to me.

Some thirty years later in New York when I stopped at Ilya's apartment for a drink on the way to a dinner party, he said that Noel with whom he was dining later, often asked about me.

"Noel who?" I inquired.

"Don't you remember how Noel Coward went with us to the gypsy party in Chicago long ago?"

I hadn't realized until that moment that our shy friend had been Noel Coward. He had been playing in Chicago in

"Charlot's Review," which I had seen, but I did not recognize him.

As I moved among the university and literary circles in Chicago everyone seemed to envy me my coign of vantage. I was aware of the strategic opportunities which I enjoyed for observing life and thought, including colorful personalities, but at first it didn't occur to me that many people would really want to travel to a home in the slums with several known gangsters as neighbors for the privilege of associating with Miss Addams and her circle.

Despite the noisy and dirty ordeal of Chicago's growth, it was emerging as an elementally important city of great beauty, unique character and dynamic energy. Its skyscrapers were the first high-rise office buildings in America. Its parks and lake front were as splendid as anything of the kind in the country. The Art Institute and the Field Museum of Science and Industry attracted visitors from everywhere. The Opera and the Symphony were supported by a white-tie group of civic leaders and attended to capacity by all sorts of plain people.

Yet, somehow around the middle of the 1920's, the Chicago literary group began moving east to New York or west to Hollywood. The city was a tremendous printing center, but not really a publishing center. Most of the famous reporters of the *Chicago Evening News,* who had produced a burst of overseas journalism unmatched even by the *Baltimore Sun,* were gone. Why the city could not hold its metropolitan appeal to creative writers and artists was something of a mystery to me.

I could not explain at the time why I, too, felt that the time had come to plant my flag in Manhattan. It was not much of a banner, to be sure, simply a figurative and invisible talisman that drew me to the heartland of the career on which I was determined—to become an editor and publisher, to discover and deploy talent in print.

I had learned in Chicago that I knew as much about the workaday world of books and magazines as many of my teachers and elders, and that the only way to fulfill my private dream was to take a chance where the competition was fierce and the sanctuary of a sheltered life, so far as I knew, was nil. I would be within occasional weekends of Maryland, too, for the healing experience of country life.

I went to New York by way of Hollow Rock Farm, and then to Europe, stopping off in Manhattan only long enough to find a literary agent—O. K. Liveright, brother of Horace Liveright the publisher—to find a little apartment that would be available in six months and, easiest of all, to land a job as an editor at the Butterick Publishing Company.

I then visited Wales to attend some of George Stapledon's lectures on grass at Aberystwyth. I had heard from friends at Cornell that he was the rising man in new concepts of grass for pasturage and forage crops including new species that were drought resistant and capable of providing a longer grazing season. I also took the opportunity to study something of the habits of the gypsies in Wales traveling highways described by George Borrow nearly a century before in his classic, *Wild Wales*.

I then visited Oxford as a guest of David Cecil at Wadham College where he was just about finished with his biography of Cowper, *The Stricken Deer*, which eventually won the Hawthornden Prize. Through introductions from Sylvester Gates I met a number of people in government, business, the press and the arts.

I proceeded to Paris, where I had never before been, and worked for a while at the old *Paris Times*, under the tyrannical supervision of H. Gaston Archambault. The newspaper maintained no genuine news reporters. We derived most of our news from the *Petit Journal* with which I suppose there was an arrangement for translation and adaptation. The franc had dropped and Paris was swarming with Americans living at bargain rates, many of them the literary exiles of the period.

The principal rendezvous for many of us was Sylvia Beach's Shakespeare & Co. bookshop. I was, unfortunately, not among those who frequented the salon of Gertrude Stein. My position was almost entirely that of a poor man on the Grand Tour. Archambault liked my style and selection of items for the paper but was rightly mistrustful of my knowledge of the subjunctive mood in French. I did a little writing and returned to New York with just enough money left for the cab driver. I quickly drew my savings account in Maryland and reported at Spring and MacDougal streets. I was welcomed by Henry Blackman Sell, general editor and assistant to the chairman of the *Delineator,* and my employment was confirmed. We shared many things in common—a love of Chicago, of gypsies, of printer's ink, of good food and drink, of stimulating conversation and of hard work. Our tastes differed on only one fundamental issue: He was a committed man of the City and I was still a Countryman in Town.

Chapter III

A VOICE IN THE CITY

A man is a bundle of relations, a knot of roots, whose flower and
fruitage is the world.

—Ralph Waldo Emerson

How it came to pass that Warren G. Harding, Calvin Coolidge and Herbert Hoover presided over and symbolized our
American destiny in the Jazz Age—a hypocritical era of false
values, outward repression and inner tension, prohibition of
alcoholic beverages and rampant stock market gambling—is
a paradox that has been variously interpreted by social historians. That corrupt decade, and not the Depression decade
which followed, almost demonstrated the perishability of our
culture.

Our country was ruled at the top by apparently well-meaning but bland, pompous, myopic, totally materialistic and
easily duped advocates of conformity. Their pseudo-respect-
ability was fronted by unwitting minions who might well
have worn the steeple-crowned hats that Rollin Kirby drew
in his *New York World* cartoons to symbolize the synthetic
neo-Puritans of the age.

The bottom of society was much more on the go—none
knew whither, except that all were in revolt against a system
that concealed its vices behind a deceptive mask of old-
fashioned rustic virtue. The new ferment among poets, art-

ists, speculators and clowns, gangsters and reformers, radicals and students presaged the not long to be delayed death of the nineteenth century.

It was little wonder, I reflected during my first week in the city, that the Bohemians, the openly pro-Soviet Marxists, the urban radicals and parasitic gangsters were equally contemptuous of rural folk and provincial values. Even the radicals were too self-centered, for the most part, to want to try to discover or respect the heritage of three centuries of pastoral life in the shaping of a nation, its language, its values, its law and culture.

While the Anglo-Saxon upper crust of New York erected an exclusive economic and social oligarchy, the also-rans were relegated to a caste apart—the masses. The Communists identified themselves with the masses; so did the hucksters and marketers of periodical and tabloid circulation, of movies, of stocks and bonds, and of most of the products that were mass-produced and widely, often misleadingly, advertised.

Sensationalism was substituted for mind and heart by Jimmy Walker, Bruce Barton, Bernarr Macfadden, Louis B. Mayer, Captain Billy Fawcett and all their pandering company from Hollywood to Wall Street. I was happily endowed with just enough common sense to be myself—a countryman in the big city.

I sensed that New York was somehow not yet really a city but a caravansary, heartless, corrupt, and, as a community, unreal as a carnival. Behind the glittering Manhattan façade were millions of simple folks, accommodating themselves to new lives in neighborhoods in The Bronx, Brooklyn, Queens and Harlem. These ordinary workaday folks were in limbo, unseen and unsung, pumped back and forth in the subway like living sludge. New York, unlike Chicago, was not a Big Home Town to the stranger.

I had found a small furnished apartment in Greenwich

Village from which I could walk to work and to which I could bring friends occasionally for lunch or for bootleg cocktails at the end of the day. I hung a few Maryland hams and bacons from the kitchen ceiling to advertise the fact that privileged friends could expect a Sunday morning breakfast, country style, from the gleaming and well-laden sideboard on special occasions after strenuous Saturday afternoons of sport and Saturday nights of touring the speakeasies. The five-and-a-half- or full six-day week was usual. The long weekend and the long holiday existed only for the affluent few.

In the little restaurants and cafes of Greenwich Village near the Butterick Building, we drank our wine in early speakeasy style from tea cups. But a little farther north, at the old Brevoort, we carried our own alcoholic beverages and bought "setups"—ice and soda water—in lieu of a corkage fee at an exorbitant price. Even the amenities of dining well were driven underground behind peepholes in phony "clubs."

The Butterick Company had been founded by Ebenezer Butterick, inventor of the paper dress patterns around which several magazines and quarterlies had been developed to promote the new home-sewn fashions, eventually functioning as general magazines for a female audience. Most of the magazines except the wood pulps, printed on the equivalent of newsprint, were dependent upon advertising.

The Butterick Company also published *Everybody's,* once a lusty, muckraking organ; *Romance; Adventure;* and several trade papers in the grocery, hardware and drug fields. As an associate editor I dealt with fiction at *Adventure* and with non-fiction at *Delineator.* Butterick literary standards under Henry Sell's purview were high. So were the standards applied to the editorial promotion of the niceties of the domestic arts—cooking, decoration and architectural design.

Dreiser had been a Butterick editor. So had Sinclair Lewis. Dreiser visited the offices from time to time, a huge, shambling, lonely figure who obviously strove to cast a shadow as poisonous as that of a beech tree upon the new saplings at the old desks. He was truculent when deriding the sex prowess and brain power of the new generation. Sinclair Lewis came occasionally to inquire about the addresses of old friends or his old ideas that might be in the files—until we published a divorce-theme novel, *Half a Loaf,* by his ex-wife, Grace Hegger Lewis.

The guiding corporate spirits of the Butterick were Joseph Moore and Stanley Latshaw, chairman and president respectively, who mingled freely with the editors, advertising staff and circulation staff when not in conference or at frequent committee and board meetings. They steered the enterprise with a light rein, giving exceptional leeway to Henry Blackman Sell who had employed me on the basis of a ten-minute interview and a quick checkup with several of my friends on the staff. A chit to the ubiquitous Mr. Evans, amiable secretary of the company and acting personnel manager, and within twenty-four hours I was reading manuscripts, negotiating with authors and agents and keeping a secretary overworked.

Like many Hoosiers whom I have known—Elmer Davis and Paul V. McNutt, for example—Henry Sell was prematurely gray and distinguished in appearance. He had started out in journalism with Roy Howard in Indianapolis, found his way to Chicago, where he invented the weekly book page of the *Chicago Evening News.* His formula there had been very simple. If financial houses would run advertisements on the financial pages, certainly publishers and book shops would advertise in the *News* if there were appropriate pages dedicated to literature to attract the attention of natural customers. I had never met him in Chicago, but we were aware of each other, despite the difference in our ages, so that I was not a suspect outsider.

Henry had come to New York at the invitation of William Randolph Hearst to edit *Harper's Bazaar,* and had instantly made a conspicuous mark on the sophisticated circles of high style by his eclectic curiosity and driving ambition to make known all that was good, new and interesting. For example, he had discovered "bleed" illustrations in postwar German magazines and had introduced the "bled" photograph in the United States over the technical opposition of the printers who insisted that it was impossible for the grippers to make room for printing plates that covered all four margins of a page. He had moved on to the *Delineator* with a franchise to make it the best and smartest of the magazines catering to women readers in the vast new urban and suburban communities.

His only concession to the farm and village was the regular publication of the homely aphorisms of Ann Bachelder, a kind of prose Grandma Moses, with a remarkable talent for combining the latest fashions in clothes and cookery with a touch of nostalgia for the warmhearted, intimate and cheery texture of the past. Henry and I became fast friends—as, indeed, we still are—and I was bitterly disappointed when he ultimately moved on to take control of an advertising agency, leaving his protégés at Butterick to their own devices. We soon discovered that he had been the actual bridge between the creative and business departments at Butterick.

The period for me was one of constant editorial concern with the excitement of the creative process—in daily touch with significant writers, artists, poets and the new architects and planners. We worked in an almost detached milieu from the America of Coolidge and Hoover. We were never complacent, never content, constantly aspiring to lure the latest and best (even shocking) writers into our pages. We succeeded beyond expectation in maintaining vast circulation for the periodicals, even when the advertising began to slip because of the unforseen effect of competition from the upstart radio and other media such as *Time, The New Yorker* and the burgeoning women's pages of the newspapers.

The old Butterick Building was reconditioned. It had to be, for the ancient presses on the lower floors had almost shaken the fourteen-story structure to pieces. Mr. Moore arranged for the printing to go to Cuneo. The composition was done in Cuneo's Philadelphia plant, but the actual printing was done in Chicago.

It was a lucky break to volunteer for the monthly chore, which most people tried to avoid, of going to Chicago to put the journals to bed. The magic quality of life with a roundtrip ticket on the Twentieth Century Limited, mingling with the film stars and tycoons who used the nation's most famous deluxe train, was to me more than sufficient extra compensation to atone for my modest pay. When it was my turn to go to Chicago, I would sometimes encourage local poets to let me have at least a few sonnets on speculation to insert and accept if there was blank space not filled at the last moment by advertising or by internal promotion copy. I became known as a soft touch for characters such as Harry Kemp who under several pseudonyms would hand me a sheaf of verses in the hope that he would achieve publication and a fifteen or twenty-five dollar check if he was lucky enough to plug a hole with a lyric "filler."

The literary life of the city circled around Horace Liveright and his group of young authors and editors; Condé Nast and Frank Crowinshield and their sophisticated group of writers and artists; George Doran; *The New York World; The New Yorker;* the *New Republic;* the *Saturday Review* and, most visibly, around John Farrar and his friends at the *Bookman.* John Farrar was for a period the whirling dervish catalyst of the literary profession and publishing industry; he was a "stringer" for the new *Time* magazine's book review department, a poet and lecturer, and appeared with apparent simultaneity at all places where writers foregathered. Like the dervishes whose toes were pivoted on a center pin for their circular dance, John Farrar's digit was figuratively fixed to the editorial blue pencil around which he spun with grace and fervor. *The New Yorker* group were usually to be found at the Algonquin for lunch, where they merged into the solvent Bohemia of that hotel's congregation of film stars, agents, critics and playwrights.

Many of us met new creative friends, too, in the cozy fellowship of the small and sometimes elegant speakeasies located in every neighborhood but mainly in Greenwich Village, in the midtown area now occupied by Rockefeller Center and in the Tavern on Irving Place frequented by Ernest Boyd and his stimulating coterie.

The pace of editorial life placed a tremendous strain upon those of us who were trying to keep up with the speculative prosperity of our friends in Wall Street.

I frequently visited the farm in the Maryland Red Lands to reassure myself that the metropolis which I had chosen was not totally a nightmare universe of the damned that would blot out all love of trees, water, animals, stars and intimate human community.

Occasional trips abroad gave me an ominous feeling that all was not well. Europe, especially England and Germany, were sick.

One really had to consort with friends at the *New Republic* or at the *Survey Graphic* to know for certain that the stimulating aspects of our professional lives in New York in the twenties were a kind of escape from serious responsibilities of the day, and that economically and culturally the nation was in peril. In 1926 the *Survey Graphic* was occupied with the planning of special publishing projects dealing with the new Negro in the new Harlem; with an analysis of Fascism—probably the first responsible examination of Mussolini's meaning for Europe and the world; with giant power and water studies to keep pace with madly unplanned urban and industrial growth; with social legislation for workers and the unemployed—leading with an incredible gift of prophecy to a very important blueprint of the Social Security Act of 1934. This project was published in April, 1929, six months before the stock market crash.

In the countryside, and especially in my native Maryland, the farmers had not shared in the prosperity of the boom. Only the most enterprising and scientific farmers earned a decent living without mining the land, without taking more than they replaced from soil, buildings and machinery.

The group at *The New Yorker,* most of whom had been educated at Cornell or who had served as county agricultural agents, were not personally taken in by the magazine's advertising slogan that it was "not for the old lady from Dubuque."

The New Yorker was run like a deluxe country weekly. Harold Ross acknowledged to me that the cartoons were an innovation derived from *Punch* rather than from *Judge* and *Life* (pre-Luce), with Rea Irvin's and Peter Arno's inspired insistence upon the one-line caption instead of dialogue to make the point. Years later I introduced Ross to Peter Agnew, the *Punch* proprietor from London, and Harold reiterated to Peter Agnew his debt to *Punch*. He hated, but tolerated, the book reviews; otherwise it was a remarkably slick smalltown paper with a wry conscience that might have derived from any capricious country editor in the hinterland.

Ross had discovered the empathy of clique editing on the *Stars and Stripes* in the American Expeditionary Force in Europe during World War I—with FPA, Heywood Broun,

Alexander Woollcott, Robert Benchley and Bob Sherwood. He had tried to re-create a civilian echo of it at Butterick after the war with a periodical called *The Home Sector*. This venture was happily killed by the great typographical strike that briefly crippled even strong magazines at the end of the war. Unfortunately, *The Home Sector* files were hauled away to the city dump when the Sixth Avenue subway excavations ruptured the storage basement wall of the Butterick Building. I read through a lot of them before the tumbril arrived but was helpless to cope without a pickup truck and a warehouse; so away they went to oblivion.

The quality magazines—except for the few years when *Scribners* serialized S. S. Van Dine's Philo Vance novels—were declining, one by one. *Harpers* and the *Atlantic* survived, but the *Century, Scribners, Forum* and others eventually failed or were transformed into something more popular or prejudiced, and less significant.

For a while *The American Mercury* seriously dominated my generation only because H. L. Mencken had apparently recanted from some of the superficial prejudices inherent in *The Smart Set* which he dropped in 1923. In a note to authors, Mencken and Nathan had emphasized that *The Smart Set* was a magazine of mere cleverness.

Mencken had the shrewdness to emerge into the Jazz Age temporarily more mature and more generally provocative just in time when, at the invitation of Alfred Knopf, he assumed direction of *The American Mercury*. *The Smart Set* had published some excellent stuff, but nothing morally significant. *The American Mercury* attempted, in Mencken's words, to "track down some of the best nonsense available and do execution upon it." The iconoclastic *American Mercury* published various articles by and about Negroes; important scientific articles; some devastating reportage—in addition to creative work by all the leading writers of the time such as Sinclair Lewis, William Faulkner, Edgar Lee Masters, Carl Sandburg, James Weldon Johnson, Eugene O'Neill and some of the finest satire by H. L. Mencken himself.

The *Literary Digest,* a scissors-and-paste publication, declined into oblivion during the period while *Time* magazine, catering to the new literacy and sophistication of the period—even before the launching of *Life* and *Fortune*—rose in influence and circulation. *Time*-style at first was based upon the Homeric hyphenization and compound adjective favored by Britten Hadden. Time, Inc., was a struggling enterprise in an untidy old loft building with cardboard partitions and, in the days before a news and research staff could be afforded, depended upon "stringer" correspondents and heavy reliance upon *The New York Times* and encyclopedias for the background information of their highly colored coverage of current events. As they prospered, they added a number of distinguished journalists to their staff and there was no question that, despite being undercapitalized, their news magazine as well as their later *Life* and *Fortune* projects would thrive. They assumed an atmosphere of omnipotence that was often comic, but they did not fall into the standstill trap of complacency.

Newsweek soon followed, polite and often more authoritative, but it did not get into its full stride until it was merged into the *Washington Post* more than a decade after the end of World War II.

One of the remarkable qualities of the Butterick Company as a publishing organization was the free association between editors of the various magazines, and also the constant and equal partnership during Henry Sell's tenure between the creative staff and top management. We were all engaged in a common venture. There was no snobbery by the Paris-oriented, high-style *Delineator* staff toward the profitable wood-pulp magazines, *Adventure* and *Romance.*

With the possible exception of the old *Black Mask Magazine* of Street and Smith, *Adventure* and *Romance* were the finest commercial nourishing organs for important literary talent. We knew that many authors would eventually escape to the book publishers, unless they were too slick—in which case they would graduate to the popular mediocrity of the formula fiction of *Saturday Evening Post, Colliers* and *Redbook*.

We strove at *Adventure* and *Romance* always to be interesting, literate and respected and to encourage the vigor and independence of American writing. We ran a comprehensive reference operation on sport, the arts, geography and natural history, and financed Gordon MacCreagh's expeditions to Abyssinia and East and Central Africa just as *Delineator* financed some of Osa Johnson's photographic explorations in faraway places. We published better sea stories than Street and Smith's *Sea Stories Magazine* edited by Lawrence Lee, the poet. We serialized nearly all of the early books of Harold Lamb dealing with Oriental conquerors, the Crusades and the rediscovery of the Holy Land. At *Adventure* we published most of the early work of Erle Stanley Gardner, when his heroes were still legally trained Western sheriffs rather than his eventual Perry Mason. We also published most of the work of T. S. Stribling, Sabatini and a great deal of non-fiction dealing with the Old West, the sea, exploration and World War I.

At *Delineator*, the fiction emphasis leaned precariously toward the standard middlebrow writers, but we did serialize Galsworthy, I. A. R. Wylie and Edith Wharton. Once we very foolishly scheduled and started to print the early sections of an Edith Wharton novel, *Hudson River Bracketed*, before the entire manuscript had been delivered by Mr. Rutgers Bleecker Jewett of Appleton.

To our horror, when the third installment was ready for

the press, we learned that Mrs. Wharton was ill in France, and possibly never would complete the novel. Henry Sell leapt aboard the *Ile de France* through the last minute assistance of Clay Morgan, who represented the French Line in New York, to intercede with Mrs. Wharton to complete the novel so that it could be serialized in normal installments. He returned a fortnight later in abject despair. Mrs. Wharton had given him only a twenty-minute interview saying, "I cannot push my work beyond the limitations of my old Rhinelander heart." We blew up the illustrations, shortened the installments, and though I do not recall the number of months during which we had to improvise, it seemed to be more than a year before the last pages arrived from Appleton's, who handled all of Mrs. Wharton's rights despite the role of Ann Watkins as titular agent.

Looking back, it is easy to see where women's magazines such as *Delineator* went wrong. Circulation did not decline. But advertising revenue flattened out long before the 1929 crash. *Pictorial Review,* a competitor, was limping along; Crowell's more conventional *Woman's Home Companion* was slowing down in importance. The *Ladies' Home Journal* tried to be folksy and held its stride through the enormous bargaining power of the Curtis Company.

The most devastating competition in the Thirties came from the resurgence of *McCall's* under the editorship of Otis L. Wiese. He was only twenty-one years old when he assumed the $50,000 job. Through his brilliant academic career at the University of Wisconsin, he had become something of a protégé of Glenn Frank, who had become president of that institution after losing his post as editor of the *Century*. Frank gave him his introductions in New York. When young Wiese detected some irregular practices by the editorial department at *McCall's,* he informed the president of the company and got the top job himself. He promptly employed

Henry Dreyfuss, the young designer, to undertake layouts and redesign the magazine. He recruited the major journalists covering foreign and domestic affairs as regular contributors, and lifted *McCall's* from an also-ran to a runaway.

Good Housekeeping occupied a special position in the competition due to the high regard in which it was held by its readers because of its unswerving and incorruptible concern with the consumer, reflected by the Good Housekeeping Seal of Approval and the medical and educational authorities whom it employed at a time when we at Butterick were too much concerned with the garniture and festoonery of life, not enough with the basic facts of family, education and community problems.

After Henry Sell left *Delineator* to make a new career in advertising—he gave the cachet and exploitation motif to the development of Elizabeth Arden's cosmetics—the heart seemed to go from the enterprise except for the certain taste and indefatigable energy of Eleanor Carroll. She had gained her first experience under the tutelage of the editorial group of the old *New York Post* and never deviated from her built-in publishing integrity.

Butterick took the first cigarette ad in a woman's magazine —Chesterfield—imagining that the heavens would fall. All they received was a handful of critical letters.

I favored the ad, but was worried by the mild reaction. It was not, I said, a sign of blasé tolerance but of indifference to the magazine as a genuine arbiter of feminine taste. Without Henry Sell's spirit the magazine lost its meaning and purpose, and soon became just another magazine.

Meanwhile, *Adventure* and *Romance* flourished largely because they were honestly intended to entertain and, in doing so, to maintain standards of style and quality. One of the secrets of these wood-pulps was the curious group of editors, the *Adventure* boys, of which I was a marginal member. They included Lawrence Jordan, who edited "The Pamphlet Poets" for John Day; Myles Tierney, an expert on Joyce and Irish Literature; Anthony Rudd, a protégé of Burton Rascoe and an alumnus of the Doubleday magazine department at Garden City; and for several years Geoffrey Hellman, who immediately after graduation from Yale reviewed books for the *New Republic*. He began covering tennis and then all racquet games for *The New Yorker* when Harold Ross became weary of John R. Tunis, and eventually Geoffrey went to *The New Yorker* and achieved a notable record as a writer and reporter.

There were others—Albert Proctor, Bill Corcoran, Henry LaCrosset and the talented Max Wilkinson. The *esprit* was dominated by devotion to the discovery, development and promotion of authors. The editors were as enterprising as a pack of fox terriers, those keen stubby-tailed dogs which handle the pursuit of quarry in terrain beyond the competence of foxhounds.

It became obvious around New York that, paradoxically, the wood-pulp group was generally more respected in literary and in social circles than the second wave of smooth opportunists at *Delineator,* and that the Butterick Company as an enterprise was ultimately going to slip downward. No one mentioned this apprehension except in the most intimate top management circles, but I began to seek other outlets for my energy—and by the time of the crash in 1929, I must have had more than a dozen well-paid sideline jobs writing advertising copy, book reviews and interviews for film magazines, besides various reportage for the serious periodicals.

Max Wilkinson was the first to leave—to become fiction editor at *Colliers* and later to serve as right-hand man to Sam Goldwyn in Hollywood before becoming a literary agent. His loss was irreparable.

The year 1928 was the year of maturity not only for myself

but for many of my friends who were deeply troubled about the future of American society as viewed from the summit of the Jazz Age. Perhaps the reflection of the most agonizing political dilemma in my life, and therefore especially revealing, was the choice offered as Presidential candidates—Al Smith and Herbert Hoover. Neither of them seemed to me to be endowed with the vision to see beyond the false values in the cities and the decline of so many stalwart virtues that one wanted to associate with a continuous culture.

To me it was a deeply personal privilege to vote for Franklin D. Roosevelt for governor of New York. He was a man who, oblivious of his crippling polio, symbolized the seriousness of purpose and the long view of a man at home alike in town and country and on the sea; a man with concern for people in terms of human values; a conscious conservationist of natural resources. He was witty about the present; grimly determined about the future. I listened attentatively to speeches by Hoover and Smith.

When I finally entered the election booth, I voted for Norman Thomas. I was opposed to socialism although not frightened by a greater degree of essential socialization, and could not help but admire the integrity, courage and spirit of Thomas in contrast to the crudity of Smith and the mechanistic sterility of Hoover. It went against the grain to cast a protest vote, but I have never regretted the decision. The time had come, I thought, to redress the wrongs of ten years of complacent and ineffectual national government.

Much as I approved of Al Smith's campaign against Prohibition, I had never been persuaded that he was a great governor. His later manifestations of churlish bad sportsmanship and reactionary tendencies confirmed my first impressions of him. What the country needed in 1928 was neither a clown nor an engineer, but a gentleman capable of evoking the aspirations of all the people, not through selfish popu-

D

lism but through dedicated, educated, intelligent, idealistic, forward vision.

Thomas was defeated for President, but we at least achieved the election of FDR as the governor of New York. In due course, Mr. Roosevelt took the measure of Jimmy Walker and then set the course through perilous times for the future.

Lest I sound disgruntled to the modern reader, I must repeat that although the latter half of the 1920's has been romanticized by some historians, actually it was a time of productive work and rich fulfillment for very few. Paper profits were to prove ephemeral. I eschewed the stock market, kept my modest savings in solid banks, and strove manfully to accumulate capital in my head, i.e. the development of firsthand knowledge of the world to the extent possible, and the cultivation of wiser and more experienced scholars, writers, businessmen, bankers, lawyers, farmers and statesmen.

On visits to Paris and London I contrived to meet H. G. Wells, Bernard Shaw and the editors of economic, literary and critical journals. In Paris I became better acquainted with Eugene Jolas, editor of *transition,* Sylvia Beach and Edward Titus. I felt it important to keep in touch with agriculture overseas, and spent several days at Aberystwyth in Wales observing more closely than during my first visit the extraordinary pioneering that Sir George Stapledon had undertaken, to the point where a few years later I was pioneering with the new grasses in Carroll County, Maryland.

In Washington I frequented the Department of Agriculture and the shabby corridors of the Agricultural Extension Service and began to become skeptical of the indispensability of such tillage crops as maize for grain or silage in the feeding of cattle and swine. I moved from timothy, the standard forage crop for horses, toward alfalfa and orchard grass for the Horseless Age which was dedicated to providing fluid milk for the Baltimore market.

This led inevitably, even while my father was on the farm, to specialization in Holstein-Friesian breeding to take advantage of the high volume of production and the declining prices for butter-fat as vegetable fat came into greater use throughout the country. As a dairyman, I was called a traitor for espousing the margarine lobby.

I was increasingly alarmed by the color of the water in the Monocacy River, which, before World War I, had been clear with only a tinge of brown from the tannic acid in the oak leaves along the shore and tributaries at the foot of the Blue Ridge. Overcultivation of the hill farms upstream meant a muddy river, faster run-off and less sustained flow in time of summer heat and drought.

It was considered something of an affectation for a city dweller to become so grimly concerned with the health of the soil and the scientific rotation of crops on contour, but eventually during the Depression the unit costs of milk, pigs and poultry at Hollow Rock Farm were low enough to make a profit at distress prices for all produce and still allow for generous application of lime, superphosphate and other supplementary fertilizers.

Perhaps my motivation was not altogether economic—perhaps equally aesthetic. To me there has never been anything more depressing, including a city slum, than a run-down farm with buildings and machinery in disrepair and nondescript rat-tailed livestock standing listlessly without attention from pitiably poor and baffled human failures.

Traveling back and forth between New York and Maryland, I came to know most of the train crews, the deteriorating menus in the dining cars of the Pennsylvania Railroad and the condition of the countryside across New Jersey, Pennsylvania, Delaware and Maryland. I was not displeased by the trend of New Yorkers to acquire and rehabilitate country estates on Maryland's Eastern Shore or in the grassy fox-hunting country of Harford, Baltimore and Howard Counties. The hunting fraternity preserved the amenities of rural life and added greatly to the vigor and classless merriment of the outdoors. For the most part, they were nonintellectuals but very respectful of good architecture, fine furniture, well-cooked food and home-grown flowers. Many a rescued mansion and meadow survived in pristine beauty due to the sportsman who would rather ride a horse than dance the Charleston and rather squat in a duck blind than in a smoky nightclub.

When I did return to New York after frequent short sojourns in Maryland, I was sometimes regarded by my literary friends as an escapist. To correct the impression, I would cut a swath through the speakeasies and nightclubs, go to all of the literary cocktail parties to which I was invited and endeavor to stand firm to my personal standards by attacking the doltish and bourgeois game of golf that was creating new patterns of cultish and uncreative leisure in every suburb.

As a young bachelor in the twenties, it was inevitable that in addition to associating with close friends in the city, in the suburbs of Long Island and Westchester County and elsewhere I should be drafted as an extra man at dinner parties, weekends and Sunday luncheon parties given by an older generation. The suburban visits, in the days before the tunnels and bridges across the Hudson, almost isolated many from New Jersey due to the congestion and delays on the ferries across the river. Westchester and Long Island were easily reached by bridges and main thoroughfares although none of the parkways was then developed except the Bronx River Parkway as far as Kensico Reservoir.

When I went farther up the Hudson, beyond Poughkeepsie, to visit friends who hunted hounds, I would usually leave

New York around three-thirty in the morning and plod my way in a Model "T" Ford up the Albany Post Road or Route 22. When visiting Long Island, I eventually learned to take the train and be met at the other end rather than attempt the journey by motor even to areas now comparatively easy to reach on the North Shore.

To avoid too many such expeditions, I found myself accepting a lot of odd invitations in the city largely out of curiosity. For a while I frequently visited the Riverside Drive apartment of Konrad Bercovici, who always entertained a remarkable group of characters. It was at his apartment that I first met Paul Robeson, a gentle giant, still free of the eventual radical reaction to the treatment of the Negro which soured him on the entire American system. He chose to disdain the patience of the reformer and to identify himself with the Revolution.

I also went to Harlem, occasionally, to the nightclubs there which attracted downtown patrons from midnight onward. There one met the new and the old, Negro intellectuals and their white friends. On one occasion I fell into a dialogue with Carl Van Vechten, who was astonished to discover that in Paris I had stayed in the Hotel de la Place de l'Odéon which had gained a kind of fame, unknown to me at the time, as the Left Bank domicile of Peter Whiffle, the hero of Van Vechten's celebrated though not widely read novel of the period.

With Otto Liveright I sometimes visited Jerome Kern on the Yonkers side of Bronxville and admired his rare book and manuscript collection. The widely creative young set of the period seemed to gravitate toward Woodstock, partly because it was a beautifully rustic haven of artists and partly, I suspect, because it was in the heart of the applejack country. In those simpler days one could hardly go anywhere without encountering academic figures from Columbia, a much more uncommon experience today except in such clubs as the Century.

When I was in Chicago I had met Professor Irving Brown, then teaching at the University of Wisconsin, who was not only an outstanding scholar in the field of Romance Languages but America's leading authority on the gypsies. He had written four notable books on gypsy life, music and dances, and was the earliest interpreter of Flamenco songs and dances in this country. Before Wisconsin, he had taught at the University of Cincinnati for a while, and it was at his apartment on Morningside Heights that I met a former Cincinnati student of his, Hildegarde Fillmore, one of the editors of *McCall's*. In a matter of less than a year we were married—an association that lasted until 1949.

As a professional woman, Hildegarde Fillmore was modern in outlook, and devoted to her career to such an extent that she and I were on separate editorial trips as frequently as we were at home. We first moved to Bronxville and subsequently to a remodeled farmhouse near Yorktown Heights, commuting from Harmon or Peekskill depending upon the trains and the weather.

A generation ago upper Westchester County was unspoiled country, much of it held in large tracts, ideal for shooting, riding and all the countryside diversions. We were near enough to Garrison to enjoy the company of the urbane aristocracy of that remarkably intelligent community, which was dominated by the Osborn family and other residents who maintained hospitable large houses. We managed with a small *pied-à-terre* in Manhattan, usually subletting during the winter months from someone going south for the season in Florida. Otis Wiese subsequently bought French Hill Farm at Yorktown Heights and other friends settled in the area, developing within a decade a most harmonious group of people in the arts and letters, business and finance, and the stage.

Crosby Gaige maintained his farm nearby in high style with a deluxe separate studio for his private printing press, and his paper making, typesetting and culinary experiments. Each individual family of our group seemed to have a separate circle of friends, in addition to the local group, so that we never developed the inbred togetherness of such distant sanctuaries as New Hope in Bucks County, Pennsylvania, or Westport, Redding and the western area of Connecticut.

The commutation down the Hudson was pleasant and in good company. Some of my happiest memories are of the homeward journey up the river in the summer, with a refreshing sense of trees, water, horses and dogs, to greet the homing evening exiles from the city. It seems incredible, but in the decade after 1928, despite the depression, we all managed to find willing domestic staffs—cooks, maids, gardeners and, as time ran on, butlers and chauffeurs—who were proudly interested in maintaining a hospitable home.

It was never difficult to find hotel accommodations in New York without notice if one decided to stay in town for a night or two. Many of us kept a spare wardrobe including evening dress—black tie and white tie—in New York.

I found the country an ideal place for extra work, writing for a dozen magazines under a dozen different names, reviewing books for *College Humor,* often writing advertising and radio copy for the new medium that was eroding the magazine advertising citadel which was my primary professional home—the Butterick Company.

Throughout 1927 and 1928—through the grim national sacrifice of the Sacco-Vanzetti execution; the heroic urge which Lindbergh's flight to Paris fulfilled; through Peaches Browning and the Hall Mills murder, and the inevitable crash of the phony prosperity of the decade—I saw a good deal of the *Survey Graphic* people. I was most impressed by their prophetic concern with the materialist and sensational spree of the period.

At last, it came—the stock market crash and the disappearance of unrealized paper profits which so many had counted as real. The debacle justified the foreboding of a grim few of which I had been a beardless Jeremiah, and made me very unpopular for a while because of my reiterated, "I told you so."

In Maryland, which I visited more frequently at this time, the stock market crash and the depression which followed were not quite as severe as in the cities and the heavy industrial districts of steel and coal and automobiles.

There is now no need to recount what happened or even to try to analyze all of the reasons. The phenomenon has been well covered by experts. From 1929 until 1934, when I left the Butterick Company to write my biography of Francis Scott Key with many other writing assignments on the side, I personally suffered from no economic penalty or sacrifice; nevertheless, I was, if anything, as moved by events as if I myself had been struck down in mid-career. The wastage and agony of frightened humanity was appalling, and the gradual disappearance of people's jobs and savings with the final indignity of the bank failures and ultimate bank closings is an experience that I don't believe another generation of Americans will ever have to endure. I simply worked hard on local matters and campaigned for Franklin D. Roosevelt for President in 1932 and 1936. The panderers to the lowest common denominator of escapism were still publishing confession magazines and selling them to bewildered daydreaming women and to some men.

In Europe, Hitler and Mussolini came into visible power, and few seemed to believe the inspired journalism of the ex-isolationist American foreign correspondents who, in their hostility to a sick Europe, had predicted Fascism and Nazism as an evil equivalent to the Soviet tyranny and ruthless liquidation of independent spirits. I knew and admired nearly all of the foreign correspondents at that time—from Dorothy Thompson, Jay Allen, Raymond Gram Swing, Louis Fischer to the younger and more radical group, some of whom seemed to be turning toward the Communists in their frustration.

I was happily preoccupied with finishing my biography of Francis Scott Key which was published by Farrar and Rinehart in 1935. It brought me an invitation to the White House and a certain amount of fanfare throughout Maryland, including the beautiful and stuffy capital city of Annapolis, where Key had been married, where his brother-in-law, Roger Brooke Taney, had practiced law and where beautiful old St. John's College, in the days before Stringfellow Barr and Scott Buchanan, was run by an ex-Federal Prohibition Administrator.

After doing a bit of writing for the new *Esquire* magazine and for *The New Yorker,* I resolved to move to a platform more congenially adapted to my philosophy. By happy accident on Decoration Day, 1935, Paul Kellogg telephoned to ask me to join him at Survey Associates.

D*

Chapter IV

A BRIGHT OASIS IN THE DISMAL
SOCIAL SCIENCES

————⦿————

While this America settles in the mould of its vulgarity, heavily
thickening to empire,
    And protest, only a bubble in the molten mass, pops and sighs
out, and the mass hardens . . .
                                —from "Shine, Perishing Republic"
                                      by Robinson Jeffers

IT WAS NOT UNLIKE moving from a sunlit mansion to a small
and smoky cottage to find oneself in the modest offices of
Survey Associates on the top floor of 112 East Nineteenth
Street. The floors were uncarpeted. The offices were small
and meagerly equipped, but the organization was mentally
furnished with magnificence. The only semblance of swank
was a private key to Gramercy Park, an enclosed private garden and greensward open only to those who lived or worked
nearby.

Paul Kellogg, who had founded and built the non-profit
enterprise, shocked all of his veteran staff by inviting me to
serve as managing editor without consultation of those whom
it became my responsibility to direct. He had, however, consulted most of the members of his board so that my appearance had the backing of a wide variety of citizens and scholars
concerned with the study of social trends and the efforts to

ameliorate the conditions of life among the third of the nation that had failed to benefit from American progress and productivity.

He had come from the Dutch district of Michigan, and his face was characteristically Dutch—florid, youthful, although curiously preoccupied in gaze, as if his delft-blue eyes were looking over the tulips to a distant dike that contained his private world. At times he appeared to be composing his conversation rather than articulating spontaneously. He had gone into journalism directly from high school, but there was only one indication of his lack of higher education—a constant dependence upon clichés of the sort that might have been inherited by rote from *McGuffey's Reader*. Despite the sprinkling of clichés, quotations, apothegms and occasional malapropisms in his speech and in his writings, he was a truly brilliant observer and an original thinker. He was a man with a message.

Everything he did was motivated by a desire to improve the lot of mankind. Fundamentally he was not a fighter but a compromiser and had assembled on his board of trustees such contrasting characters as Edward L. Ryerson and Sidney Hillman, Felix Frankfurter and Harold H. Swift, and two lovely ladies who were almost faery queens, Mrs. Henry Goddard Leach and Mrs. August Belmont. The gyroscope for the board was Professor Joseph P. Chamberlain of Columbia, whose wise counsel and practical knowledge kept the enterprise on a semblance of a budget with a plan which combined purposefulness and practicality.

Paul Kellogg was never affiliated directly with Marxists, leftists or Communists, but he liked to give them their say in the pages of the *Survey* and the *Survey Graphic*. His position derived from a conglomeration of the philosophy of Jane Addams, Theodore Roosevelt and the early social researchers of the Russell Sage Foundation. He had an unconcealed admiration for the Russian Revolution as a modern phenomenon, though he was critical of the dictatorial excesses and cruelties. He had, in the fashion of college presidents, a mixed fascination with men of money and men of ideas. Above all, however, he was a patient reformer in the general framework of capitalist development.

Paul, like the Quaker who was once reported to have said that "No money is tainted after I get it," spent a great deal of his time appealing to foundations and individuals to support the general inquiries and investigations of Survey Associates and occasionally to underwrite special projects in the fields of health, education, conservation, labor relations and social work. He had a genius for enlisting the assistance of those industrialists who were likely candidates for investigation. In every instance he seemed to win them over to policies recommended by the editors and their expert advisors.

He was fundamentally an optimist who catered to the best instincts—and the vanity—of powerful interests that might otherwise have slowed down in their progressive social and employment policies. For example, in dealing with the Wage Stabilization Plan of Procter and Gamble, he emerged with a title that was widely quoted: "The payroll that floats." Like Ivory soap! He especially enjoyed challenging the creative philanthropy of the new foundations such as the Rosenwald Fund, the Twentieth Century Fund, the Rockefeller Foundation. When approaching these organizations, he mobilized not only logic and rhetoric but people who could push at strategic points of decision.

There was never, in any sense, a tendency to whitewash or superficially expose deplorable conditions without the beginnings of a solution. His preoccupation with fund raising placed upon me, almost immediately, more responsibility for planning than I had anticipated.

By good chance, I was, in 1935, very well acquainted with

a great many leaders of American life in finance, business, academic circles, the literary professions and the labor move- ment—so that it was a pleasure to demonstrate my knowledge- ability of the world, whether it be in Detroit or Chicago, California or the TVA, Washington or London, Paris or Geneva.

Within a month of my joining the staff of the *Survey* as managing editor, I went to Washington to have a reunion with a number of friends in the New Deal. At a luncheon of some twenty people I was half-sneeringly introduced as hav- ing now become "the hired conscience of capitalism." To the best of my ability I attempted to justify the expression, saying that I was proud of the description. This was in the period of the Black investigation of holding companies, particularly Howard V. Hobson and the AG&E companies. I was hard put to hold my own in a witty but devastating attack by Paul Y. Anderson of the *St. Louis Post-Dispatch*.

Anderson soon afterward wrote for *Survey Graphic* a violent but largely documentary account of AG&E in which he stated that they had "failed." The libelist implication of the piece escaped me when editing the article for the printer. Immediately after it appeared we were threatened by a suit, and on the advice of Morris L. Ernst, had to run a retraction. I learned then and there that no matter what economic de- cline of a company or an individual one wanted to describe, one could not use the word "fail" unless there had actually been conclusive bankruptcy proceedings. This article also proved embarrassing to Federal Judge Julian W. Mack, a member of the board, who at one stage had been involved in federal handling of aspects of AG&E in the courts.

It was an extraordinary training ground in editorial re- sponsibility to work under the tutelage of Paul Kellogg. He soon came to count on me to get our various inquiries and conclusions over the hurdles of research and checking without the risk of unfair, untrue or libelist statements.

We had, of course, many differences of opinion and strove to reconcile them by discussion and debate. For example, Paul Kellogg had covered in a series of articles the great floods in the Mississippi Valley, when Herbert Hoover as Secretary of Commerce had endeavored to substitute earth-moving machinery to strengthen the levees in place of the ineffectual mules and men plodding with scoops that had been traditional in such emergencies, sometimes for local political reasons. He never swerved from his admiration for Hoover, the engineer, and often tried to persuade me that Hoover had anticipated the New Deal in his approach to relief of the cities, especially Detroit, and in the stimulation of RFC loans which would not be repaid and which was the beginning of federal relief to the unemployed.

"Hoover just didn't go fast enough for the size of the job," was Paul Kellogg's feeling. He never converted me on this point. I derived more background for my attitude from Frank Murphy, who served as mayor of Detroit and governor of Michigan before he was named to the United States Supreme Court.

On one great development of the period, however, we were joyfully in agreement: the Tennessee Valley Authority. We published Dr. H. A. Morgan's *Benchmarks in the Tennessee Valley* first as a serial and subsequently as a book. I covered the dedication of Norris Dam and of the subsequent dams and power-generating stations as they were completed with special attention to the related revolution in agriculture, ecology and local industry, and the benefits which transcended even flood control in the creation of an inland fresh water sea in the area from the Clinch River near Knoxville to the Kentucky banks of the Ohio.

In microcosm, Survey Associates reflected the national

division of opinion on NRA and the Blue Eagle. Paul was pro-NRA, but I was much less favorably inclined, except as a distasteful emergency measure. I felt that only one perpetual advantage had been derived from the codified and rigid authority of the National Recovery Act: the almost universal establishment of the five-day week for most white-collar workers in most cities, enabling us to escape to the country for the healthy experience of a proper weekend.

When the NRA was declared unconstitutional by the U. S. Supreme Court, I undertook a hasty survey of the industry which had precipitated the case that reached the Supreme Court. It was the Scheckter case, appealed by a representative of the kosher chicken industry who claimed not to be involved in interstate commerce. Paul was so dashed that he asked an ardent NRA protagonist, Professor Walter Whittlesey of Princeton, to write what proved to be an angry masterpiece of political polemics facetiously entitled "Back to the Confederation!"

The wonderful quality of our association was that there was never any personal acrimony when we differed. We were as cool and polite as advocates in a courtroom as we shaped up the pros and cons of issue after issue. Occasionally, to clear the air, I did emerge with an idea with which no one could possibly quarrel. One such idea was of far-reaching significance. It derived from consultations with DeWitt Wallace of *Reader's Digest*, who had become disenchanted with some of the original material he was developing as an alternative to reliance upon the periodicals and magazines which furnished his primary reprint source material.

In this period, *Reader's Digest* paid generous first-option money to many publications which gave the *Digest* exclusive first chance at such desirable material as "The Talk of the Town" and "Profiles" in *The New Yorker* and the nonfiction of *Harpers,* the *Atlantic* and most of the general periodicals.

Eventually, the *Digest* inspired original articles, some of them not even planned to simulate reprint condensations.

One such series dealt with swindles practiced on the consumer by a wide variety of manufacturers and merchants and service industries—radio repairs, spectacles, automobiles, etc. During the heated ideological hearings in Washington on the consumer movement, which was described by a right wing critic as part of "the transmission belt from Moscow," Richard Berlin of the Hearst magazines became convinced that espousal of the consumer movement, including consumer cooperatives, was inimical to the interests of the general publications whose advertising subsidized their editorial content which was then used and effectively distorted or exploited by *Reader's Digest*.

Berlin, possibly in association with other magazine publishers, threatened to block further use of periodical material by *Reader's Digest* unless they stopped criticism of nationally advertised products. Albert L. Cole, who had recently joined *Reader's Digest* to give it general circulation beyond the mail subscription list, and who has been largely responsible for its astronomical circulation in the years since, prevailed on Wallace to run a broadside attack on the consumer movement.

With his incredible journalistic perspicacity, Wallace realized (soon after publishing this diatribe) that it was not popular to pick on innocent consumers who, after all, were his readers. One day at Pleasantville he was searching for a target without a friend. The man-eating shark was mentioned, but the winner of all ideas was a nearly taboo target, and certainly without friends—venereal disease.

By a series of happy coincidences, we at Survey Associates with our medical editor, Mary Ross, in charge, developed an article by Thomas Parran on leave from the U. S. Public Health Service to the New York State Department of Health and an outspoken crusader for social hygiene. Dr. Parran's wife was a gifted writer with experience in an advertising agency, and it was she who wrote, or edited, her husband's historic article, "Stamp Out Syphilis," which was to appear in *Survey Graphic* and to be picked up simultaneously by *Reader's Digest* as a worthy, if shocking, crusade. To add to the strategy, the article was published at the time when Dr. Parran was slated, with the knowledge of insiders such as ourselves, to succeed Dr. Hugh Cummings as head of the U. S. Public Health Service.

I had been aware of Edward W. Bok's courageous coverage, despite taboos, of venereal disease in the pages of the *Ladies Home Journal* a generation earlier. I had noted in Chicago while at Hull House that Colonel McCormick of the *Chicago Tribune* had not minced words about venereal disease in a valiant newspaper campaign. The Metropolitan Life Insurance Company had been conducting a modest information program, but until the combined effort of Survey Associates and *Reader's Digest,* there had never been a realistic and professional report without all the smugness which had contributed to the increase of venereal disease in the period before wonder drugs were invented.

"Stamp Out Syphilis" was the first illustrated article ever published by *Reader's Digest.* Charts and diagrams were done for me by Rudolph Modley, an American disciple of Otto Neurath, the famous graphic designer of Vienna. At the time of the release of the article, telegrams were sent to all newspaper publishers, radio broadcasters and public health administrators.

One of the responsive recipients who promptly commented on the article was General Hugh Johnson, only recently relieved from his job as director of the defunct NRA. As a writer, and the author of many boys' books, he was an immediate success as a radio broadcaster. His remarks on the article were so personal and so descriptive of venereal disease among the young men he knew in his youth and in the Army that the National Association of Broadcasters had to pass an immediate ruling that the subject of venereal disease could not be discussed on the air except by members of the medical or welfare professions.

The publicity was so great that, for the first time, *Reader's Digest* had to go back to press to fill the demand for copies. If this had been simply a single effort, it might have been dismissed as sensational. We followed up with further articles, some of them written by Dr. R. A. Vonderlehr, which called for premarital examinations and periodic examinations of those likely to be infected. The result was ultimately the adoption by many states of premarital examinations and the establishment in certain areas, particularly the South, of mobile medical units for free examinations and Wasserman tests.

In this entire experience I doubt very much that more than one percent of the readers realized that the *Reader's Digest* articles were reprinted from *Survey Graphic*. We were content to diffuse information through others, since our impeccable authority was the primary factor which enabled the campaign to be effective.

The expansion of public welfare in the early days of the New Deal had given Survey Associates a unique role in reporting developments, through close contact with all of the major social agencies of the nation. We were, by 1935, in frequent and intimate contact with Harry Hopkins, Eleanor Roosevelt and the major welfare executives of the Federal Government. When Thomas Parran became Surgeon General, his agency was still under the jurisdiction of the Treasury, a vestige of the old days when maritime quarantine was, naturally enough, associated with the administration of the customs service.

The directors of the Children's Bureau and of the Women's

Bureau of the Department of Labor were all graduates of Hull House and personal as well as professional friends. I had met most of the top civil servants in the Treasury when doing research for my biography of Francis Scott Key who, as a brother-in-law of Roger Brooke Taney, had brought Taney to President Jackson's attention, and who led the Jackson assault on the Biddle dynasty and the Bank of the United States.

We all knew Frances Perkins, Secretary of Labor; Harold L. Ickes, Secretary of the Interior (a former Chicagoan who frequently came to Hull House during my sojourn there) and many of the young lawyers in the new administration and independent quasi-judicial administrative agencies. I followed with special interest the transition from crop control toward conservation in the Department of Agriculture, and felt at home among all of the old friends conducting these vast experimental schemes.

The rehabilitation of beautiful old, though often small, Georgetown houses kept pace with the addition of sophisticated people to the federal establishment, so I was never at a loss for access, in charming surroundings, to friendly legitimate sources of information on statistics, economic trends and pilot programs. Since my farm in Maryland was only a little more than an hour from Washington, I could easily entertain my contemporary government official friends in the country, and through this propinquity I occupied a strategic publishing advantage.

The White House and its staff of "passionate anonyms," as FDR had dubbed his young men, was a friendly great house, accessible and responsive and to the best of my knowledge never indiscreet on matters that were not suitable for immediate publicity. These friendly connections led inevitably to a new and close liaison with the younger congressmen and senators, all of whom had a very high regard for the integrity and reliability of Survey Associates as an objective medium for the most authoritative coverage of social, cultural, economic and political trends.

Washington did not seem to be as aware of the rising tyrannies in Germany and Italy as we were in New York. The center of gravity of the nation was no longer the Northeast, but an area which, further west and south, was the figurative hub of vast programs in the South, the Dust Bowl of the High Prairies and the irrigation and power plans for the Northwest reflected by Bonneville and Grand Coulee.

Although millions of Negroes had migrated northward toward the cities during World War I and after, the Negroes were still preponderantly rural and southern rather than urban. I was in close touch with Gunnar Myrdal and his remarkable research aide, Ralph Bunche, in those days; and we published many of the preliminary findings of *An American Dilemma* in *Survey Graphic*. Sometimes we worked with subordinate researchers on Ralph Bunche's staff, notable among them George Stoney, a white southern graduate of the University of North Carolina at Chapel Hill, who was often of great assistance to us on research projects involving Negro migration, health, education and social ostracism in the North as well as in the South.

Although I had been, long before, a friend of Walter White of the NAACP, I did not fully appreciate his genius until the height of this ideological period when Communists attempted to infiltrate Negro organizations as they had infiltrated some labor unions and universities. Walter White resisted all influences that would divert him from helping to cope with Negro disadvantages except in ardent and zealous use of the finest American traditions of law, order, persuasion and information. He was only one of many extraordinary Negroes whom I knew well, saw frequently and counted as intimate friends from then on.

One, for example, was Alain L. Locke, professor of philosophy at Howard University, an early and discriminating collector of primitive African art and a fastidious gourmet. He was the third generation of college graduates in his family, and I believe that he was the first Negro Rhodes Scholar when he went on from Harvard to Oxford. Frail, gentle and charming, he frequently advised government, industries and labor unions to speed their consideration of the place of the Negro in American life.

Mayor La Guardia named him to conduct an inquiry into the Harlem riots, and he did so with the stipulation that he would like to publish the essence of his findings in *Survey Graphic*. He took his report to La Guardia at the old Pell Mansion, then the summer home of the Mayor, on the far shores of the Bronx, and telephoned me in the Mayor's presence to say that he had presented his report, had written his briefer article based upon it and could meet me with it in time for lunch—provided I was prepared to celebrate with champagne. I debated in my mind whether to suggest that we meet at the Algonquin which certainly had no anti-Negro policy, but decided suddenly to suggest the Brevoort which at that time still boasted a great cellar, elegant French cuisine and a distinguished luncheon clientele. It was one of the finest and most agreeable luncheon occasions in all my life.

I took him to the office after lunch. We brushed through the article and dispatched it to the composing room, then spent the rest of the afternoon window-shopping in Fifth Avenue. I was keen to demonstrate to Alain that I was not functioning as a publisher to an author but as a friend with a friend. If Locke had not been so delicate and almost effeminate in appearance, he would personally have achieved a tremendous position outside academic circles—but even from his citadel at Howard he had a great qualitative influence on the aspiring students whom he taught, many of whom achieved more highly visible positions in the effort not only to establish equal rights for Negroes but to establish for Negroes the economic, educational and social privileges that would accelerate the obliteration of prejudice. Locke had discovered and publicized the cultural ferment in the new Harlem of the 1920's, but unfortunately, he did not live to celebrate and contribute to the progress of the new Negro emancipation in the 1950's and 1960's. Even his last book, *The Negro in American Culture,* had to be completed for me by his researcher, Margaret Just Butcher.

During the New Deal we covered labor union developments more objectively, I believe, than any other publication in the country. Beulah Amidon of the *Survey* staff maintained an incredible relationship with industrialists and union leaders, members of the Labor Mediation Board and with Louis Stark, labor expert for *The New York Times,* whose advice and writing were often at our disposal. I covered the turbulent earlier years of the United Automobile Workers in Detroit and elsewhere, until the final capitulation of the Ford Motor Company. My visits to Dearborn were exceptionally felicitous because of the circumstance that my brother-in-law, Leroy Manning, had been chief test pilot for Ford in the days of the tri-motor plane, the only man whom Henry Ford would accompany as a passenger. When Manning crashed and was killed on a test flight, Ford immediately decided that he would give up the making of planes and have nothing more to do with supplying the Army with such weapons of destruction as the bombers which were then on the drawing boards.

This was in 1932 when the N. W. Ayer Advertising Agency persuaded Ford to advertise widely for the first time. They stipulated that the company must have an advertising manager and Manning's good friend and mine, Fred Black, was named to the post of advertising and public relations director. He usually offered to put me up in his beautiful house when I visited Detroit, but since I also wanted to see Ford's labor relations lieutenant, Harry Bennett, I did not want to compromise either myself or Black. However, at Dearborn, I had many opportunities to visit with Henry Ford and with Edsel Ford.

On one occasion Henry Ford asked me the time and, discovering that my watch was four minutes slow, volunteered to repair it. It took me a year to recover it from his little workshop, partly due to my hypocritical flattery when in the executives' dining room I told him that I really liked the soybean mush that he had prescribed on the menu that day. I was no longer an independent stranger. Mr. Ford seemed to rely on Harry Bennett more than he ever had on W. J. Cameron, his former editor of the *Dearborn Independent,* who was demoted to a radio functionary on the orchestra program of the "Ford Sunday Evening Hour." It was incredible to me to observe the quiet and countrified atmosphere of the top Ford offices in the Engineering Building with the Old Man—as they called him—occasionally striding unannounced into any of the unwalled but glass enclosed offices.

Once he asked me if I wanted to come on a tour of the plant in his car which he drove himself, up ramps and along the assembly lines and then on to Greenfield Village where he proudly pointed out to me one of his treasured collections of nineteenth-century life—at least a thousand chamber pots that had been purchased at country auctions for ultimate display in the museum.

Mr. Ford was a warm-hearted and likable man, but ignorant and often ruthless. He was flagrantly defiant of theory. He considered himself a scientist, like his applied science friends Burbank and Firestone, and in a strange fashion some of his technology leapt from theory to practicality through channels of thought or instinct known only to himself. I went with Fred Black one Saturday night to the folk dances in Greenfield Village and was horrified by the thought that perhaps the Old Man liked folk dances because he had a captive harem of the wives of young executives to swing round to his heart's content.

It was a strange transition to move on to the basement citadel of Harry Bennett and his squad of goons and spies. When I asked him why my late brother-in-law should have been afraid to subscribe to the *New Republic* when he was still at the Ford Motor Company, and had asked me to send him copies along with other literature first-class, he frankly told me that the periodical literature ordered by top Ford employees was scanned in the post office by his representatives.

I candidly told Bennett on several occasions that I was also interviewing Walter and Victor Reuther and other United Automobile Workers officials while in Detroit, and he assured me that he was aware of the fact. He then recited the entire masthead of *Survey Graphic* as if to let me know that there was not much that escaped him. It was a strange paradox to find the builder of the greatest American enterprise owned by an individual, and perhaps the most admired industrial figure in the entire world, headed for oblivion—only to be bailed out by World War II, which he opposed, and ultimately by the extraordinary respect of his grandson for sophisticated, professional business brains when the war was over and Henry and Edsel Ford were gone. Somehow, I sensed that the UAW people realized all this and that time was on their side, and that nothing on heaven and earth would ever throw the Ford Motor Company into the control of Harry Bennett or alien interests when the founder and his son had passed.

One of the appalling complications of Ford policies was

created by the lay-off during the Depression of employees who lived outside the Dearborn tax jurisdiction where the Ford River Rouge plant and offices were located. Ford was against relief or any sort of dole for the unemployed. He could easily scuttle those responsibilities upon the city of Detroit. He admired big industry, such as his own, but was fearful of big government and high finance, locally or nationally. Harry Bennett reflected his prejudice against the UAW. General Motors and Chrysler were only a little more modern in their concept of employer responsibilities, but they appeared to be more humane because their top management was exposed to frequent contact with bankers in New York, the Du Ponts in Delaware and the Federal Government in Washington.

As in all labor relations of the period, the situation was worsened by the attempt of Communists or Communist sympathizers to seize control of critical unions. The Wagner Labor Act was especially disliked by the automobile and steel industries. We covered the evolution of collective bargaining through a series of *Survey* inquiries in nearly every major industrial area of the country.

We at Survey Associates were deeply disturbed by the Communist activities in the mid-1930's. But in many instances it was impossible to ascertain who the extreme left-wing leaders were. The Spanish Civil War eventually smoked them out because they could not resist taking sides with the Spanish Government after the Fascist and Nazi supporters of Franco, and then the Soviet support of the Republican Government. But before that occurred, the influential Communists were very much under cover. Paradoxically, honest and patriotic Americans who were critical of domestic social conditions were often described and denounced as Reds.

At first, the Spanish Civil War had enlisted the sympathy and support of progressives and liberals on the side of the established Republican Government which Franco was endeavoring to overthrow. There was no question in my mind that, prior to substantial intervention of the Soviets, the Government deserved full support. Certainly no American could conscientiously espouse the Falangist cause. However, by the end of 1936 it became apparent that not only the Government of Spain but the relief organizations attached to it were subservient to their Moscow allies. They were not Communist, but they were too far to the Left for comfort. America and Britain were criticized for nonintervention, but in my opinion they were justifiably aloof from any all-out commitment at the time when opposition to the embryonic Fascist-Nazi Axis demanded full support of the Communist opposition.

Perhaps the Spanish Republican Government and their courageous troops were duped, but on balance that was no reason for the United States to become officially involved in a military showdown, alongside the radical International and Lincoln brigades that were preponderantly pro-Russian rather than limited to support of the Government of Spain. It was primarily the responsibility of the Spanish Republican Government to demonstrate its hold upon Spaniards. The United States, at the time, had a problem in dealing with Communist infiltration of campuses and labor unions, without the awesome commitment that could have swung the country into an ideological cleavage that might have precipitated violent obstruction to the half-finished programs initiated under the New Deal.

The wonder to me was that the most disadvantaged large groups in the country—Negroes, miners, migratory farm workers, and so on—were more sensibly immune to Communist doctrine than the highly paid and organized workers in the cities seemed to be. The rise of Hitler and the anti-Semitic programs in Germany drew a great many Jewish workers into a deeper sympathy with Russia and even with the Communists until the Russian-German Pact of 1939 halted their faith in the USSR. The German-Russian confrontation had been nowhere more dramatically displayed than in the pavilions of the Russians and the Germans at the Paris Exposition of 1937. The American pavilion in Paris had been a pathetic and shabby affair, featuring Rural Resettlement photography of the poorest one-third of the nation and, of all things, a fountain of second-rate California wine. As a footnote to that year, the Spanish Civil War provided a laboratory for the testing of Nazi and Soviet war planes and machinery. America and Britain remained well on the sidelines.

It was my feeling that the Roosevelt Administration, anti-Communist as it was, eventually tended to be more tolerant of Russia because of the idealism that had been reflected in the aims of the Revolution and the feeling that Russia and America were moving into position as the world's dominant powers and would have to learn to live together somehow, no matter how suspicious of one another, in the challenging world of the future. Even the press and foreign correspondents in part reflected something of this attitude, not because they were Marxist or even leftist, but because there seemed to be some hope for Soviet Russia, but not for Nazi Germany.

I was bitterly criticized in the summer of 1937 for sailing to Europe on the old North German Lloyd liner, *Columbus,* and returning on the *Europa* which happened to be the only trans-Atlantic passages that could be booked in a hurry, the vacancies being caused by the boycott of the Germans by many Jewish travelers. Upon my return I reflected on the wisdom of using Nazi-German transport and finally concluded that it had not been an immoral gesture. But I don't believe that Paul Kellogg ever quite forgave me.

By 1938 it was apparent to most of us at Survey Associates

that war was inevitable, but for at least a year we labored under the premise that although isolationism was impossible and indeed suicidal, we should hammer hard in favor of the domestic programs initiated under the New Deal. We made the *Survey Mid-Monthly,* our periodical specializing in social work, the major journal in the field of public welfare under the brilliant direction of Gertude Springer.

In the *Survey Graphic,* a more general periodical devoted to social interpretation, we focused on the unfinished business of the cities, the states and the Federal Government— ranging from fiscal and taxation policies to resource development and decentralization of industry. We covered thoroughly the migration of drought-stricken farmers from the Dust Bowl to California and to other areas on the West Coast. We dealt extensively with water pollution and water and soil conservation. We collided with Wendell Willkie in our studies of rural electrification.

Although I traveled widely, from coast to coast and from Canada to the Gulf, I spent many of my weekends in Maryland, and for the first time felt that I had made a local contribution not only to the prosperity of Hollow Rock Farm but to the welfare of the countryside. The farm programs of the Government, which stimulated conservation practices and mechanization of dairy operations, created a general atmosphere of prosperity under the imaginative and dynamic leadership of the county agricultural agent, Landon Burns, a man who undoubtedly would have gone on to larger tasks if he had not had the good fortune to be married to a local girl and to live in a magnificently remodeled old house on the edge of Westminster. He worked closely not only with the principal commercial farmers of the area but with the schools and with the 4-H Clubs and participated in all of the cultural activities such as the annual Eisteddfod and the formation of a County Symphony Orchestra. He adopted as his students the occasional city families who bought farmsteads as country retreats and assumed the role of part-time farmers. He found herdsmen and machinists for those in need. His home economist staff campaigned for roadside planting and flower gardens in every farmyard. He wooed light industry and avoided further migration of redundant laborers and tenants by providing instructions in new manufacturing processes.

Simultaneously, James M. Shriver, who farmed some three thousand acres, emerged as a financial man of more than local importance, ultimately becoming a Federal Reserve Bank governor of the Richmond District. All of this renaissance of the community and its prosperity were manifest to visitors as well as to local citizens. The era of ghost towns and abandoned tenant houses was at an end. A pack of foxhounds at Westminster added to the autumn and winter amenities of the countryside. Subsequently, Charles Rogers developed the Timber Ridge Bassets which sometimes were followed by a field of eighty or one hundred people, young and old, on foot, mixing town and country folk in a happy atmosphere of social equality.

In the period between the great wars, there were a few very wealthy men who lived multiple lives—in Maryland and Virginia in the seasons of spring steeplechasing, and fall hunting; Newport in the summer; the Scottish moors in August and September; New York in the late autumn and early winter; then Palm Beach; and then all over again. This sort of life, led by some of my very rich friends, with time out for financial and private affairs, is more than I could ever have contemplated fiscally or in terms of limited human energy for self-indulgence. I did, however, manage to create a happy double life, with a few personal trimmings—New York and its nearby pastimes, alternating with Maryland and its handy access to Washington. From time to time, travel—domestic and foreign—provided a bit of embroidery, usually somber in tone because of my preoccupation with the fate of a world bent on turmoil and destruction.

It is almost impossible in retrospect to see how I summoned the vitality on top of exhausting and varied publishing work to rise at dawn and walk puppies before commuting to New York, keep a Westchester garden and grounds flourishing, then dash to Maryland on Friday afternoons on the old Congressional Limited to face the multiple decisions of a modern farmer keeping up with the line breeding of cattle and pigs and the care of soil which ranged from heavy arable loam to light sandy slopes which were sensitive to erosion and unsuitable for ordinary tillage.

My preoccupation with the fertility of Hollow Rock became so obsessive that, blindfolded, I could have analyzed the soil's chemistry and condition by the sound and feel of the ground beneath the hoofs of the horse which I rode over the fields every week. In contrast, the superficial care which I gave to my compact grounds north of New York through the week was, although concentrated, careless of all concern except the appearance of grass, trees and garden.

The impending war, after Munich and the German takeover of Czechoslovakia, made every moment seem more precious and every aspect of the countryside more significant. In the summer of 1939, as if subconsciously impelled to have a farewell view of the United States, I embarked on a leisurely automobile journey to the West Coast and return. Accompanied by Uncle Ray, my mother's brother, I aimed first for a tour of inspection of the Tennessee Valley, then on to New Orleans to explore the remarkable writers' project under the final vestiges of the Works Project Administration in Louisiana. Lyle Saxon, director of the Louisiana Writers' Project and editor of the *Louisiana State Guide,* was ensconced in the old St. Charles Hotel, hospitably sharing his Sazerac cocktails and displaying his collection of early nineteenth-century imported mechanical French toys—dancing figures and tiny animated metal animals from France brought over during the transient prosperity of the cotton days before the Civil War when the *nouveau riche* of the period enjoyed a splurge of elegance not even matched by the later prosperity of the local petroleum speculators.

There was an unreal atmosphere from New Orleans westward. In San Antonio, my friend Maury Maverick, defeated for another term in Congress, had been elected mayor. He startled his native city by displaying an interest in the welfare of the impoverished Mexican pecan pickers who lived in huts and sheds on the edge of his picturesque and beautiful city, far from the historic glamor of the Alamo which had faced haughtier armed Mexicans nearly a century before. We drove down to Uvalde to survey the domain of Vice-President John Nance Garner, who had become disgruntled with the New Deal.

We visited Indian reservations in New Mexico and Arizona on the eve of the eventual establishment of Los Alamos near Sante Fe. The picturesque old Spanish capital of the state was preoccupied with the sudden prosperity caused by the filming of Louis Bromfield's novel, *The Rains Came,* in the upper Rio Grande Valley.

Westward at Flagstaff, Arizona, the Chamber of Commerce had imported trainloads of water, watermelons and corn meal to attract the Navajos from their hogans on the Reservation to put on a giant pow-wow and rodeo as a tourist attraction on the Fourth of July. During one of the evening performances I found myself seated by an anthropologist from the University of New Mexico who shocked me with the observation that the most energetic Indian dance was not traditional, but a complete imitation of the African dances that the Indians had seen in the film, *Trader Horn.*

Route 66, the highway of the Oakies escaping from the

drought-stricken plains, was almost entirely preempted by ancient junk-laden jalopies of poverty-stricken families hoping to reach California. The California State frontier attempted to stop every Oakie on the ground of plant quarantine, but anyone who appeared solvent was passed without inspection. It was just a bit too soon for the manpower requirements of the defense and aircraft industries to be crying for more men to work in the outdoor assembly lines.

It was not until we turned northward from Los Angeles to San Francisco, where the World's Fair was a tremendous attraction on Treasure Island, that one sensed a West Coast awareness of the threat of Hitler in Europe. Japan was equally feared. At Portland, Oregon, however, the giant development of the Bonneville Dam indicated the electric power needs of the West Coast were put on a calculated regional basis within a national plan. This was more dramatically demonstrated at Grand Coulee in the state of Washington where the Columbia River water was about to be harnessed not only for the benefit of the rural population but for the necessities of industry—ultimately including the vast Liberty Ship Program under the dynamic direction of Henry J. Kaiser.

I had been to the West Coast many times before but never in a mood to appreciate fully the contribution of the New Deal to the Great Northwest, then being described only in occasional articles by Richard L. Neuberger of the *Portland Oregonian*. He was still without personal political ambitions, unmarried and dedicated to the glories of the New Deal and of such regional Republicans as Norris, Borah and McNary.

As the tension rose in Europe, we sped eastward rapidly through Yellowstone, Cody, Cheyenne and the prairie route across Nebraska and Iowa to Chicago. I drove day and night to reach New York before the European explosion occurred. I arrived home as the Polish invasion started.

Thinking that the war was upon us, I invited a number of old friends, some of them military, for the Labor Day weekend—by which time England was in the war and the *Athenia* was sinking from a German torpedo. One of the men who was present and whom I did not see until later during the war in London was Howard Snyder, a brilliant medical officer who ultimately became White House physician. Others present included: General Hampton Anderson, then a colonel, Colonel Sherlock Davis, and our great and good friend, the painter Thomas E. Stephens.

Stephens was a portrait artist and was there by appointment to paint my portrait. He had come to the States a decade before in 1929, with several portrait commissions from businessmen, nearly all of which were canceled after the Wall Street Crash. After years of striving, he had been commissioned to do a portrait of Edward VIII for the Seventh Regiment Armory in New York, only to discover, upon landing in New York, that the King had abdicated and that the Seventh Regiment was reluctant to accept and pay for the portrait. Through Colonel Snyder (later General) he had painted Justice Vandervander who lived in the same apartment building as Snyder in Washington, and from that moment his commissions included military and political figures as well as the board room portraits which he had painted for General Motors, Ethyl and other corporations. He was an ardent beagler who had hunted with the West Surrey and Horsell Beagles in England. By the time of his death in 1966, he had painted scores of the outstanding men of affairs in the United States. In 1939, however, he was still comparatively obscure. He sensed that he must complete my portrait over a single weekend and he would not even permit me to move from my melancholy sitting pose, riveted to the radio, even to change or shave. The result is a remarkable, although incomplete, painting that I would never permit him to finish in detail. It symbolized too much of an historical moment in all our lives.

In the winter of 1939–40 I took over from my father the total responsibility and ownership of the farm in Maryland, and just before Dunkirk was fortunate enough to have it completely equipped with new tractors and implements, including new milking machines for the dairy, so that it could withstand a man-shortage siege. By the time of Dunkirk and the fall of France I was convinced that, because I might never again manage to live a normal life, I should squeeze all of the experience possible out of the farm. I went to Maryland, drove the tractor or rode the combine, hoisted the bales of hay and then, the main harvest over, resolved to face the larger responsibilities of a citizen in a world of crisis.

Was the farm a retreat from harsh reality or was it an effort in microcosm to demonstrate in the age of urbanization that the basic resources from whence came all our food, fiber, metals, timber and power must be cherished? I have never been able objectively to analyze my motivation. Certainly, I was alarmed by the remote catastrophes of flood and drought as dramatically as I was ever concerned with the patient corrective conservation of my own streams, fields and forests. There is a mental and spiritual quality about a pleasant countryside, not a stately park, which displays evidence of purpose, and which creates out of soil, water and love, beauty and substance for the benefit of the eye as well as for the satisfaction of hunger, and gives gracious warmth beyond the power of the automatic steam radiator.

Indeed, thirty years after my involvement in conservation, we have achieved many things—but our streams are still polluted, our water tables are still falling; our cities face water famine and our air is laden with pulverized waste and garbage.

In March of 1940 many of us who were concerned about

the waste and exhaustion of the surface of our native land met at the Wardman Park Hotel in Washington to found an organization that would carry the conservation message to the unconverted and especially to the cities more effectively than had ever been done by the government departments, the land grant colleges and the crusaders who were primarily addressing themselves to farmers and foresters. It was one of the most fundamentally satisfying occasions of my entire life. A manifesto was prepared and promulgated by a working committee prior to the meeting: Morris Llewellyn Cooke, Charles W. Collier, Bryce C. Browning, Charles E. Holzer and Russell Lord. Cooke, a great engineer, had been closely involved with the earlier work of Gifford Pinchot. Collier, the son of John Collier, Commissioner of Indian Affairs, was a farmer; Browning and Holzer came from the Muskogee conservancy district in Ohio from which emerged our ultimately most effective prophet, Louis Bromfield.

Russell Lord, with the exception of Liberty Hyde Bailey, the most eloquent agrarian writer the United States has ever produced, was a natural candidate to create whatever bulletin or organ should be needed to diffuse the gospel of Friends of the Land.

I lived and worked with these dedicated men prior to, during and after the Washington meeting, although *The Land*— a quarterly magazine—was not finally launched until the winter of 1941. Each of us met with groups of people across the country and in Canada for months, whenever we had a free day or weekend, to promote the organization and its cause.

Like many pioneers, we were in the long run so successful that we were overtaken and superseded by vast foundations and educational programs, but I am convinced that the formation of Friends of the Land marked the turning point in the effort to save our hinterland—to rescue our farms, forests and streams from mining and looting of precious and often irreplaceable ingredients of civilization, including microscopic trace elements in the soil. Dramatization of sustained forestry and contour tillage, retirement or reforestation of eroded hills—these and other related programs, which are now taken for granted—were our crash crisis causes at the time.

It was a paradox to discover that many of our first and most zealous disciples were conservative businessmen and bankers and that some of the most difficult people to persuade were the labor union leaders in the cities. This may not have been any reflection upon the character of the union leaders, but it was a reflection upon their education and their bland concentration on issues which seemed to benefit labor exclusively, immediately and directly. In 1940 most factory workers—except the employees of the automobile factories in Detroit who came primarily from the South with a natural love of hunting and fishing and, consequently, prone to take days off at the beginning of the hunting season—were over-urbanized and heedless of the implications of waste and reckless misuse of natural resources.

In the autumn and winter of 1940–41, throughout the Presidential election campaign, the blitz of London and the awesome decisions which faced the United States, it was difficult for me, as a solitary individual, to cover all of the responsibilities which faced me as a publisher, a citizen and a farmer-conservationist.

Among other activities I organized a special issue of *Survey Graphic* to dramatize the necessity for Western Hemisphere solidarity: the Americas South and North. Nearly every Pan-American authority enthusiastically contributed articles and advice, including A. A. Berle, Jr., Juan T. Trippe, John G. Winant and a variety of Latin American experts who were at that time responsive to the emergency program of Nelson A.

Rockefeller as the coordinator of Commercial and Cultural Affairs between the American Republics.

The volume was widely acclaimed from Cape Horn to Hudson Bay and I have no doubt that it left a permanent mark upon the thinking of policy-makers and educators who were baffled by the prospect of a new and unknown balance of power in Europe and Asia. We partially failed in the effort, I think—in our zeal to preserve amity—by portraying too uncritically the challenge of poverty in such countries as Cuba and Chile. I dashed to La Guardia Airport with the first copy from the press for John G. Winant who, as our new Ambassador to the Court of St. James's, was taking a Pan American Clipper across the Atlantic on the way to his new post.

I could not anticipate that within a year Mr. Winant would be requesting me to serve on his staff in London. Indeed, I find it difficult now to recall what I did anticipate, in personal terms, as I contemplated the fate of a beleaguered Britain before the German invasion of Russia. I knew within my heart that Britain could not fall to a military conquest, but I was sure that a British victory with or without the eventual military aid of the United States would leave Britain an exhausted island without a dominant economic or political position in the world. The important thing was that the values which Britain cherished and fought for should survive, like the ideals of ancient Greece, and that the English-speaking world should retain a powerful moral and independent material position in the future affairs of all mankind.

At that time, however, the United States was living in something of a false paradise as "the arsenal of democracy" and we immediately began a number of studies for a special volume of *Survey Graphic:* "Manning the Arsenal of Democracy." The primary thesis was that we must speed diverse production and at the same time preserve free capital and labor relations.

I personally covered the Ford Motor Company under the title "Ford Puts on the Union Label." It represented more than a Labor-Industry agreement when on Labor Day, 1941, Ford Local No. 600 of the UAW-CIO took first prize in the Detroit parade. Only a few weeks previously the first Ford car to bear a union label was exhibited on the platform of the Buffalo Convention of the UAW. The biggest banner in the parade flaunted the message:

> Ford Workers, 120,000 strong, present to the CIO and to the Nation, the First Union Shop Contract, the First Union Label Car in the automoblie industry.

One could only speculate on the reasons for Ford's acceptance of the demands of his workers. To be sure, the Ford-wide union shop was to Ford's advantage. It emphasized the totality of the entire Ford manufacturing operation—including the railway, glass, steel, electric power and lake transport industries which were a part of it. Designed to prevent strikes over dues or jurisdiction or branch plants, despite all concessions to the union, it gave Ford the initiative which he had lost in relations with his employees. Indeed, several of the more generous provisions of the contract were regarded by some friends of labor as dangerous to independent unionism—especially the forcing of twenty-two thousand people over from one union to another; the company payment of full-time union committee chairmen's wages at the rate of their Ford job when elected; and the inclusion of the branch plants in the CIO entirely upon the basis of NLRB elections in Dearborn and Detroit. Unless the UAW-CIO actually could hold a majority in each plant included in the contract and win elections in some of the branch plants where the AFL had requested NLRB elections, it was not likely to be able to administer satisfactorily the provisions of the contract. As it was, Ford had taken the initiative.

Ford had not made large profits for a decade. In some years Ford had lost money. There was a significance in the fact that an important Ford sales official had been active in the formulation of a contract. At no time was Charles E. Sorenson, Ford production chief, involved in the negotiations. Nor had Henry Ford himself dealt with union officials. Edsel Ford, although he did not sign the contract, closely followed its application. Edsel Ford had been in active discussions with Washington officials on the transition to defense employment and production as auto curtailment went into effect.

History was bunk. Bygones were bygones. The UAW-CIO expected every Ford worker to do his duty in defense production. The left-wing element of the UAW had been smashed and Harry Bennett was left without any choice except to sign the contract with the necessary elements of the union which had won the company election.

This was really, with one exception at the end of the war, the last major research and editorial assignment which I undertook for Survey Associates. The arsenal of defense was in high gear on production three months before the Japanese bombing of Pearl Harbor.

Chapter V

FOUR YEARS IN GROSVENOR SQUARE

———◆◇◆———

Bastard. O, let us pay the time but needful woe,
Since it hath been beforehand with our griefs.
This England never did, nor never shall,
Lie at the proud foot of a conqueror,
But when it first did help to wound itself.
Now these her princes are come home again,
Come the three corners of the world in arms,
And we shall shock them. Nought shall make us
rue,
If England to itself do rest but true.
—Conclusion of "King John"
by William Shakespeare

ON DECEMBER 7, 1941, the St. Peter's Foot Beagles met at the Anna Held, Jr., Tavern, a remodeled farmhouse on the edge of Yorktown Heights. Although we hunted on the Sabbath, we felt sanctified by the presence of Father Leeming, the parson who functioned as headmaster of St. Peter's School, a small Episcopal institution where hounds were kenneled and cared for as part of the field-sports program for the students under the direction of the masters.

We found a hare and had a fine run over Foxden, the estate of Mr. and Mrs. Mortimer Fox. Mrs. Fox was a sister of Secretary of the Treasury, Henry Morgenthau. Foxden House was surrounded by gardens, including a world-famous herb garden, and the interior was adorned with many me-

mentos of Mrs. Fox's youth in Turkey with her father when he was Ambassador to that country.

It was a chilly and gloomy afternoon. Some of the field returned early to the inn for the hot tea which would be served when hounds came in. We were greatly alarmed as we approached the inn by the waving and shouting of a group at the parking lot. The confusion was so great that no one could guess what was the matter until we were within a hundred yards of one of the cars which had the radio turned on. It was the news of Pearl Harbor. To many of us, and to me in particular, the shocking broadcast came as a catharsis. I felt a sense of relief that the long suspense was ended. The hunt breakfast was forgotten. Students were hurried back to the kennels with hounds, and everyone hastened home to his own radio. I remained listening for hours to the repeated broadcasts, too dazed by the implications of the moment even to telephone friends who might not have been tuned in and who might still remain in ignorance of events. I hurried to New York the next morning at daybreak, determined to enter the armed forces as promptly as possible.

I was advised by highly placed friends to apply for a commission as an officer and went to Washington on the night train to see where my experience and aptitudes might best be used. Washington was so hopelessly confused that I could not get near the old War Department Building or any other military headquarters. I stood up in a crowded day coach all the way back to New York.

My colleagues at Survey Associates persuaded me not to dash to Governor's Island to enlist as a private. Within a few days I had two feelers from those who would like to recruit me as an officer. I was in the midst of the formalities, including an option on uniforms, when a most fortuitous series of circumstances and coincidences followed so speedily that I was completely bewildered. .

E*

I was told by Robert E. Sherwood that the Coordinator of Information, COI, agency of the Federal Government was going to be split into two operational agencies (which later evolved as the Office of Strategic Services, OSS, and the Office of War Information, OWI). He hinted that I might be wanted for what turned out to be the OWI even though it had not yet been established and might somehow be partly derived from the Office of Facts and Figures, OFF, under Archibald MacLeish. Then came an overture from Edward S. Stanley, and another from Harold Guinzburg of the Viking Press, both then at COI, and still another from Elmer Davis, who was later to head the OWI with Robert E. Sherwood as his deputy for overseas information.

The result was that I was persuaded to hold myself available for the new agency. Eventually I asked permission to make a quick swing around the Tennessee Valley and Detroit, to refresh my knowledge of the hinterland. By the time of my return I was told that I would probably be sent to London. Apparently, five names had been submitted to Ambassador Winant. While he was anxious to have J. Wallace Carroll, he especially wanted to have me on the London staff. He was keen, I was told, not to let any OWI activity in the United Kingdom get involved in matters outside of the jurisdiction of the American Embassy, so that psychological warfare and intelligence would be once removed from any informational program for the British. The whole matter was shrouded in such secrecy that I kept no notes, even in my diary, during that period of shuttling back and forth to Washington.

When I was finally ordered to report to a Pan American Clipper flight at La Guardia Airport, the admonitions of secrecy were so strict that I did not dare inform anyone, including my family, in what direction I was vanishing into the maw of the war machine. My final papers were handed to me in Washington by Evangeline Bell, Bob Sherwood's assistant, a charming and talented young lady who later turned up in London and was married during the war to David Bruce, head of the OSS in London, and now (1966) Ambassador to London.

At La Guardia, to my great surprise, I ran into Justice Felix Frankfurter accompanying three delightful children and what was obviously an English nanny. We chatted a moment, and then he informed me that the two girls were stepchildren of my old friend Sylvester Gates and that the young boy, Oliver, was Sylvester's son by his present wife, Pauline Newton, who had married Sylvester after her divorce.

I had encountered two of the Newtons (Joy and Robert) in London before the war, not unmindful of the rumor that the Newtons were the family depicted with ribald affection in the best seller, *The Constant Nymph*. Felix had persuaded the Gateses to send the children to him in Washington during the 1940 blitz, and now Sylvester and Pauline had insisted that they return. I was delighted to serve as family escort. The three children and their nanny enlivened the journey for all aboard the Clipper.

We put down in Nova Scotia and then at Gander before the long but comfortable flight to Foynes, near Shannon. Then we flew to Poole, England, in a British Sunderland Seaplane and I took the afternoon train to London. It was a unique gesture to deliver the Gates children to their flat in Lowndes Square where I learned that Sylvester—of all coincidences—was at his office in the Ministry of Information, where he was Home Controller, a vital position under the Ministry headed by Brendan Bracken.

The OWI was so new that few in the Embassy were aware of it. All except the Ambassador seemed ignorant of the fact that a modest unit would be attached to his offices in Grosvenor Square. Accommodations had been arranged for me at a hotel, but after several days I found a flat in Kensington through the courtesy of Alan Dudley, who had been attached to the British Information Services in New York and whose wife, Isabel Brunton, I had met a decade earlier at Aberystwyth, Wales, where she was studying at the University College.

Alan—now Sir Alan—Dudley was uncertain of his Foreign Office assignment and suggested that I take over the flat, which had been beautifully equipped, complete with a curious enemy alien cook-housekeeper, Teresa, by the late Patrick Kelly, head of General Electric in London. The one stipulation was that a bedroom should be available for Donald Kelly, a son who had joined the Royal Canadian Air Force and who was stationed at Biggin Hill.

So until the spring of 1945, when Mrs. Kelly came to London with the Clark Minors to use her flat and settle the affairs of her husband and of young Donald who died in 1944, I was comfortably ensconced in wartime London. I had thought that my assignment to London was top secret but soon after my arrival I read on the front page of the London *Sunday Times:*

> New arrangements for informative contact between British and American scientific societies, social services, and similar bodies are planned by the United States Office of War Information now being set up in London. Mr. Archibald MacLeish, assistant director of the office in charge of policy development under Mr. Elmer Davis, is to control the scheme.
>
> Preparatory work has already been begun by Mr. Victor Weybright, who has preceded Mr. MacLeish to London. The Office will undertake for the first time the supply of information about the United States to Great Britain and may deal with requests for American speakers at British gatherings.
>
> These new arrangements are a result of President Roosevelt's decision to concentrate all American information and propaganda services in the one office under Mr. Elmer Davis.

It soon became obvious that although one was obliged to be trustworthy, discreet, and to handle all matters in confidence, I was not destined to be blotted out by the hush-hush practices which seemed to be an obsession in Washington. I had established immediate liaison with the Ambassador, which was not difficult because of long acquaintance and professional friendship over more than a decade ever since he had been governor of New Hampshire. He had won a Republican primary race against Frank Knox, who at the turn of the century had served under Theodore Roosevelt in the Rough Riders and later became a top executive of the Hearst newspapers. Knox went on to acquire the *Chicago Evening News* and then to serve as Secretary of the Navy under Franklin D. Roosevelt.

A haunted Lincolnesque man, Winant often looked disheveled, despite his English tailoring, because of a large frame for his lean body and often a sort of hulking Frankenstein stance. As a public speaker he was hesitant, his low-pitched voice sometimes difficult to understand, but in intimate private discussions he was nimble-witted and loquacious, a gifted conversationalist. He was always genuinely interested, never shy, but often appeared to be inattentive and perplexed. He possessed an excellent memory for dates and places in history and in his own experience, but sometimes had difficulty in recalling the married name of one member of his own family—his daughter who had married a Chilean with a multiple Spanish-style surname.

Many members of his professional foreign service staff were at first mildly resentful of the Ambassador's affinity for the wartime amateurs of his staff. They should not have been annoyed. Winant was an experienced public executive from his early days as Governor of New Hampshire, through the period when he was the first administrator of the United States Social Security Administration and on to the chief executive position of the International Labor Office in Geneva. He had an understandable dread of the individual getting lost or, even worse, destroyed by the mammoth and sometimes bewildering bureaucracy of government. We temporary wartime aides were his favored prodigal sons, so to speak.

Some of the regular State Department Foreign Service staff in London seemed to regard Winant as naive, but they knew that he enjoyed the full approbation of President Roosevelt and of Secretary Hull. More important, in wartime, his sometimes brooding and moody atmosphere gave the British, from the Prime Minister and War Cabinet down to the old ladies in blacked-out bomb shelters, a sense of dedicated understanding and sympathy. This pervasive atmosphere of caring deeply enabled Winant to maintain his position as *the* Ambassador, even though two other ambassadors were assigned to special duty in London—Averell Harriman, later succeeded by Philip Reed, in charge of lend-lease with the rank of Ambassador, and in 1944, Tony Biddle with the status of Ambassador *near* the Governments in Exile. Not even the ultimate Supreme Commander of SHAEF, General Eisenhower, managed to dilute the status and standing of John Gilbert Winant at the Court of St. James's.

My first tutor for several days was Ritchie Calder (now Lord Ritchie-Calder) on leave from his post of science editor of the *News Chronicle* and working in the Political Warfare Executive Offices in Aldwych. After discussing my duties with the Ambassador, I made my first call on the Ministry of Information which was lodged in the new and modern University of London building in Malet Street. I first had a cordial reunion with Sylvester Gates in his office, then was introduced to Brendan Bracken—one of the most remarkable men I have ever known and one of the ablest.

A large loose-jointed man with a shock of light red curly

hair, at first glance Brendan seemed to be a man concocted in the manner of a patchwork comic—but this impression was soon effaced by his charming and authoritative discourse, personally or in Parliament, his self-confidence buttressed by his extraordinarily close relationship to Winston Churchill. The two men were so close that, naturally enough, occasional rumors were repeated that Brendan was an illegitimate son of the Prime Minister. This was disproved by documentary counter-evidence, but it persisted throughout the war. I don't believe that anyone was closer to Winston Churchill throughout the war than Brendan Bracken, not even Oliver Lyttelton (later Lord Chandos), General "Pug" Ismay or Lord Beaverbrook.

As Minister of Information, a post which Bracken had assumed after others had failed, he was the perfect minister—loyal to his wartime staff, no matter how Bohemian or mistaken they might be on minor matters or how much he might secretly loathe some of them who had obviously more talent for neurotic self-justification than for mature conduct as civil servants. In Parliament it was a joy to hear Brendan Bracken reply to questions on MOI matters. He was unfailingly patient, courteous and accessible. In the late evenings he often made the rounds of White's and other clubs of which he was a member to indicate buoyant confidence in the progress of the vast wartime effort which it was his duty to explain at home and abroad.

I discovered many old friends in the Ministry of Information. Robin Cruikshank, who had been the London *News Chronicle* correspondent in Washington and New York, headed the American Division, a unit which dealt with the relay of information to the United States and also dealt with American correspondents and visitors and the American Armed Forces in conjunction with the press division headed by Jack Brebner.

Within a week I managed to secure a private office at Number One Grosvenor Square near to that of the Ambassador. It had been occupied by representatives of Averell Harriman's lend-lease staff, and then, when he moved next door to Number Three Grosvenor Square, by a few residual COI (Coordinator of Information) executives who had not yet been transferred to the new OSS headquarters nearby in Lower Grosvenor Street.

I then implored Washington to expedite the formation of a library to supplement the Embassy library, which was a specialized collection of books and documents restricted for the use of the Ambassador and secretaries of Embassy. Archibald MacLeish proposed several names of men whom I diplomatically blackballed as too narrowly equipped. By a stroke of good fortune, Archie then came up with the name of a man whom I had not previously met but whose credentials were exactly right for the job, Richard H. Heindel, now president of Pratt Institute in New York but then a professor of history at the University of Pennsylvania and former fellow of the Library of Congress. He was the author of a remarkably fine and scholarly book dealing with American influence in Britain, rather bluntly entitled *American Impact on Britain*.

His book, published in 1940, had been based upon first-hand study for nearly a year in the United Kingdom and wide contact with universities, industries and organizations of all sorts.

Richard Heindel had been graduated from Harvard after spending several years at Gettysburg College, twenty-odd miles from my birthplace. It was easy to check on Dick Heindel's wholly admirable background and to clear his name with the Ambassador in less than a minute. Later, in October, when he arrived in London I suggested that he might like to share my large apartment as a paying guest. He lived with me in

Abington Court until his departure for home in the summer of 1945.

I soon foresaw the need for additional staff, and when Christopher Morley's daughter, Louise, came to London, at the time of Mrs. Franklin Roosevelt's visit in August 1942, to make a speech at a giant youth congress, I drafted her as a helper. Her father and two uncles—Felix and Frank—had been Rhodes Scholars, which meant she should feel at home in England.

While I was working single-handedly and as inconspicuously as possible to establish a quietly useful informational and cultural office at Number One Grosvenor Square, I found myself swamped by appeals for urgently wanted information from every British Ministry, including the War Cabinet, and from every branch of the British Armed Forces, as well as by members of Parliament, schools and universities and social, industrial and civil organizations. At the time, no more than a half-ounce letter could be accepted for trans-Atlantic airmail, and the airborne Embassy pouches often took a week to reach us from Washington—except for those carried by special couriers on top-secret missions. The American Lend-Lease Mission attached to the Embassy referred at least a dozen queries a day to me. One of my functions was to coordinate certain areas of relations with the American Armed Forces, a responsibility which came very easily to me because of an instant feeling of fellowship with General J. C. H. Lee who was commanding the Services of Supply and Communications Zone.

I remained close to General Lee throughout my assignment in London until he went on the Continent after the 1944 invasion in a blaze of publicity for the Red Ball Express—truck convoys which, although not as logical or economical as rehabilitation of railroads and canals might have been, heartened everyone with the noisy and visible certainty that the hardware was on its way to the receding front, and that food, fuel and ammunition would keep up with our advancing troops.

General Lee was responsible not only for supplies but for the morale and welfare of the troops in the European Theater of Operations. At times he seemed in league with the American Red Cross as an invading conqueror of England, requisitioning facilities and hostels under reverse lend-lease until finally the Embassy had to take a discreet hand to intercede and preserve a few spots for British civilians to eat and sleep when traveling on business, and above all to prevent the Red Cross from taking over the best hotel in every town adjacent to American military installations and training areas. I had to work secretly on this assignment with the Home and War Offices. General Lee never guessed that I helped crush the American Red Cross's well-meaning but greedy claim to the best of everything, everywhere in Britain.

Lee had come practically direct to London from his command in Oregon, soon after the death of his wife in an automobile accident when he had accidently speeded with her through a lowered barrier at a railway crossing. It was not uncommon for him to fix morning committee meetings as early as 6:30 A.M., by which time he had already spent a half hour in meditation and worship in the nearest Anglican Church. Lee was attended by a remarkable staff—efficient, hardworking, but always immodest about their master's performance. His chief publicity officer was wise, able, dapper, cheerful, Broadwayish Colonel Jock Lawrence who before joining the General had been chief public relations executive for Sam Goldwyn. Jock would not have known how to work with a blushing violet, and his zestful optimism always reflected the dynamics of General Lee's entire organization.

I kept none of my most perplexing problems (except the predatory Red Cross) from General Lee on any matter which was relevant to his responsibility in the European Theater of Operations. He knew my background and I knew his, through a vast network of previous friends and acquaintances including General Fred Osborn in charge of Special Services in the Pentagon, which included morale, nontraining education and recreation. I introduced General Lee to many British civilians in and out of the Government who were later useful in preparing the United Kingdom to accommodate over two million American Armed Forces in a blacked-out, rationed and weary nation, whose own menfolk were overseas in the British Forces or prisoners of war, from Africa and the Far East to the German-occupied territory across the English Channel on the Continent.

General Lee's early hours effectively put me on a daily sixteen-hour basis; for with double daylight saving time in Britain the time difference with Washington was six hours, the consequence being that if one waited for all cable signals from Washington until three or four o'clock along the Potomac, it was nine or ten o'clock at night in London.

As an illustration of some of the urgent and awkward problems which I cheerfully undertook to solve without embarrassing the State Department and Foreign Service staff of the Embassy, I recall one in particular while I was working alone soon after my arrival in Grosvenor Square. It was a request for a positive statement on the status of the Negro in America, made by a brigadier in the British War Office. He thought it would be useful to have prepared for the Army Bureau of Current Affairs a pamphlet making it clear that the Negro was a "hewer of wood and a bearer of water" not fit to associate with the general population and, therefore, to be excluded from pubs, clubs and British amenities that were not off limits to white G.I.'s.

Shocked by this assertion of "the white man's burden," I gave the brigadier a lecture on the ideals, as distinct from the

realities, of American society and said that any such statement promulgated to the British Armed Forces would create
political havoc in the United Kingdom as well as in the
United States and do irreparable harm to the war effort. I
told him that I would cooperate in the preparation of a
pamphlet on the position of the Negro in the United States,
and that I should like to discuss it with William Emrys Williams, civilian director of the army educational programs
under General Sir Ronald Adam, the adjutant general at the
British War Office. I reminded him that Walter White of the
NAACP was about to visit Britain as an accredited correspondent, primarily to observe the treatment of American colored
troops in the United Kingdom.

I thought that my chore would be comparatively simple.
In confidence, I informed General Lee through Colonel
Lawrence that I was cooperating through the OWI in Washington on the preparation of a British Army Bureau of
Current Affairs pamphlet. The British program was universally known by its initials as ABCA. The ABCA program
had been developed by the adjutant general as a compulsory
fortnightly hour of orientation on duty time with an authoritative pamphlet for the junior officer who conducted the
discussion, using supplementary material when available.
During the vigil in England after the fall of France, when the
country was bewildered and underarmed and in peril, the
ABCA hour had become a fundamental contribution to
the understanding of the war, the issues, the enemy and the
friends and potential allies. Billy Williams, as he was known
in those days—now Sir William Emrys Williams—had been
active in adult education and the Workers Education Association in Britain as well as advisor to Penguin Books on
their educational Pelican series.

He functioned in close relationship to General Sir Ronald
Adam. They often skated on thin ice because of the Prime

Minister's aversion to educating the troops on matters not directly germane to fighting or preparation for fighting. I had a word with Ronald Adam, a Cromwellian figure, often restive under the absolute directives from Number Ten Downing Street. He understood at once the subtleties of the assignment which I had assumed. I cabled Washington requesting that the OWI or the embryonic Writers' War Board prepare a pamphlet which would state the position of the Negro with respect to education and general opportunity at the federal level, with some description of state and local exceptions to national policy. To my amazement I was told that Washington preferred not to cooperate because of the sensitivity of vital Southern senators and congressmen to the color issue.

At that time James P. Warburg was in London, where he had been assigned by the Coordinator of Information, but not quite formally transferred to the Office of War Information. He volunteered to supplement my request with an imperative cable. Again I was turned down. I thought it wise to inform the Ambassador and ask his advice. He courageously responded by saying that if I had committed myself to deliver a pamphlet that I should do so even if I had to write it myself, and that he would not disavow it; indeed, he did not even want to read it, so great was his confidence in the outcome.

I did not have time to prepare a pamphlet myself, so I drew on the talent of two British scholars who were familiar with the United States but who, because they were working in the Political Intelligence Department (PID), could not sign such a pamphlet. I informed Billy Williams that I could not produce the pamphlet from Washington by the deadline requested and that, therefore, it was being undertaken by composite authors in England. My British friends were Professor John A. Hawgood of the University of Birmingham, a distinguished historian, and Professor E. J. Dingwall, an anthropologist from Cambridge. Dingwall actually wrote most of the pamphlet. It was based upon a flow of information and statistics which Hawgood and I provided as well as upon his own knowledge, except for such documentary evidence as the Federal Fair Employment Act which had established a committee to function under the War Manpower Commission in cooperation with the United States Employment Service.

I sent the manuscript to the War Office by messenger. Within twenty-four hours I received a galley proof, with a hint that the War Office might want to submit an abstract to Sir John Anderson, Minister of War. Sir John (later Lord Waverley) actually took an abstract of the ABCA pamphlet entitled "The Colour Problem as the American Sees It" to a War Cabinet meeting where, although it was not part of the proceedings, it did—I heard in confidence from a member of the secretariat—elicit a noncommittal grunt from the Prime Minister.

By chance, however, Brendan Bracken was present when the pamphlet was referred to and requested a copy as possibly of great usefulness to him for the purposes of his ministry in learning more of the most complex internal problem in America. Brendan took the galley proof to the Ministry of Information. Almost immediately he had use for it. A journalist from the West Indies came to interview him on the position of colored people in Great Britain, where many West Indians were already present. It was very easy for Brendan to hand him the galley with a statement that it represented the position of the United States, with which he was in concurrence, pointing out the fact that it dealt only with the national attitudes despite any regrettable local deviations from national policy.

The West Indian paper, *Gleanings,* in Kingstown, Jamaica, published almost the entire ABCA pamphlet. By one of the coincidences of a world woven close together by the shuttle of wartime travel, a London journalist delayed in Jamaica on a Pan American Clipper saw the extensive news story which quoted the Minister of Information as in approval and immediately cabled his newspaper, which ran a sensational and bold headline, "*No Colour Bar in Britain* Says Minister of Information," followed by much of the text of the pamphlet.

Although the ABCA pamphlets were restricted to military personnel only, they were not confidential or secret, but so far as I know this was the first ABCA pamphlet to achieve widespread attention by the general public. Moreover, it established wartime policy supported by a statement of a minister of the Government. Certainly the Home Secretary, Herbert Morrison, could not or did not demur or quibble over the intrusion into matters that fell under his jurisdiction. It was a most remarkable accident with far-reaching consequences, and enabled the British to halt at once tendencies in many parts of the country to define as off-limits to Negroes, American or Commonwealth, areas and amenities that were tending to be proscribed, sometimes with the connivance of American Air Force Officers, many of whom were Southerners.

My role had been simply that of an informational executive and not that of a propagandist, but I was proud to have participated in a constructive effort to make clear the policy and attitudes of my Government at home.

One of the guiding principles of my work was, whenever possible, to remain totally in the background and give responsible British agencies and individuals authoritative information which they might use as they saw fit. It soon became obvious that I would have to make myself responsible for liaison with book publishers, periodical publishers, His Majesty's Stationery Office and other publishing organizations which were frustrated by the slow movement of news and their hopelessly inadequate access to current American published material. We soon evolved one vital but simple setup with the Ministry of Information, Publishing Division, headed by Robert Fraser: An American arbiter could secure extra quantities of paper for book projects which were judged to be of vital interest to the United States. The Ministry of Supply Paper Control at Reading relied upon Robert Fraser and Robert Fraser relied upon me, so that for the next four years, I made all decisions on such quotas for book publishers without consultation or approval from any committee or other Government official. It is a source of tremendous satisfaction to me that not once was any paper quota decision ever questioned or criticized.

There was one project which was the cause of a lot of gossip a little later in the war. Joseph C. Grew had written *Ten Years in Japan* published by Simon and Schuster, which immediately became a best seller in the U.S.A. Simon and Schuster consented to the placement of Ambassador Grew's book with Angus and Robertson in Australia, where interest in the war against Japan was intense. As a result of Australian publication independent of London—i.e. a subdivision of the British market—no member of the British Publishers Association would accept the book; indeed under their membership pledge no member of the British Publishers Association could accept without breaking his pledge. Laurence Pollinger, a leading London literary agent, had the manuscript on offer. He was very disappointed by the negative reaction from publishers who belonged to the PA. He and I had the same idea: It would have to be published by a nonmember, which really meant one of the struggling German Jewish refugee publishers who had come to London during the previous decade and had not yet become members of the "club."

At last it went to Peter Guttman of Hammond and Hammond, a publisher who had ventured into business on his own in London. After clearing with my opposite-number British authorities, I assured him he would not only have all the paper he needed at the fixed price but top priority on production. Moreover, I told Ambassador Winant and Robert Cruikshank of MOI that I thought we should have a foreword by the Right Honorable Sir Robert Craigie (G.C.M.G., C.B.) who had been the British Ambassador in Tokyo at the time of Pearl Harbor. By this time Grew had become annoyed by waiting. Like many deaf people, he was suspicious. He impatiently asked us to uncover what influences in England were suppressing his book. I doubt that he ever fully appreciated that publishing his book was delayed and nearly thwarted by a rigid and, considering the times, petty trade practice. However, he was thrilled by the final product handsomely manufactured by Morrison and Gibb, Ltd. of Edinburgh. All ended happily. Guttman had a best seller. The PA immediately invited him to join, and he did.

Toward the end of 1942, I had one of the greatest inspirations of my London assignment. I encountered Herbert Agar, then a lieutenant commander in the United States Navy working with the Economic Warfare staff at 40 Berkeley Square. A scholar and author, winner of two Pulitzer Prizes and former editor of the Louisville *Courier-Journal,* he had served in London with Ambassador Robert W. Bingham, proprietor of the paper, and later in Louisville with Barry Bingham who eventually turned up in London with the Navy. My inspiration was very simple: Why not persuade the Ambassador to borrow Herbert from the Navy and establish him as the chief of the OWI in Britain so that he could deal with Fleet Street and the press while I devoted myself more effectively to what I came to call "slow media," i.e. every sort of channel except urgent news.

The Ambassador managed to take Herbert back with him on a quick trip to Washington during the Christmas season of 1942 and to return with him in mufti. Meanwhile, James Reston had set up an OWI news room and found a man to run it before he returned to *The New York Times*—James Oldfield, an experienced Fleet Street journalist. Scotty Reston had managed to establish a new cable channel for fast London reception of American statements on policy and developments so that full texts of White Papers and important speeches could be delivered not only to the press (which under rationing had not the space to render them in full) but also to members of the Cabinet, the House of Commons, the House of Lords and others who without such texts would never have been aware of 90 percent of the urgent material orginating in America. Simultaneously, Richard Heindel arrived, and we established him in the American Library attached to the Embassy. The Library had a remarkable collection of books and magazines which attracted a throng of elite readers and researchers, day and night, most of them highly placed Government officials, scholars, and industrial and educational representatives.

One thing led to another. The Ministry of Information requested money to facilitate a few more key American visitors to deal with specialized audiences on activities in America from which the British might learn not only about the United States but about improvement of techniques in agriculture, industry, management, labor, etc. We usually managed to have these visitors invited by a British organization, our only expense being the round-trip transportation and sometimes a modest per diem fee. However, in order to cope with this activity, I needed help. Since it was almost impossible to find and bring help from America, I scanned the

available people in England and found in the American Red
Cross Miss Ruth Dowling Wehle from Lexington, Kentucky.
She was a beautiful girl with an M.A. in political science.
She said she would be willing if the Red Cross would release
her. The Ambassador quite rightly said he didn't want to be
involved in raiding the Red Cross, but if I had the courage
to face Commissioner Harvey Dow Gibson, I had his blessing.
It was a rather stormy session. The Commissioner in Great
Britain was a good deal tougher on such matters than William Stevenson who was holding the Red Cross fort at the
time I arrived.

Commissioner Gibson gave me a long and detailed account
of the arrangements that had been made at great cost and
effort in the case of every Red Cross girl in the European
Theater of Operations. I thought I had lost my case, but at
the last moment, as we digressed into a discussion of fox
hunting, he relented and said,

"After all, we are all part of the same team and your case
persuades me."

Miss Wehle immediately assumed responsibility not only
for visitors and speakers, but assisted every wartime agency
in the Embassy in dealing with officials and experts who arrived expecting a hotel room and some place to work and
receive messages.

In the autumn of 1942, while I was working alone except
for a secretary, I was informed by Ritchie Calder that the
long awaited Beveridge Report on postwar social security
and welfare services was complete and ready for release at a
date to be fixed by the Government. Until that time it was
a secretly guarded document with no copy available to anyone except, I suspect, the London *Times*. The *Times* would,
by tradition, be entitled to quote generously and comment
upon it on the day it would be released by His Majesty's
Stationery Office. Ritchie and I agreed that it would be most

unfortunate if Washington had no advance inkling of the
Beveridge Report's contents. Therefore, it was decided that
I should make an effort to secure the report in draft and relay
in a top secret cable the principal recommendations with
enough background for officials in Washington to comment
upon it as evidence of England's humane concerns, not only
in overseas shortwave broadcasts, but also domestically.

I rose to the challenge and made a date with Frank Pakenham, secretary of the committee appointed by the Ministry of Reconstruction. Pakenham—now the Earl of Long-
ford—was a man of complete integrity and at first reluctant
to divulge anything about it to me. Although he was a
Socialist he was also a financial man; in the course of our conversation I confided to him that I had been involved in welfare and social service, had served as Jane Addams' secretary
and had published John Gilbert Winant's first statement
when he became Chairman of the Social Security Board. I
further said that I didn't want to involve the Ambassador in
any calculated leakage of a high security matter and that I
would like simply to transmit to Robert E. Sherwood in
Washington a top-secret abstract, the security of which would
be observed, but which would permit some advance preparation of coverage of the Beveridge Report in the United States
for overseas purposes.

I emerged from his office with a tattered galley proof in a
civil service envelope. I hastened to my office, digested the
report and prepared a comprehensive cable which I filed with
Fred Frick, chief code clerk. The response from Washington
was immediate and grateful. I had confided my advance access to the report by arrangement with Pakenham to only
three people: Ritchie Calder, who had recommended that
I cope with it; Ambassador Winant, who was naturally sympathetic; and Dr. Stephen Taylor (now Lord Taylor), who
was in charge of Home Intelligence of the Ministry of In-

formation and would be in a position to let me know if British Censorship had tuned in on my audacious, if indiscreet, helping hand on a matter of utmost significance with respect to postwar planning.

In those early months in London I endeavored to cement my relations with the various secretaries of Embassy as well as the ministers and counselors of Embassy. I struck an immediate friendship with Dorsey Gassaway Fisher, press attaché; Loyd V. Steere, agricultural attaché; Samuel Berger, labor attaché who was at first attached to lend-lease; Allen Steynes, economic attaché; and all the others. I never intruded on their normal liaisons with British individuals and agencies without their knowledge or consent, which was always willingly given. For example, as a farmer I was most interested in wartime agriculture in England, and through the kindness of W. H. D. McCullogh, who was public relations officer for Robert Hudson, Minister of Agriculture and Fisheries, I came to know Rob Hudson and, whenever possible, other representatives of this vital ministry which was dependent upon American fertilizers and machinery so as to produce foodstuffs effectively and thereby release tonnage for military shipment. Lord Woolton, Minister of Food, was one of the men whom I came to admire mightily; his training as a merchant had given him incredible insight into human nature. He liked, for example, occasionally to announce little surprises that would relieve the monotony of austere rationing, such as three ounces of raisins the week before Christmas or an extra ounce of chocolate at Easter.

When it became obvious that due to the shortage of fats, potatoes would increasingly have to be mealy for mashing rather than harder varieties for frying into chips, the Ministry of Food and the Ministry of Agriculture (frequently with the advice of my dear old friend, André Simon, the world's leading authority, then as now, on food and wine and the amenities as well as chemicals and calories of nutrition) encouraged a drive to use more American recipes. André Simon's attitude toward the Americans was one of special appreciation. The fact that I was a close friend and neighbor of his old gourmet colleague, Crosby Gaige, immediately led him to put me into his select and trusted circle of austerity improvisers of better eating habits. I suggested to Mac Kriendler of "21," at the Eighth Air Force, that they invite André Simon out to Bushey Park to inspect their mess, and he made a great many recommendations that improved the taste of their food as well as the variety of their meals.

In the spring of 1943 André, who lived in East Grinstead, appeared at my office one morning with a little basket full of pokeberry greens. *"Mon Dieu!"* I exclaimed. "How in the world did you find this Southern delicacy, and how did you know that I had smuggled from my smokehouse in Maryland, through a visiting friend, two of my old hams, a few slices of which would add savor to the spring greens?" He explained that in Colonial days before cochineal had been discovered as a cosmetic for ladies' cheeks and lips, an early traveler in the American Colonies had brought a clump of pokeweed and planted it in East Grinstead, using the red autumn berries for the preparation of lipstick and rouge. I immediately invited him to a potlikker feast at my flat, preceded by mint juleps and accompanied by some excellent hock which I procured from the Britannia Pub around the corner, where all things German were still taboo to the locals.

My flat, at Number Six Abington Court, just off Kensington High Street at Allen Street, became known as a source of excellent food with many surprises. This was partly due to the foraging proclivities of Teresa, my cook-housekeeper, who had a remarkable instinct for finding delicacies that were off-ration, and partly due to the advantages of her Italian heritage in the kitchen and at the greengrocer. I suspect that she often swapped our farina rations for meat rations with the Gibraltar refugees who were housed nearby and who were known as "Scorpions from the Rock." I lived on regular British rations happily stretched by many meals outside and by occasional packages from Hollow Rock Farm or from friends such as Crosby Gaige, who believed that we were all starving to death in England during the war.

Actually, those of us who had access to military messes such as the officers mess at Grosvenor House—known as Willow Run—fared well on an ample diet. The workers in Britain who were fed at factory canteens were adequately nourished. The really deprived were civil servants and white-collar workers who could not afford outside meals and whose rations were hardly adequate for sustenance.

When Dick Heindel moved into two rooms of my apartment, we shared our rations without ever any awkward striving for advantage.

Soon after Heindel was installed I added several other people to my staff: Dorothy Crook, to deal with the informational requirements of women's organizations and welfare agencies; and Ernestine Carter, wife of John Carter, the distinguished authority on rare books and manuscripts, as coordinator in charge of traveling exhibitions. Mrs. Carter, an American girl from Atlanta, Georgia, had had great experience with circulating exhibitions at the Museum of Modern Art in New York before going to London before the war.

British factories, schools and armed forces units made constant requests for photographic and even more elaborate exhibitions that would portray the American war effort and various aspects of American life. They were keen to know the details of American conscription, rationing, wartime transport regulations and especially to have more information on the war in the Pacific. We frequently persuaded the American Army, Navy and Air Force to help us with military material—but we had to have someone to design such exhibits for circulation throughout the United Kingdom.

Isolated British military units in restricted coastal zones were especially persistent in clamoring for American exhibits and speakers. We found many articulate men and women in the American military establishment in England who were happy to give their leave time to visit British factories and military units. By the end of the war the Embassy staff alone comprised nearly a thousand people, including those in the OSS, economic warfare and the psychological warfare staff of OWI engaged in propaganda to the Continent. As time ran on we recruited visitors who were requested by the Ministry of Information, Ministry of Supply and other British Government agencies as well as private organizations such as the National Council of Social Service.

Such visitors included the superintendent of schools in Seattle who was wanted by the president of the Board of Education, R. A. (Rab) Butler, who was working on postwar educational plans for England and Wales. When Dexter Keezer, a prominent educator, economist and journalist, arrived on a lend-lease mission, we prevailed on him to lengthen his stay by a week and lecture to significant groups. An extraordinarily capable and versatile man, a son-in-law of Lowell Mellet, special assistant to the President, Dexter had served as chief editorial writer of the *Baltimore Sun* and as president of Reed College in Portland, Oregon.

One of our prize occasional additions, deployed about the United Kingdom by Miss Ruth Wehle, was David Cushman Coyle. He had come semi-independently on an invitation from the Ministry of Information. It was issued prior to my arrival in London. When his visit ended he preferred to stay on in England for the duration, so we put him to work on a very modest per diem basis as a one-man brain trust. He advised the entire Embassy, and my office in particular, on history, economics, engineering and nautical matters. From time to time he would disappear and serve gratis on small British cargo steamers which dodged the mines in the Channel. David Cushman Coyle had written many books and articles and at the same time remained a typical Maine downeaster, at home on any sort of boat or ship, despite the fact that one of his legs was artificial.

In due course, the National Council of Social Service became concerned about the crowded American military installations in hundreds of British communities and wanted more advice than we could give on everything which could contribute to better understanding of Americans in provincial British towns and villages. The answer was simple: Bring over Margaret Mead, the anthropologist, and let her diffuse through the welfare agencies the kind of information and interpretation that would be conducive to harmonious understanding.

Her visit to England was a triumph of educational effort. She spoke, she wrote, she visited industrial towns and tiny villages that were often completely surrounded by our Army and Air Force, and enabled the British to understand why Americans were different from the British, why they chewed gum, why they walked with their hands in their pockets, why they seemed to enjoy playing with children more than British adults do and, above all, how American attitudes toward women differed from those of the British.

James Reston, meanwhile, left the news operation in charge of James Oldfield, and for a while Thomas S. Eliot, ex-congressman from a Massachusetts district that had been gerrymandered, occupied a plateau position with us, but the real completion of our operating group came with the return of Herbert Agar from Washington early in 1943 as special

F

assistant to the Ambassador and chief of the British Division. I was glad to abdicate from daily involvement in the news operation and henceforth devoted myself to the subtler channels of cultural and informational transmission. All of us endeavored to deliver the information that was wanted and let British individuals or agencies proceed without any overt propaganda on our part. Herbert Agar was at home in Britain. He remarried during the war and remained there—but he was fundamentally as American as the Founding Fathers and almost as eloquent and well versed in the articulation of political science and the ideals which give it life and meaning.

Soon after Herbert's association with us in the Embassy, the OWI established a compact service office in the United States headed by Ferdinand Kuhn, who had been London correspondent for *The New York Times* before the war, aided by Chester Williams, an educator, and Miss Mina Turner, a photographer and author. They provided us with every nuance of Washington policy not only from the OWI but from the Pentagon, the State Department and the White House, and unfailingly complied with our never unreasonable demands for information, speakers or news. The news cable at the Washington office was headed by E. W. (Ned) Kenworthy, now at the Washington bureau of *The New York Times,* who was extraordinarily skilled in sorting out the vital minimum of urgent documentation to relay to London.

It would be impossible and redundant to recite all of the significant and often unpublicized relations which led to the natural desire for authoritative knowledge about the United States during the war. One of the most influential men with whom I set up an early partnership was Sir Norman Scorgie, controller of His Majesty's Stationery Office, who out of the goodness of his heart and the boldness of his spirit (with the blessing of his Minister, representing the ubiquitous Treasury) not only turned out notable official publications for Britain, but actually reprinted a number of American Government Printing Office documents in such attractive format that they became best sellers in the bookshops of the United Kingdom.

We started off with *Target: Germany*, one of the early expositions on precision bombing prepared by the Eighth Air Force to give Americans, as well as others, a clear understanding of the relationship between American bombing and the British Bomber Command, which dealt with wholesale night targets to a greater degree than the Americans who aimed at critical targets where the German war effort was most vulnerable. This little book, of which Simon and Schuster sold less than one hundred thousand copies, sold over three hundred thousand in the HMSO edition. It paved the way for HMSO to undertake and print and circulate United States Government White Papers and other significant documents, entirely on my recommendation, as punctually and efficiently as if they were British documents. The range was enormous, including State Department documents, periodic reports by the lend-lease administration, the war mobilization office reports by James Byrnes and copies of significant wartime legislation as released in Washington through the Government Printing Office.

I enjoyed equal cooperation from Robert Fraser, chief of publishing at the Ministry of Information, who worked closely with Robert Cruikshank of the American Division on publishing projects deemed of special interest to the British and which, without such cooperation, would never have become available in the slow convoyed cargo-carrying fleets which were laden with strategic materials, food and a minimum of surface mail.

Few Britishers could secure currency exchange for renewal

of their subscriptions to American magazines, but they could find them at the American Library under the direction of Richard H. Heindel. Before the war I had known many of the leading British book publishers, but during the war I came to know nearly all of them extremely well. I helped them sort out the best American material that was awaiting publication, recommending additional paper quotas only when necessary. I usually favored Penguin Books for material which was deemed most useful if widely diffused. At that time Penguin was the only specialized paperback publisher with a large paper quota, so that Penguin could be more flexible in publication schedules than most of the hardcover publishers.

I associated myself very closely with the editors of the leading weeklies—*The Spectator* under Wilson Harris; Kingsley Martin of the *New Statesman and Nation;* Aneurin Bevan of *The Tribune;* Lady Rhondda and C. Veronica Wedgwood of *Time and Tide* and many others.

I found it useful to make frequent trips to the universities —not only Oxford and Cambridge, but Edinburgh, Glasgow and the provincial university and college centers in England and Wales. I was led to cultivate Chatham House—the Royal Institute of International Affairs—by an anecdote told to me by one of their learned staff. It seems that when the raids and sinkings were most severe, and no overseas magazines or newspapers had arrived for intelligence analysis, Professor Arnold Toynbee, director of Chatham House, came into the working area with a startling announcement: "I say, there is nothing in the hopper!" I did my best to fill the hopper with certain vital publications wanted by Chatham House from Latin America and the United States.

For a while J. Wallace Carroll was with us as a top executive of the OWI in London, and his wife, Peggy, ultimately became a member of the Embassy staff, working closely on matters affecting relationships with the American armed forces. I added one other member to my staff, Ruth Hooper, to coordinate intelligence so that everything we sought to do was demonstrably necessary and not a boondoggle. We imported practically no literature of information material except for deposit in the American Library for the voluntary use of researchers.

When my first secretary, Diana Horton, decided to leave, I recruited a remarkable young lady, Honora Bruère McIver, whose father, Henry Bruère, was president of the Bowery Savings Bank in New York and whose uncle and aunt, Robert and Martha Bruère, had been frequent contributors to the Survey publications. Honora was married to a Scottish officer and managed to keep a household running with a nurse and child and at the same time put in ten or eleven hours of work, sometimes seven days a week. She was an imaginative assistant and administrator and assumed many duties and responsibilities without being reminded or instructed to do so.

This enabled me to increase greatly my efficiency and that of all the others who were working under my direction. Fortunately, I seldom had to trouble the Ambassador about minor details of policy or procedure, nor did I have to worry Herbert Agar, Wallace Carroll or Washington with workaday matters. Herbert and I worked as a happy team, always in step and always in quick and cheerful consultation on essentials.

Unlike most Americans in Britain, I detected by 1943 that when the war ended the election would undoubtedly bring a labor government into power. Herbert was not so sure, and the Ambassador was very skeptical of my prediction. Nevertheless, both of them encouraged me to seek out the potential labor candidates from the trade unions, from the Fabians and from the socialistically inclined intellectual community, and to make certain that they were informed on the nature of the American political system and the personalities likely to emerge in the United States when the war was over.

I did not neglect the conservatives. Indeed, I could not neglect many of them who were firmly in Parliament or in the Government or potential candidates for Parliament. I refer to such old friends as Sir John Rodgers, Bart., M.P., at that time involved deeply with the Foreign Office on leave from J. Walter Thompson, Ltd., which he had helped to found in London after serving an apprenticeship under Stanley Resor of J. Walter Thompson, New York; or John Foster, now Sir John Foster, the eminent barrister who ultimately joined SHAEF as a brigadier. On one evening my flat in Kensington would seem to be a branch of the extreme right wing society of individualists; the next evening it would be a gathering of laborites including the eloquent Aneurin Bevan.

When special visiting professors such as Henry Steele Commager, Walter Prescott Webb or J. Frank Dobie assumed their posts at Cambridge or Oxford, they tended to make my office and my flat their headquarters in London, which in turn drew British scholars in every conceivable discipline to Abington Court. Denis W. Brogan of Peterhouse, Cambridge (now Sir Denis), probably knew more about the United States than any of us or our experts and was a veritable Dr. Johnson in his capacity for thoughtful but voluminous discourse. Denis's gift of inspired conversation on one occasion saved my life when I was dining with him at the Reform Club. At his insistence, I tarried for a nightcap of vintage port. I arrived in Kensington High Street by the last bus and found the traffic at a standstill. A high explosive bomb had dropped in Adam and Eve Mews just back of my flat, knocking in the windows and shaking most of the plaster off the ceiling of my bedroom. From the amount of glass that

had been violently hurled across my bed, I am certain that
I would never have survived if I had gone home a half hour
earlier and gone straight to bed. I never went to shelter
throughout the war.

Chapter VI

THE PEN AND THE SWORD

Time, gentlemen, please
—The classic closing cry of
English bartenders, marking
the beginning of a new night
and day ahead.

MY PRIVATE and professional concern with the affairs of authors and publishers was consistent with my assignment in London. We had to do what we could to establish the means to keep the flow of ideas through publications, mainly books, running in both directions across the dangerous wartime Atlantic. I was thus destined to become a strategic controller, and even selector, of this traffic.

Through Denys Kilham Roberts of the Society of Authors, I was invited to serve on the committee of management of the Society to keep *au courant* with the concerns of creative writers in England and to do anything possible to expedite normal relationships with their opposite numbers in the United States, as well as with their American publishers. On rare occasions I agreed that I would see that their heavy booklength manuscripts were flown to America in the heavy nonsecret pouch—otherwise, with airmail limited strictly to the half ounce in weight and with the slow movement of convoy ships, it sometimes took up to four or five months for heavy mail to cross the Atlantic by surface post. This gesture was blessed by the Ambassador and by the State Department as well as by OWI.

Actually, I did not leave the management committee of the Society of Authors until toward the end of the war when they put on the agenda the question of BBC fees for material, and I thought it unwise for me, as a member of the American Embassy staff, to get involved in knowledge of, let alone support of, negotiations aimed at a better settlement from a quasi-governmental agency, which the BBC was and is. I was sorry to miss the regular meetings with Osbert Sitwell, Rosamond Lehmann, John Strachey, Graham Greene and a dozen other eminent men and women of letters.

In connection with my agricultural interests, one of my fondest recollections of comfort during the war in England is of the occasional weekends with Lord Portsmouth at Farleigh Wallop, among the grassy acres and well-tilled fields, watching the great herd of British Friesians being cared for in modern barns and stables by elderly but faithful farm workers and young dairymaids. Late in the evening we would dine simply but with the embellishment of vintage claret and vintage port afterward, shared generously with whatever guest might be present—landed gentry, nobility, veterinarians, farm machinery repairmen and harried bureaucrats working for the Ministry of Agriculture. Portsmouth has now carried this marvelous atmosphere to his farm in Kenya. It is still a joy to reminisce with him in Africa, in London or in New York on our kindred views of high farming and conservation throughout the world.

It was the Ambassador's idea that if I were to reflect knowledge of developments in the United States, I should go to Washington and even visit war production centers in the hinterland from time to time. In the spring of 1943, I was instructed to return for a month to Washington and New

F*

York to consult with the OWI, the Department of State, the Pentagon and, while in the country, to gain as much knowledge as possible of political and economic and manpower trends as well as to explore training and education and post-war plans. I was delighted at the prospect and took off with as much mystery as I had been instructed to display when I left New York a year before.

This was the first of a number of quick executive returns to Washington. In each case I had to conclude my business by getting a new set of medical shots for transportation clearance and a new release from my draft board. Because I was slowed down on the 1943 flight to the United States, the Ambassador quickly up-graded my AGO status to the equivalent of a brigadier, which was useful not only in priority but in the amenities when delayed along the route of the Pan American Clippers. I always spent several days at the operating offices of OWI in New York, getting acquainted with the new personnel, as well as in Washington. Eventually, Bob Sherwood was succeeded by Philip Hamblett. James A. Linen, now president of Time, Inc., was responsible for the world-wide communications of OWI in cooperation with the Pentagon and the Department of State.

Elmer Davis seemed preoccupied with the domestic informational program and, so far as I can recall, even though he had been a Rhodes Scholar at Oxford, made only one inspection visit to London. He seemed to have confidence in any setup under the wing of Ambassador Winant and our small group of employees in the British Division. Always when in the United States I visited with General Frederick Osborn and with the Writers' War Board and the group in charge of the Armed Forces editions in New York. As the Ambassador stated in *Letter from Grosvenor Square,* posthumously published in 1947 and covering his experience as Ambassador in England up to the time of Pearl Harbor, "I tried to make as many contacts as possible with all people everywhere and in all localities. I visited the university towns and the larger cities, and covered all those areas in which there had grown up traditional loyalties to particular sections of the country. This included the south of England and the port towns, the Midlands, the North Country, the North of Ireland, Wales and Scotland."

So carefully did we hew to this dedicated line that one afternoon the Ambassador summoned me to his office simply to say that he had been rereading *Tom Sawyer,* and that he had to let me know that I reminded him somewhat of Tom when he artfully enticed his friends to whitewash the fence. I jokingly replied, "Do you remember the opening sentences of the *Adventures of Tom Sawyer?* —'Tom.' No answer. —"Please," I said, "don't go any further and borrow Aunt Pollie's phrase, 'Drat that boy.' " His appreciation of the fact that we relied on British individuals and agencies to multiply the precious information that we commanded was one of profound understanding.

To revert a moment to one of the significant episodes of 1942–43: Wendell Willkie in his *One World* tour—accompanied by Gardner Cowles and Joseph Barnes—was, despite President Roosevelt's blessing upon his journey, subtly diverted from visiting India by the British. They were obviously worried by Willkie's total conversion to global "liberation" as reflected in his speech of October 7, 1942 in Chungking, which was generously reported in the British press. In that provocative speech Willkie said:

> We believe this war must mean an end to the empire of nations over other nations. No foot of Chinese soil, for example, should be or can be ruled from now on except by the people who live on it. And we must say so *now,* not after the war.
> We believe it is the world's job to find some system for

helping colonial peoples who join the United Nations' cause to become free and independent nations. We must set up firm timetables under which they can work out and train governments of their own choosing, and we must establish ironclad guarantees, administered by all the United Nations jointly, that they shall not slip back into colonial status. . . .

On November 10, 1942, Prime Minister Churchill responded to Willkie's statement in China in the following statement at the Lord Mayor's Day Luncheon,

I have not become the King's First Minister in order to preside over the liquidation of the British Empire . . .

It was not our function to argue the points raised in this remote debate between Willkie and Churchill.

I don't believe that any of us could have predicted the postwar dissolution of the Empire and Commonwealth at the actual pace which occurred. But all of us, including staunch English, Scottish or Welsh friends, were aware of the exhaustion of the Mother Country and the inevitability of vast changes to come about when the war with Germany and Japan was ended. Some of our socialist friends seemed to be looking forward to a "cozy little England," but even they would not have been capable of spreading alarm and despondency by prophesying the constriction of Britain to its present actual dimensions. We had to think of Britain as what it was and what it represented in the fight for survival against insensitive brute force.

In the spring of 1943 when Dick Heindel received the first copy of *One World* as published by Simon and Schuster, he joined Wallace Carroll and me in taking it to the Ambassador a month before publication. Wally reports that Churchill handed the book to one of his aides and said, "Mark all the pages that will make me mad, so I'll read them." According to Wallace the Prime Minister expressed a variation of his November speech, "I did not become the King's First Minister to preside over the liquidation of the British Empire by Adolf Hitler—or by that other German, Wendell Willkie."

As testimony to the honesty and integrity which Britain represented, HMSO, in the course of reproducing and making available American White Papers under the imprint of the King's Printer, never hesitated to circulate even those documents that occasionally in detail, in essence or in intent were critical of British policy or proceedings or questioned Britain's future as a Great Power.

The war produced in Britain, as the gods had done in tiny ancient Greece, an army of heroes in and out of uniform who were giants on the world scene with Winston Churchill leading all of them. Whatever the future of the Empire, they loved their native land.

In the spring of 1943 the battle of North Africa was won, but the war in the Pacific was in the balance with desperate naval and air action indicated for a long time. While the military action in Europe proceeded from Sicily to Italy, the aerial action from Great Britain by Bomber Command and the Eighth Air Force grew in intensity and in numbers of planes involved—as well as in casualties. Generals Eisenhower and Spaatz and their staffs began the consolidated buildup of SHAEF for the ultimate invasion of the Continent. It sometimes seemed incredible when visiting English cities or isolated areas filled with troops that the countryside remained as beautiful and bucolic as before the war, except for the increasing plowlands and cultivation of ancient grassy areas that had not been stirred for centuries. The close coordination of the Ministry of Agriculture, the Ministry of Food, the various agencies engaged in shipping and economic warfare enabled Great Britain to take care of her own citizens and provide for the multitudes of Americans, Canadians and Poles (the latter mainly in Scotland) who were all a part of the effort. London became more cheerful with the crowded discomfort, although the underground stations were occupied at night by thousands of people who had not slept at home since the blitz of 1940. Rationing was strict and adhered to. Occasional alerts brought up the barrage balloons throughout the city, often simultaneously with the din of anti-aircraft fire. The most ominous subject of the time in England—and not excepting the war in Asia and in the Pacific or in the air—was the timetable for the European invasion of 1944. Secrecy became stricter than ever. Gossip was taboo except in the upper reaches of the Supreme Command which was taking shape and, curiously, in several of the upper-class clubs with their carefully selected membership that were often visited by members of the War Cabinet and, occasionally, by the Prime Minister himself.

Sometimes, with John Rodgers, I met with the Pyramus and Thisbe Club, a club of Americans and British who "talked through a wall." No breach of American security or of the British Official Secrets Act ever occurred at these gatherings, but we did manage to exchange views on overall developments of the war and on the occasional, almost unaccountable, shifts in highly placed personnel in the United States and in the United Kingdom.

A more intimate and eclectic forum for occasional discussions—mainly of postwar problems—was the PEP (Political and Economic Planning) Club in Queen Anne's Gate. This was an organization supported mainly by Israel Sieff and his colleagues at Marks and Spencer and devoted to general economic and cultural surveys as a basis for future plans and decisions. About fifty of us would meet monthly and sometimes discuss a particular topic such as agriculture, birth control, refugees, postwar reconstruction, the future of Japan and, above all, the future of Germany.

In due course, there was established in the Dean's yard in Westminster, the Churchill Club, a special club for members

of the American Armed Forces, including members of the
Embassy staff. There was always a Churchill on exhibit,
usually Major John Churchill or Pamela Churchill, then the
wife of Randolph Churchill, helping to serve the food and
drink.

These gatherings, multiplied a thousandfold in other parts
of the United Kingdom, brought us into a feeling of unique
comradeship. In the autumn of 1943 I was asked by General
Lee and the Ambassador to work with Colonel Jock Lawrence on plans to bring the American Army show written by
Irving Berlin, *This Is the Army,* to the British Isles. It
was obvious to Jock and me that the show could not be taken
on tour simply as a fantastic diversion for only our own
G.I.'s. We struck upon the idea of having a third of the seats
reserved for allied soldiers in addition to several appearances
throughout the country exclusively for allied troops with two-
thirds of the seats to be handled as a benefit. Through the
imagination and kindness of Mr. B. E. Astbury of the Charity
Organization Society, a British Service Charities Committee
was established with Lady Louis Mountbatten and Lady
Ward as co-chairmen and including Mrs. Ernest Bevin, Miss
E. M. Acton, Mrs. A. V. Alexander, Mr. B. E. Astbury, Mr.
George Black, Hon. Mrs. Jack Crayshay, Mrs. Dunderdale,
Lady Gordon Finlayson, Lady Jardine, The Countess of Lime-
rick, Hon. Mrs. Sydney Marsham, Mrs. Edward R. Murrow,
Mr. Robert Nesbit, Mr. Val Parnell, Mrs. Abel Smith, Lady
Strathallan and myself. The difficulty was to find a group of
theater owners or managers who would make their facilities
available during the Christmas season—sacred to the British
even during the war as the season of pantomime.

Due to the persuasive charm of Lady Louis Mountbatten,
who telephoned the most prominent British citizens in every
community, including Lord Abercorn at Belfast, regional
theaters were persuaded to cooperate after the grand opening

at the Palladium in London, where we had the wholehearted cooperation of George Black and the assistance of Val Parnell. Since Irving Berlin had written a special song for the British presentation, *My British Buddy,* we wanted to print that sheet to music. I prevailed on Louis Dreyfuss of Chappell to print it, and I gladly arranged for several hundredweight of extra paper quota for the purpose. The biggest problem faced by Jock and myself on behalf of the committee was to select the guests for the opening night.

We sat down with Lady Mountbatten and worked out an eminent guest list for the opening night, making certain to space out the top command so that if by any chance a bomb should drop on the Palladium there would be surviving talent to carry on the war. It was a wonderful show, and slightly ribald, especially one act which portrayed an American female officer ordering her sergeant husband about after a brief reunion and lovemaking before their respective leaves were ended.

Everything was planned in the greatest of detail except for the essential approval of the Lord Chamberlain, whose office is required by statute to censor theater performances in England before they are shown to the public. Fifteen minutes before the curtain went up we had to dispatch a courier to point out the juiciest number of the show so as to win with open candor Lord Clarendon's okay. It was forthcoming, but the curtain was late. This sudden bit of theatricals by uniformed Americans who were soon due to train for the invasion did as much good for the morale of the troops and civilians as any event of the somber autumn and winter of 1943–44. When the show went to Bristol, sections of the troupe visited Queen Mary, the Queen Mother, where she was staying with friends nearby, and she was enchanted, requesting so many encores that the contingent nearly missed their curtain at Bristol in the evening.

Lady Mountbatten was active throughout the war in a dozen causes, including the Red Cross and Toc-H, lending a touch of gracious dynamics to every occasion. I had known Louis Dreyfuss professionally, but we became fast friends as a result of the myriad details with which we had to cope together in connection with *This Is the Army*.

We arranged for Irving Berlin to be invited to Ten Downing Street to dine with Winston Churchill. This was prior to the opening of the show. The Prime Minister had him confused with the other I. Berlin, Isaiah Berlin, the philosopher at Oxford who for a while during the war was stationed with the British Embassy in Washington and whose voluminous dispatches to the Foreign Office became the most desirable reading of the period because of his incredible gifts of perception and expression. It was something of a joke in London that the Prime Minister had confused two visitors, because of typically inadequate and mumbled British introductions, with Isaiah Berlin. On another occasion Adolf Berle was wrongly identified by the Prime Minister. Since he was an assistant secretary of state, Berle was shocked when the Prime Minister looked up and said, "Mr. Berlin, I always ask to see all of your cables. They are irresistible in their appeal and in the accuracy of their political information."

Although it was not really my responsibility to deal with the American military establishment, after the success of *This Is the Army*, I was besieged with requests for Embassy cooperation by the Army, the Air Force and the Navy. Sometimes they wanted to imitate ABCA, with voluntary—not required duty time—educational programs based on prescribed subjects with a specially prepared pamphlet for orientation on respective themes. I always replied that all I could do would be to try to provide a qualified author—and from mimeographed beginnings this effort grew into a program supervised by Special Service, called "Army Talks."

Nearly every day British book publishers, with no thought of paper quotas, sought my advice on postwar priorities for putting books back into print, especially those dealing with American themes or written by American authors. I found myself a free counselor on a dozen or more publishing programs. Although periodical publishers were not permitted extra paper quotas and no new periodical could be launched under the wartime regulations, one exception was made. It grew out of conversations with Allen Lane and John Carter, then in the Ministry of Information. It was suggested by Morris L. Ernst, the New York lawyer, that the Writers' War Board in the United States would be happy to make material available or to write it specially, provided a vehicle for the material could be found. Brendan Bracken and the Ambassador both agreed that it was of sufficient importance to create a special exception to wartime regulations, provided that the Ministry of Supply Paper Control would not object. We started it in 1943 with Geoffrey Crowther, then editor of the *Economist,* as our editor. He and his brother had lived in America, had married sisters in Delaware, and he had been graduated from Harvard. Allen Lane leapt at the idea.

In 1946 when I opened an exhibition of British books produced in the previous two years, my memory went back to wartime London as I told the postwar audience what I had observed of British book publishing in London. It was interesting, looking backward, to note the content as well as the design of books under preparation during the war for a clue to the character of the people who produced them.

From Sir Osbert Sitwell's charming autobiography to the amusing little Tom Thumb chapbook, from such a utilitarian volume as *Cast Iron in Building* to Plato's *Examination of Pleasure* in a new textbook translation, and from the latest Penguins to Harrap's two *Home Guard* volumes, they reflected the humane society that Britain was fighting for when the volumes were in production.

There was a dearth of novels. There was an avalanche of printed material from His Majesty's Stationery Office. Without for a moment questioning the selection of volumes, I felt a little disappointed that, for overseas purposes, our British friends did not give Americans a chance to see some of the magnificent wartime work done by the King's Printer.

The poignant intimacy whereby the war brought about a more kindly consideration of one another in England was reflected by the exhibition.

Practically all of the books were planned for the common reader and priced within reach of his purse. This was not wholly due to the austerity of wartime, which tended to make everything, including books, a utility model. It was induced by the urge to communicate with—to commune with—the ordinary man. The squire in his manor, the lord in his hall and the industrialist in his midland villa never before in Great Britain partook of the same necessities and minor luxuries at the same price as the workmen or village housewife, until the war.

During the four or five months prior to the invasion, German Intelligence must have been extraordinarily inept insofar as England and SHAEF were concerned. Notable Generals could not conceal their presence—Bradley and Patton, for example, recognizable by even uninformed newspaper readers. Except for journalists who were covering the Pacific, outstanding newspapermen from America began to converge upon England. The inflow of troops was tremendous, and the growth of SHAEF headquarters almost a match for the Pentagon. I had a general pass to restricted coastal areas but seldom used it during this period—although I encouraged my staff to proceed normally when invited to speak in the banned zones.

The flow of men and material continued throughout the spring, and then, one day, none of the war correspondents could be found in London—they had vanished to join the invading forces, not to return until they had covered the Normandy beaches. Even our staff meetings took on a guarded atmosphere lest anyone would reveal anything exceptional in his everyday experience. A few days before D-Day we were briefed in top secrecy, and soon the whole world suddenly knew even more fully than the Germans, at first, that the landings were not a feint, but the real thing.

All of us in the Embassy lost a few friends with whom we had been associated for several months or for several years, but our concern for others was suddenly punctuated by concern for ourselves. The buzz bombs began to descend upon London. They came with a buzz while still following their trajectory and then a mighty explosion when making impact on the city below. They were followed a few months afterward by the V-2's, the giant missiles which were more powerful but less deadly unless they made a direct hit on a crowded building or area, since they drove a deep hole in the ground before exploding and catapulting less glass and debris horizontally than the V-1's.

The year 1944 was an election year in America, and it was decided in a meeting between the Ambassador and myself that I should return to the States for six weeks, coming back to London immediately after the election with as good firsthand impressions as I could gather on Thomas Dewey, John W. Bricker and Senator Harry S Truman.

I heard all of the candidates speak and had a rather dismayed view of Franklin D. Roosevelt's preelection campaign, looking older and less buoyant and not in the full vigor of 1940. I went as far west as Iowa to visit Alan B. Kline, later head of the American Farm Bureau Federation, who had come to England the year before on an invitation by the British Ministry of Agriculture.

In Detroit I did my best to get a grasp of present and post-war thinking in the automobile industry and among the United Automobile Workers, spending one long evening with Walter Reuther in his modest bungalow with a group called together for discussion. In Des Moines I stopped long enough for lunch with Bill Waymack of the Des Moines *Register and Tribune,* then wove my way eastward in time to vote and return to London.

I recommended that we lay down as much background material on Harry Truman as we could, not realizing how urgently important it would be. I had a brief session with Henry Wallace and felt relieved that neither he nor James Byrnes had been nominated and elected as Vice-President. No one in England at that time seemed to want to know anything about Harry Truman, but Dick Heindel and I kept discreetly reminding people that he was possibly going to be President of the United States during the next four years.

On the way to the American Thanksgiving Service at Westminster Abbey with the Ambassador, who read the morning lesson, he was morose and preoccupied. "F.D.R." is not a well man, he said, and he added even more dolefully the same observation later when he returned from the Cairo Conference which preceded Yalta.

After the suspense of the Bulge during the Christmas season of 1944, we all knew that victory in Europe was in sight. The Ambassador as chairman of the European Advisory Committee was frequently inaccessible. Pentagon characters began to appear in increasing frequency, obviously to survey the transfer of the war effort to the Pacific and to deal with urgent problems of occupation.

Among those who came to London during this period were Governor Lehman of New York, as chairman of UNRRA, and experts on sanitation, transportation, medicine, nutrition and other specialized matters essential to the future. Russia suddenly became a more suspicious ally than hitherto. People were frightened by the advent of European peace, in a strange sort of way. We did our utmost to promote greater comprehension of and interest in the war against Japan, but the main concern of the British—after six years of war—was with the reconversion of Great Britain to a peacetime life with a future.

On April 12, 1945, at about 11:15 in the evening, the telephone of my apartment rang while Dick Heindel was coming in the door. I suggested that he take the call and tell anyone who wanted me that I was not available. He hung up the phone and said:

"I'm afraid it is now the big two-and-a-half." He was breathless. "Roosevelt is dead," he said, "and the Embassy wants us to return to Number One Grosvenor Square."

We got a taxi in Kensington High Street, and when we arrived we found that the Ambassador, who had dined out, was walking home on a balmy spring evening unaware of the President's death. There was an atmosphere of shock, disbelief and grief.

Dick Heindel was the first man in action. He dashed to the Library, organized his Harry S Truman material—speeches, statements, biographical accounts—then priority was received for immediate printing, and by morning every editor and notable person of influence in London had his extraordinary compilation in convenient form before him. It was Heindel's quick and correct judgment that most news would be concerned with the late President and that the new President seriously needed more attention than he would get from the press.

Dick Heindel emerged at dawn from his labors a self-converted admirer of Truman whom he had been prone to belittle a few hours earlier. I confirmed his attitude from first-hand evidence while I had been in the States on my preelection assignment the autumn before.

My first telephone call the next morning was an inquiry from Madame Tussaud's Wax Works. The speaker wanted President Truman's measurements—shoe size, hat size, preference in colors—for immediate action. Madame Tussaud's Wax Works figures, like living people, were subject to clothes rations, but the speaker said he had an American suit in storage if it remotely adjusted to the effigy that was already in preparation. Within an hour I received the requested information from Washington and later learned that Elmer Davis personally had taken charge of gathering the new President's measurements.

Then came a second call from Madame Tussaud's saying that they had no photograph of the back of Mr. Truman's head. I said I would try to locate a picture, but it seemed that Mr. Truman was a very able politician with sense enough to face the camera when photographers were present. Several photographs of Mr. Truman from the rear were located, however, in Washington and speeded to London.

That curious episode was scarcely over when I was informed that the British were preparing a memorial service in St. Paul's on April 17, and that only three hundred American guests could be accommodated. Dorsey Fisher, the press attaché, and I worked day and night sorting out the list and getting the invitations and tickets into the right hands. The outcome was nearly perfect with very few disappointments except on the part of junior members of the Embassy staff and some of the Red Cross people in the London area. The service included all the Royal Family, the Prime Minister and all of his Cabinet and nearly every chief of the British and American Armed Forces. When the service was over, I realized what a tremendous psychological help it had been to be working under total pressure without a moment's rest, around the clock, and above all with a staff and associates who had swung into action as if prepared in detail for the emergency.

There is no point in describing the effects of V-E Day and the preliminary drama and the effect of Hitler's death in Berlin. But to me one of the highlights of the occasion was the personal experience of mingling with the joyous throngs in London. A group of a half dozen of us, holding hands so as not to get separated, managed to get through Birdcage Walk from Whitehall. Finding that we were very near to Wellington Barracks commanded by Colonel John Vigor, an invalided guardsman and a close friend, I decided to call upon him. To my amazement, he was available, although he confided that he had just been requested by Buckingham Palace to send over several guardsmen to escort the Princesses out of the Palace to join the crowd, where they could observe the King and Queen and the Prime Minister waving from the balcony where they themselves had recently been part of the pageantry. It was especially significant because the Royal Family had firmly refused to leave Buckingham Palace for safer headquarters during the war. Presently, the Princesses and three officers of the guards appeared and joined hands with our group and for fifteen minutes milled through the throng without anyone recognizing the Princesses, so that they had a full view of the scene on the Palace balcony from the point of view of the jubilant celebrants in the Mall.

The next day we went early to a service of Thanksgiving and then the routine was resumed without a break. The Prime Minister in jocose fashion had canceled the regulation making it a crime "to spread alarm and despondency."

Meanwhile, a general election had been called for July 5, 1945, with the final results to be withheld until the service vote, by mail, was in hand on July 26. This meant, of course, that the coalition Government functioned until July, with

Deputy Prime Minister Atlee accompanying Prime Minister Churchill to the Potsdam Conference to meet Stalin in the company of President Truman and Secretary of State Byrnes. In that period, although it seemed unbelievable to most of my associates in the Embassy and incredible and preposterous to the Ambassador, I had predicted that the outcome would be a strong labor victory.

This certainty on my part was not due to any special prescience, but to faith in objective scientific observation. First of all, the Gallup Polls published by the *News Chronicle* and meticulously compiled under the direction of Henry Durant were available to all. Second, the mood of the armed forces, many of them mobilized for a period of six years, was apparent. Most of them did not trust the Tories to reconstruct civilian roles for them in a framework of jobs, adequate housing, health and social security. They were not socialist despite their years of custodial care in uniform. But they were skeptical of Winston Churchill as a peacetime leader.

I watched Churchill on the hustings, noted that he was greeted with cheers then interrupted with harsh boos when he began to expound on the brave new world to be constructed in postwar Britain. The generation of 1945 were not aware of Churchill's social programs in the Lloyd George Liberal period prior to World War I. They evaluated him as a pugnacious John Bull, too Shakespearean in his love of England to be concerned with mundane hopes and fears in the workaday world.

I went to the Ambassador with a cable for the State Department predicting the Labor victory. He hesitated, then refused to send it under his name. He seemed convinced that the Liberals, who still occupied a substantial position in the frozen political pattern of wartime, would hold the balance of power or swing the election decisively toward the Conservative Party. When I spoke to a prominent member of the

Conservative Party in Parliament, he warned me that he hoped the Conservatives would not win the election, predicting that the result would be strikes and a government impasse as the necessity of stringent economic controls and rationing were essential in the economic adjustments at the end of lend-lease and the American support of the British economy under wartime mobilization.

I sent my cable personally and direct to a friend in Washington who assured me that he had brought it to the attention of the highest levels of Government as well as to the Office of War Information.

I was not surprised when the outcome was known and Clement Atlee formed a Labor Government. I knew some forty of the new Labor M.P.'s, as well as half a dozen Conservative war heroes who were elected, and soon managed to bring them into acquaintance with the Ambassador and my associates of the Foreign Service. There was an orderly transition in relationships, mainly engineered by Herbert Agar and myself, with the full cooperation of Ambassador Winant and the permanent secretaries of Embassy.

The Ambassador was concerned lest all of his temporary helpers would take the end of the war in Europe as a signal for return to their civilian lives. In a heart-to-heart talk, I gave him my pledge not to leave until the war against Japan was won. He then suggested that before I leave I recruit a successor. This was an impossible assignment in London, especially since the State Department was planning totally to take over my functions and wanted me to remain and join the Foreign Service as a regular overseas officer. We compromised by agreeing that I would return to the States for some of the authoritative meetings that were scheduled during the summer and that if that time coincided with the fall of Japan, I would return for a brief period so as to leave no gap in my work.

Herbert Agar and the OWI officers in Washington concurred. So, by adeptness in understanding the complexity of
traveling orders, I was able to head for Washington the day
that the first atom bomb was dropped on Hiroshima. We were
delayed by weather in Ireland, and the Nagasaki bomb was
dropped while I was there. By the time I reached Washington, the V-J Day Parade was in full swing.

The war was over. Like twelve million other men and
women in direct wartime service, I was as good as demobilized, *almost*—I had promised the Ambassador and Herbert
Agar I would not forsake my battle station in Grosvenor
Square until I had produced a successor. So I knew that after
the Washington conferences and the indoctrination of my
successor, I must return to London. Unlike many of my countrymen I was not troubled by any professional or personal
problems of peacetime. I had a flourishing farm in Maryland
and three auspicious offers for well-paid postwar positions,
two of them with an assured future. The third was the appeal
by Allen Lane for me to join his limping American Penguin
enterprise as chairman of the board and editor-in-chief to
build it into a counterpart of Penguin Books Limited in England. Allen Lane said that he had informed the caretaker in
charge of the tiny enterprise in New York, Kurt Enoch, a
German-Jewish refugee who had reached America after the
fall of France, having moved his comparatively small English-
language continental paperbound publishing activities from
Hamburg to Paris and finally escaped to New York.

The State Department had billeted me in the Dodge Hotel,
near Union Station, an un-airconditioned hostel which, in addition to other disadvantages, was a temperance hotel without a bar. I frightened an ancient spinster secretary of the
State Department by offering her an evening's employment
in my modest hotel bedroom. Despite her qualms, she was

'tempted by the offer of fifty dollars for twenty-four hours work, plus restaurant money, for my assignment.

My special task, for which I took official leave, was to observe firsthand the state of the paperbound book industry in the United States on the basis of a spot check of what was available for sale in Washington. I had purchased some three dozen titles and had them laid out on the bed when my helper arrived. I suggested that she go to a dozen drugstores and newsstands and book shops and purchase specimen copies of books in every category under every imprint which she could find. Three hours later, close to midnight and obviously under suspicion by the hotel staff, she arrived in my bedroom with her purchases. Supplementing the volumes which I had bought, we arranged them, and by quarter to two had made a tally of what seemed to be the essence of American paperbacks produced at that moment.

I dismissed my helper and asked her to contrive a half day's leave if possible the following day to transcribe my notes.

I could not sleep because of the heat and because of the excitement of my discovery. A hundred-odd paperbound books revealed that the highest literary level was probably represented by Pearl Buck's *The Good Earth,* and the most pretentious effort at nonfiction—except a few topical wartime orientation volumes—was Joseph Davies' *Mission to Moscow.* There was one collection of Erskine Caldwell's short stories but not a trace of Faulkner, Farrell, Hemingway, Fitzgerald, Lewis, Wolfe, Cather, Joyce, Proust or James. The whole array was a pale reflection of the splendid literary fare available in the Armed Forces' Editions and devoid of the taste and vision which had characterized ten years of Penguins and Pelicans in England.

By the time my frightened female recruit returned in the morning, my mind was made up. I hastily dictated letters of regret to two of the big publishing enterprises which had wanted to employ me, and which had continued to implore me to join them, while I was in London, in strategically high positions at the end of the war. I wrote a brief note to Allen Lane, by way of an APO aerogram letter to a friend in London, saying that I was proceeding to New York and would cable after inspecting the situation at Penguin Books, Inc. I had been asked by Allen Lane to get in touch with Morris L. Ernst, the attorney to whom I had introduced him in London and whom he had enlisted in May, but I decided instead to go first of all to 245 Fifth Avenue and meet Herr Dr. Enoch.

The journey to New York in a dirty express car, apparently the only passenger accommodation with space for a standee, marked the last wartime humiliation of my life as a traveling official. Fortunately, I had telephoned Hollow Rock Farm to ask my farmer to pick up my luggage and laundry in Washington, and I had telephoned my house in New York so that fresh linen and clothing were available at my club. Carefree and unencumbered, my decision made, I hurried to 245 Fifth Avenue at 28th Street and presented myself, only to discover that I was a complete stranger and that Dr. Enoch not only had never heard of me but was determined not to see me.

I waited for two hours, and finally Enoch agreed to see me. Meanwhile, I gather, he had been on the telephone with Morris Ernst, Harriet Pilpel and his personal attorney, a fellow refugee from Germany who had found his way to America as an émigré from Nazi threats to the Jewish population of his unhappy country. It was not an auspicious commencement of my new incarnation, but I resolved that, having endured a good many German bombs and burnt my bridges behind me, I could endure a bit of German rudeness in New York.

Chapter VII

PARNASSUS—AT LAST

Parnassus has its flowers of transient fragrance, as well as its oaks
of towering height, and its laurels of eternal verdure.

—Samuel Johnson

IT IS STILL, after more than twenty years, like recalling a
Kafka nightmare to try to reconstruct my week's leave in New
York in August, 1945, before going back to Washington for
conferences and then to London to conclude my assignment
at the Embassy. In London I had become a friend and admirer of Allen Lane. We were of the same age, with a genuine interest in publishing, art, public affairs, gardening and
farming.

By 1945, when the wartime pressures had eased, Allen frequently invited me to Silverbeck, his spacious house at Stan-
well Moor, to chat and work along with him in the garden
—alternating between the roses, the greenhouse and the vegetable patch. I was early that summer godfather of his second
daughter, Camilla Christine. Like his uncle John Lane—who
had come up to London as a Devonshire farmer's son at the
age of fourteen, precociously literary enough before the age of
twenty to sponsor the Yellow Book, to found the Bodley
Head, a distinguished publishing enterprise, and to establish
himself with a flat in Albany—Allen was endowed with the
energy, charm and brains of an exceptional country boy in

the big city. His brother John had lost his life in the African landings. His brother Richard was in the Royal Navy until he was demobilized after the Japanese surrender.

His paperbound books, initially priced at sixpence, had achieved sufficient volume between the beginnings of the enterprise and the outbreak of the war to command a substantial paper quota, often supplemented by the Government for special purposes. In 1935 Allen had left his uncle's firm, The Bodley Head, when its fortunes declined and was later only saved by the support of a group of British publishers, including Jonathan Cape and Sir Stanley Unwin. Allen with pioneering foresight had thrown his entire energy into his struggling new Penguin enterprise, which was a large organization in a new building at Harmondsworth, Middlesex (near the present London Airport) by the time I had arrived in London in early 1942.

Unlike myself, Allen Lane was not an avid reader. Indeed, he was not widely read, but was proud of the schooling he had received in the Bristol Grammar School and of his bold and compulsive affinity for writers, scholars and leaders in the book trade. Aware of his literary and scholarly limitations, he had surrounded himself with a remarkable brain trust.

One of his early advisors had been Krishna Menon, a radical Indian barrister and an occasional Labor Party candidate for Parliament and the London County Council. In a way, Krishna Menon really invented Pelican Books, the imprint parallel to the more popular Penguin series, consisting mainly of scholarly, scientific and political works. Krishna Menon, a member of the Fabian group in London, came to the old abandoned church which was the first Penguin headquarters with the brief written consent of George Bernard Shaw to produce a paperbound Penguin edition of *The Intelligent Woman's Guide to Socialism*.

By an odd coincidence, Allen Lane had that very day called

on the Bumpus Book Shop in Oxford Street, driving his own van and wearing a workman's overall. Doffing his overall and looking very smart in his Savile Row suit, he then requested payment from Mr. Wilson, the manager. At that suspenseful moment, Allen observed a woman customer admiring the new Penguins and requesting a shop assistant to wrap up a package of the "charming little Pelican Books" as a gift for a sick friend.

As Allen recounted that experience, he had a moment of dismay that some competitor might adopt the Pelican imprint and collide with his Penguin symbol. When he returned to the office-warehouse, he promptly told Krishna Menon that he would issue Shaw's book under the Pelican imprint. Krishna Menon protested that he had secured permission only for the Penguin imprint. "I'll jolly well take care of that," said Lane.

The book was published as the first Pelican. This led onward to the aviary imprints which developed—Puffins for children, Ptarmigans for crossword puzzles and games, and ultimately other P-Birds, including Peacocks.

It was obvious that these two proud and determined men, Lane and Krishna Menon, could not work together for long. Some people ascribe Krishna Menon's aversion to Europeans and even to Americans to the experience of being dominated by Lane. On his first official visit to the United Nations in New York after the war, Krishna Menon vehemently assured me he would never trust any English or American publisher.

Lane then recruited H. A. Beales, a reader in economics at London University and, subsequently, W. E. Williams, first introduced to him by Krishna Menon, who functioned throughout the war as an advisor while at the same time running British army educational schemes. When Penguin reprinted Agatha Christie's mysteries and Lane discovered that her husband, Max Mallowan, was an archaeologist, he quickly turned to Mallowan and his friends for the planning of books in the fields of prehistory and archaeology. He was an early discoverer of the genius of Nicolas Pevsner, the remarkable authority on architecture.

Before the war was over he had recruited E. V. Rieu, an able amateur classicist who had once represented Methuen in India, to plan and edit Penguin Classics. Restless, possessive, Allen Lane seemed determined not to let any promising literary or scholarly figure elude his grasp. He was aided by Eunice Frost, who had commenced as his secretary and soon had become an indispensable general aide, and William Glover, a fantastic "inside" editor, tattooed from head to foot including his hands, so that he habitually wore gloves in the office.

Lane had bought a farm near Reading, Old Priory. His friends helped him to renovate the premises and the old farmhouse while tenants cultivated his arable land and stocked his grazing meadows with cattle. By 1944 it had become apparent that in a not quite firm but persistent fashion Lane was endeavoring to lure me into his organization as chief of Penguin Books, Inc. in New York. This operation was then in charge of Ian Ballantine, who, while studying at the London School of Economics, had written an essay on the economics of book publishing. When Professor Beales brought the essay to Lane's attention, Lane summoned Ballantine and, without bothering to read the essay, impulsively said,

"We want you to represent us in New York. We'll send you books. You sell them. Eventually we shall develop capital enough to expand in America; after all, Penguin Books Limited, began with one hundred pounds capital."

Not long after Ballantine returned to New York, the war commenced. Shipments were delayed or sunk due to German

G

submarine action, and under British Government regulation no long-term credit could be granted in the dollar area.

Obviously, Penguin Books, Inc. could not exist as an import agency. Ian Ballantine was not then professionally qualified to produce books and was averse to going into book publishing. It was then that Dr. Kurt Enoch appeared and, functioning as production manager, produced books, helped to secure paper quotas and when cash was low, persuaded fellow refugees to invest on a percentage basis in some of the books that were produced.

In May 1945, when Lane visited New York, he had cabled me urgently requesting me to return to America and head the company. I refused to entertain any such idea until he returned to London, and until I had an opportunity to see the situation firsthand and to remain faithful to my commitment not to leave the Embassy till the Japanese War was successfully concluded.

Upon Lane's return to England in June 1945, we had many talks about his American plans. I learned that Ballantine had left the company, taking a modest payment for his minority shares, and was organizing a rival concern to be called Bantam Books, owned jointly by Curtis Publishing Company and Grosset and Dunlap. The Grosset investment had been precipitated by the purchase of Simon and Schuster and Pocket Books by Marshall Field after an unsuccessful overture to Grosset. The Grosset owners who had saved the company from Field were Scribner's; Harper's; Little, Brown; Random House and the Book of the Month Club.

These merger developments meant that the struggling and nearly defunct American Penguin Books enterprise was in competition with powerful Curtis-Grosset-Bantam and the Marshall Field-Simon and Schuster Pocketbooks combinations, not to mention Dell (Western Printing) and Avon. Having inspected and appraised the product of all these rival gentry, I was not in the least worried by competition. I knew within me that a careful but dramatic plan to emerge with a first-class product would win out in the long run, provided that a national distributor could be found to handle the distribution of the books through the magazine wholesalers who were essential for the mass market.

Morris L. Ernst and Kurt Enoch had been in touch with Fawcett Publications, who years earlier had briefly handled token shipments of Penguin Books from England and who were keen to include books among the paper products, comics and periodicals which they circulated on the foundation laid a generation earlier by Captain Billy's *Whizbang*. I was told by Elliot O'Dell, who had successfully developed the Fawcett magazines as advertising media, that my visionary description of the future of Penguin Books as relayed by him to the Fawcett brothers was undoubtedly more persuasive than Enoch's and Ernst's presentation.

However, before I could exert myself on behalf of Penguin Books, I had to pass the hurdle of Enoch's unwillingness to see me or discuss prospects with me. It was his claim that Allen Lane had bestowed total confidence upon him to run the enterprise single-handed. From the cables and communications which I had seen in Allen Lane's office and at the office of Lane's solicitor, Ronald Rubinstein, in London, I realized that this was not an accurate or maintainable statement of his position.

Morris Ernst and Harriet Pilpel were legal counsel for Penguin, and Rudolf Littauer, a fellow refugee, represented Enoch. I was unrepresented. Enoch wanted to avoid catastrophic litigation and removal, so he finally had to agree to associate himself with me in a situation of absolute parity, or sue. I would be chairman of the board and editor-in-chief. Meanwhile, in a last-ditch gesture which could hardly have been accidental, he had put out a press release which was printed in *Publisher's Weekly* stating that I had been taken into the company as a vice-president. This was beaten down back in London with the support of cables and letters from Morris Ernst, but it took me quite a while in the winter of 1946 to make it clear that in no sense was I subservient to the already dictatorial presidential office of Dr. Enoch.

Now, to return for a moment to my two-hour vigil outside Enoch's door in August 1945. When he condescended to see me, he stated that Lane had not ever mentioned my name or my visit to America, that he did not intend to give an inch or to allow me on the premises. He regarded me as a stooge for Lane and an intruder, and said so. For most of the week of the talks which followed, he refused to speak to me or to make any concession, relying upon the spokesmanship of Littauer to Ernst and Ernst to me.

I emerged unbeaten. I was not even worried, for I knew that the company could not thrive or grow under such stubborn Germanic management. I insisted that Enoch be retained to specialize in production and distribution, while I planned the publishing program, working jointly on financial matters. Just before my return to London, Enoch capitulated and conceded that my ability—of which he knew nothing and wanted to know nothing—might be useful. From that concession we reached the formula of *absolute parity*.

I was acquainted with the publishers from whom titles were licensed, with members of the literary profession and their agents, and my standing was known within the American publishing establishment. It was obvious to all, and ultimately conceded by Enoch, that his gifts might well be applied to production and distribution, but certainly not to the evolution of a publishing program or to public relations in the United States. His prewar, Albatross, continental English-language editions based upon licensing of best sellers, in the days before American book exports to the Continent were generally profitable, had not taught him anything of American tastes and trends except to follow the best-seller lists for reprint candidates.

I began with the preparation of a scholarly Pelican program for America. I lined up E. C. Lindeman, Professor of Philosophy at Columbia and a sort of adult education opposite number of Penguin's W. E. Williams. We also enlisted at Ernst's suggestion my friend Jerome Frank, the jurist. It was they who recommended the scope of our first Pelican reprint titles in America which, against Enoch's opposition, were issued commencing in January, 1946, the first being Walter Lippman's *Public Opinion,* followed by three of Gamow's science volumes, Ruth Benedict's *Patterns of Culture* and Ortega y Gasset's *The Revolt of the Masses.* The Pelican series two years later, when we acquired the company from Lane, became the Mentor Series.

I had privately if not publicly won my own battle, but the franchise included the challenge of creating from it a totally new thing in twentieth-century America—publishing books of genuine quality at a low price, including important and educational nonfiction as well as the finest fiction.

I briefly conferred with Charles W. Ferguson of *Reader's Digest,* whom I had persuaded to succeed me in London, and then I returned for two months to wind up the work of my office in the Embassy. This was at the period when the activities with which I had been identified were emerging under State Department auspicies as public affairs and cultural affairs offices. My wartime operation was adopted as standard equipment for American missions overseas. I was told by many State Department officials that my pioneering office in London provided the pattern of the future, which has survived through the years since then.

It was almost inconceivable to Gil Winant that his Embassy family of the wartime years was, with the exception of Herbert Agar, disappearing so suddenly.

Winant was a haunted man. The week of my departure from London in November, he came to Claridge's for a large farewell party and for an hour was his jovial self, chatting from group to group with authors and publishers and enjoying especially his reminiscences of wartime days with such members of the new Labor Government as Ernest Bevin, Stafford Cripps, Aneurin Bevan and others of the British Cabinet. Regardless of the austerity of the period, Allen Lane had prevailed upon Claridge's to loosen up their cellar and their pantry for the party, and we had a difficult time terminating the cocktail gala with a desperate flashing off and on of the lights in the ballroom. I was busy making the rounds of old friends during that week and bidding fond farewell to my colleagues, my own immediate staff and my old and new friends in London.

Every day included an hour with Allen Lane to discuss the prospects ahead of us in America. For the first time it dawned upon me that perhaps he had deliberately forced Enoch and me to the cockpit for a showdown, since he was not prepared to commit himself about the ultimate release of controlling shares and earning shares in the American enterprise.

For the first time, too, I noted that Allen Lane deep underneath was a "little Englishman" as only a Welshman can be, worried that the American Penguin Books might fail but even more worried that it might succeed and outdistance his parent organization in Britain. He seemed to sense that when wartime paper and other controls were removed the United States would become the master nation of the English tongue, and he did not want to lose the capacity for total control that he had thus far been unable to exercise because of the breakdown in communications with New York during the war. He was especially suspicious of Enoch's possible infidelity to

Penguin standards and repeatedly advised me to keep him fully informed through private correspondence channels on the course of our relationships as they would subsequently develop.

The night before my return to America on the first overseas American Airlines flight between London and Washington, the Lanes gave an extraordinarily lavish party at Silverbeck. In a glow of good fellowship from many toasts I bade farewell with the warm assurance that all must go well.

Upon arriving in Washington I checked out of the Government and without even visiting my nearby farm in Maryland went immediately to New York on the night train and appeared at the Penguin Books offices in the morning.

They were located in a building mainly occupied by rug and toy companies, overcrowded and ill-kempt. It was no time for swank. The company was practically broke. I shared my office for several months with Eunice Frost, on loan from Penguin Books Ltd. in England, who had arrived while I was in New York in the summer. Except for overloading the publishing schedule with a dozen dreary out-of-date English country-house mysteries, her literary and scholarly taste had paved the way for my active beginning in the best Penguin tradition.

Under my earlier instructions from London, Eunice Frost had recruited two exceptional editors and commenced to train them in the Penguin approach to softcover publishing. They were Arabel J. Porter and Donald Demarest, who in turn had enlisted the temporary service of Saul Bellow as a reader. They had accumulated several hundred books for me to read as candidates for reprint if negotiations with the owners of the rights could be managed.

I was desperately anxious to get to Maryland to see my farm and my parents and to discuss with my wife the sale of our house in Westchester and the total transfer of country quarters to Hollow Rock Farm. It was even more apparent than before my absence during the war that my wife and I were not destined to remain together. She was increasingly preoccupied with her own magazine career and, although sympathetic to my new venture, not inclined to understand my total concentration upon it. By Christmas time we had found a buyer for the house in Westchester and arranged to move the contents to Maryland, meanwhile rushing redecoration of the farmhouse so that it would be in impeccable condition as a home within reach of Washington and Baltimore and not unhandy for weekend guests from New York.

It was not until New Year's Eve of 1945 that I really had an adequate opportunity to visit Hollow Rock Farm and to study the crops and livestock program in detail. To my amazement, my notes from London during four years of absence—except for a half dozen quick appearances when I was in Washington on special brief missions—had been meticulously observed. The farm was flourishing, the dairy herd obviously headed toward prizewinning potential in conformation and in milk production. The machinery was well stored under cover, the fences in good repair and the garden and grounds so well tended that they did not appear bleak even in winter.

I could hardly believe that in four and a half weeks in New York, where Professor E. C. Lindeman had found us a modest *pied-à-terre,* I had managed to read several hundred books, to negotiate reprint rights on perhaps a dozen volumes of high quality and commercial potential, and at the same time to participate in constant discussions on print orders, distribution, cover design and advance schedules.

At long last I had achieved the dream of younger days as a latter-day Cincinnatus and book publisher. I found that it was a beneficial experience to spend two or three days a week in the country, even though most of my time was devoted to publishing matters. In no sense did Hollow Rock Farm divert me from my profession in New York. On the contrary, it reinforced my judgment by providing the essential hinterland perspective necessary to weigh trends of commerce, of thought, of education outside of New York. For example, to read William Faulkner in a rustic setting, even though not in the deep South, confirmed my judgment that this comparatively unread author (at that time) could have the same sort of universal appeal as an author with a simpler style, Erskine Caldwell. My Negro butler, a wonderful lad, handsome and intelligent though with only a high school education, told me that he enjoyed Mr. Faulkner's style. When I asked him if the long sentences and complicated language didn't tend to confuse him, he assured me that it was like the flowery style of his father, a local Negro Baptist preacher and headwaiter at the Charles Carroll Hotel. I went to his church to hear his father preach a sermon and was convinced that there was a remarkable resemblance to the imaginative style through which Faulkner achieved much of his effect, so fancy yet understandable.

To digress a moment from the New York publishing scene and to describe life at Hollow Rock in those days—we were within an hour of College Park and all of the experiments going forward there, including the early use of penicillin for veterinary medicine. I could resume my relationship with the men I had known and with whom I had worked in the Department of Agriculture and the Department of State, and at the same time function as an active member of the Friends of the Land, occasionally working with Louis Bromfield when he came east on special projects to bring the newest practices in grass culture and resource conservation to the attention of businessmen and bankers of Maryland.

There was hardly a weekend that the luncheon table on Saturday or Sunday was not circled by eminent Washingtonians, economists, politicians, authors, artists and scholars. Sometimes these groups were joined by visiting Englishmen, sometimes by Russell Lord and his wife, Kate, who edited *The Land* magazine in Belair. Often on a Saturday I would go out with hounds and enjoyed helping Charles Rogers to build up his notable pack of bassets at Timber Ridge. They attracted a large field at fixtures ranging over a country which included the domain of the Green Spring Valley foxhounds, the Howard County foxhounds, the Elk Ridge-Hartford and Carrollton hounds.

I recruited some twenty-five nonresident subscribers in Washington, and from time to time they would add a touch of political sophistication to the hunt breakfast which would follow the meet. Our field master and sometimes whipper-in was Thomas E. Stephens, the portrait painter, who was gradually achieving an extraordinary success and who was painting a series of portraits of General Eisenhower and the principal American military leaders of the war, including General MacArthur in Tokyo.

These pastoral pursuits were a source of considerable annoyance to Enoch in New York, but delighted my New York publishing friends and authors who came to Hollow Rock Farm for weekends with me. On weekends Enoch retreated to the Catskills, actually no more accessible before the New York Thruway was built than my more distant farm.

I had designed a nicely isolated study at Hollow Rock where I could, with the aid of a dictaphone, conduct publishing business as well as superintend the management of the farm and undertake all the essential planning of a country squire. I maintained a close relationship with my neighbors in the Monocacy River Conservancy District, with the county agricultural agent and his technical staff, with cattle and swine breeding associations, and with the local bankers, businessmen and educators.

As I check my records of the postwar weekends at Hollow Rock, there were no more than half a dozen over a period of four years without stimulating guests. Due to the fact that I had written a biography of Francis Scott Key, I was soon adopted by the county historical society and the garden club organizations which conducted tours of the old or historical houses and shrines in the vicinity. I made it a point to take all visitors from abroad to Gettysburg—only twenty miles away—and if they evinced special interest I also took them on to Antietam and Harper's Ferry nearby.

I always walked or rode across the fields to Terra Rubra, where Francis Scott Key had been born, passing the little Keysville school where a monument marks the spot where I had practiced youthful oratory in commemoration of the hundredth anniversary of the writing of "The Star-Spangled Banner" in 1814. It startled some of my sophisticated friends to discover that in the Red Lands of Maryland I reverted to provincial ways and exhibited enthusiastic pride in my heritage in historic territory.

I can recall Henry Steele Commager's first visit when, after introducing him to a large audience at Westminster High School, I took him on a tour of the Gettysburg Battleground and polished off the evening with a coon hunt which lasted until three o'clock in the morning, when the whisky keg went dry. It was his first acquaintance with the border and buffer area of the Civil War in Maryland. No one was told that in town and country I rose at four, seven days a week, to put in four hours of concentrated reading and publishing work before breakfast.

In the late winter of 1945–46, Allen Lane wrote me confidentially that he was sending his brother Richard to New York with the expressed intention of liquidating Penguin Books, Inc. If I could persuade Dick that the company had a future in conformity with the policy of Penguin Books Ltd.,

Dick was instructed to relent. I was warned not to breathe a word of this to Enoch, but I decided never to go behind Enoch's back and told him all. Although Dick's purpose had been described as urgent and desperate, he chose to come to New York on a slow freighter and arrived not only out of touch with his brother but bewildered about his mission.

Richard was a tall apple-cheeked countryman, not really deeply involved with the dynamic publishing plans of his brother. I decided that the best thing to do was to find a sanctuary where we could talk uninterrupted by any distraction that was unique to him or to me. I reserved a couple of rooms in the old house of Hans Zinsser which his widow was conducting as an inn, and we carried on most of our conversations walking over the lanes and fields in the neighborhood of Garrison, New York, where the inn was located, happily only a mile from the Bird and Bottle, a mellow country tavern which had maintained its standards through the wartime period.

On three consecutive mornings during a four-hour walk I made it clear to Dick that Penguin Books, Inc. had the greatest potential of any publishing house in America. True, we were barely solvent as a company, but we had arranged distribution with Fawcett and temporary printing credit with W. F. Hall in Chicago. This enabled us to launch a publishing program thus far without counterpart—providing a wide range of literary entertainment in inexpensive form but, above all, issuing inexpensive books that would be geared to the new trends in education.

I gave him the statistics on college matriculation, on the ultimate high school increase that would ensue from the baby-boom of wartime marriages, on compulsory attendance in high schools through the country and the G.I. Bill of Rights, which financed vocational and higher education for veterans.

Despite the fact that I had many misgivings about the secretive authoritarianism of Enoch, I loyally supported his prowess as a production and distribution man. Finally, on the last night of our enforced comradeship at dinner in the Bird and Bottle, Dick confided that whatever his instructions from Allen, he had no intention of turning the key on the American branch. He was not only vague but uninformed on the corporate setup of the branch, so that he could give no practical suggestions on the implementation or the share-holding understanding on which we could proceed.

I advised him to talk to Morris Ernst and Harriet Pilpel, but said that we were becoming impatient about formalities. We were being put in the position of making publishing and printing contracts in good faith on the assumption that Enoch and I were in full authority and in a position of absolute parity, but that we had no assurance that Penguin Books Ltd. would approve of our decisions. To most intents and purposes, we were more or less on our own, except for Allen's frequent questions and hesitations on legal formalities.

I made it plain to Richard Lane not only at Garrison but later during several weekends at Hollow Rock Farm that I could not represent myself to be a mere stooge for Allen Lane, that it was very awkward to take the vast risks of launching a business with the overhanging threat that, at the whim of Penguin Books Ltd., the business could be folded overnight. I gather that my sermonette sank in deeply, for I soon had a long private letter from Allen expressing appreciation for my kind hospitality to his brother and making it clear that he agreed with my theory of operations as relayed to him by Richard.

On the assumption that all was well, I expanded my editorial efforts in an accelerated attempt to plan four or five years ahead and to secure for reprint the kind of books that would make money and at the same time establish the distinctive, qualitative purposes of our imprint. Where there was a need for a book in the nonfiction field which did not exist or could not be negotiated by contracts for reprint works, I commissioned originals.

Allen seemed annoyed by the fact that during the paperbound slump which developed in early 1946, we had a boost from a best-selling author of whom he did not approve: Erskine Caldwell. *God's Little Acre* became a runaway, as I had predicted when I recommended that it be signed up while I was still in London the year before. Lane's facetious reaction was that we should have a pornographic imprint detached from Penguin—perhaps Porno Books—for such material. He was still far from being a convinced general publisher of serious modern literature that might offend the parsons and squeamish readers of the United Kingdom. He was equally annoyed when, despite the fact that Pocket Books had published *The Postman Only Rings Twice,* I persuaded Blanche Knopf and Joe Lesser to license James M. Cain's *Serenade* and *Mildred Pierce* to us. *Serenade* was too gamey for Allen's taste. Allen Lane had no use for James T. Farrell's vulgar realism.

In due course, when we published Faulkner's *Sanctuary* and *The Wild Palms,* I was told he had no use for Faulkner.

As the years ran on, of course, he changed his mind, but too late to keep in step with us in New York. By reprinting Faulkner in England and later by reprinting *Lady Chatterley's Lover* and conducting a successful legal case for the right to do so against the censorship statutes, he eventually acknowledged his indebtedness to my more advanced taste and, perhaps, even my courage.

Dick Lane delighted in salty stories of the sort that he had picked up in the Royal Navy but was an undiscriminating prude when language or the depiction of human behavior in contemporary literature reached the flagrant stage of appearing in print. Dick was equally fussy about cover designs in the United States which, in contrast to the typographical Penguin covers in England, were sometimes revelatory of female anatomy and amatory desire.

In terms of publishing, Richard Lane's visit had amounted to nil. Personally, it was most enjoyable to have him about, in town and country, after it became obvious that he had no intention of shutting down the business and that if he had wanted to make such a decision, he might not have been empowered to enforce it. He was neither an accountant nor a lawyer and was easily puzzled by legal and accounting jargon. The one thing I succeeded in persuading him was that Westerns were not necessarily trash—he recommended that Penguin in England enter the field, which they did with three of our titles under license from Harper's by Evan Evans, pseudonym for the prolific Frederick Schiller Faust.

Dick had read little American literature and seemed most familiar with nineteenth-century British poetry, the novels of H. G. Wells and plays by Bernard Shaw. He knew something of typography and called on the Donnelley family when he went to Chicago to see our printing and dispatching at W. F. Hall. He seemed surprised at an obvious revolution which we had wrought by introducing Times Roman type to W. F. Hall—a marvelously compact and beautiful type designed by Stanley Morison for the agony columns of the *Times* in London during the war and earlier adapted, especially by Penguin, to book use because of its spacious and legible effect with the low ascenders and descenders. It saved some 15 percent on paper in the manufacture of a book with normal margins.

Tutored by Allen Lane, Dick conspicuously deplored some of our cover designs, but at the same time had no contribution to make to the development of book designs for display when exposed in racks far outside of traditional book shops. In England, Penguins were usually displayed with the spines exposed or stacked on tables with only the top book visible. Dick Lane had no concept of the vast changes we were creating through the use of magazine wholesalers, pioneered by Robert DeGraf of Pocket Books and refined by us to give certain titles special displays in educational, high culture and heavy traffic outlets.

I was not shown the letters which Dick wrote to Allen, but usually he summarized them to me after he had carefully made notes and written them by hand, disdaining the use of a secretary.

When I told him that Enoch arrived early in the office and read all the mail, including personal letters, before it was distributed, he managed to have some of his post sent to him in my care at my apartment or at Hollow Rock Farm and, I believe, also in care of Morris Ernst and Harriet Pilpel.

Dick was a lovable man, so accustomed to reflecting the buoyancy and energy of Allen Lane that he was generally accepted as a mysterious partner full of deep and unutterable wisdom. I cultivated this impression as we mingled with American authors, publishers and agents. He went back to England as something of a hero having, he thought, saved Penguin Books, Inc. in New York from extinction.

With stolid grace and a cheerful smile he often reminded me more of a Russian than an Englishman; but for the life of me, with no direct acquaintance with Russians, I could not entirely explain why. Perhaps it was because at Hollow Rock Farm he moved among the workers and talked with the farmer in the manner of a beardless Tolstoy, never so happy as when his boots were muddy and his sleeeves rolled up to the elbows as if he were about to perform a mighty task that never quite appeared to summon his ready muscles. After Dick returned to England, Allen wrote a typical letter saying that my therapeutic efforts had been successful, that Dick was out of his demobilization trance and spending a lot of time straightening things out at Priory Farm. There was not a mention of Penguin in the letter.

However, Allen Lane's Penguin correspondence soon afterward became very rapid and critical. One day Allen would write a long letter commending all that we were doing with such books as Rieu's translation of the *Odyssey*. The next day would come a tirade against American taste in literature, book design and marketing practices. Some of Allen's criticism was most useful, some of it was remote and uninformed and some of it was calculated to build up a record of close supervision on all details. When he announced that he was coming to America in the spring of 1947, primarily to join a conclave inspired by Thomas Beck of Crowell-Collier, it became apparent that I should plan to visit him in England first—and I carefully arranged my work so as to go to England in the winter of 1947. I had to make certain that he would come with all the documents essential to the credit, management and shareholding of the New York affiliate. In the meantime, I felt very pleased by the general progress of our publishing program, in spite of the fact that undercapitalization was greatly cramping our ability to meet current bills unless credit could be extended by the printer for a longer period than called for by our printing contract.

We stalled off the W. F. Hall Company by saying that all problems would be solved when Allen Lane came over personally in early 1947. The Hall people were not too disposed to patience, but their imaginative sales vice-president, Carl Braun, was persuaded that we would be a major company with substantial printing requirements and that Hall would be better off if we continued, since they would not then be at the mercy of the existing giant in American paperbound publishing, Pocket Books, who were known to be flirting with other printers. At that time Hall was installing new presses and binding machines adapted to high-speed paper-bound book manufacture, and certainly would not want to lose the business if our enterprise should fail and Pocket Books should move their manufacturing elsewhere, leaving them with only Bantam and Avon as softcover book customers. Dell Books, mainly mysteries and Westerns, were manufactured by Western Printing and Lithographing, who controlled the reprint contracts as well, with Dell at that time functioning as a distributor.

The principal asset of our enterprise was that we were different and were recognized as more bookish and more versatile, with the acknowledged respect of the academic world as well as of the critics and the book trade. This distinction was not confined to editorial excellence but also applied to our design and typography under Enoch's detailed supervision.

Lane was under the impression that our books found their acceptance because they bore the Penguin and Pelican imprints. I had discovered that most readers were not oriented on imprints nearly so much as on the titles and authors that we provided. The wholesalers and retailers understood the imprint long before the public did. I, consequently, decided that the imprint buildup had to follow rather than precede the full development of a comprehensive series of books in various categories. You had to publicize good works, not rely on unachieved faith in good works. Our editorial policies derived from Penguin in England, adapted to American tastes and requirements; but in order to secure a dominant position in the mass market, I was determined to establish a more eclectic range than Allen Lane might have sanctioned.

I drew a great deal of mental and moral support from Jerome Frank, E. C. Lindeman and, for a period, from John Mason Brown.

An urbane Kentuckian, Brown had come to New York in the 1920's as an associate editor and drama critic of *Theatre Arts Monthly* and had prevailed upon Edith Hamilton to undertake a series of articles on the great Greek dramatists which ultimately was published as a book: *The Greek Way*. He was a gifted lecturer, a good critic and, above all, a perceptive cultural observer and a wise counselor, when available. His traveling lecture engagements made it almost impossible for him to remain an advisor, but even when he had to relinquish the assignment with us he remained a close friend.

In July 1946, when George Bernard Shaw's ninetieth birthday was celebrated under the leadership of the Dodd, Mead Company, Shaw's American publisher, we issued three Shaw plays, at twenty-five cents each, under direct license from Shaw through Penguin in England. When I told Howard Lewis of Dodd, Mead that I thought we should be in on the celebration which was to take place at the Waldorf Astoria, he looked at our paperbound editions of *Saint Joan, Pygmalion* and *Major Barbara* and suggested that we have our own party at the Automat. I told John Mason Brown the story. He acted as official toastmaster at the Shaw celebration, and he repeated it at the high table with embellishments and high praise to Penguin Books, Inc. for taking a table for ten at the formal occasion.

The Shaw occasion, dramatized by Brown and repeated with relish throughout the women's club circuit in which he lectured, did a great deal to give us special visibility.

It was E. C. Lindeman who piloted appreciation of our books into the educational world. Having observed the usefulness of W. E. Williams to the Penguin program in England, I had in 1945 suggested that the New York company enlist the services of Professor Eduard C. Lindeman, almost an opposite number of Williams, as an advisor.

After I had made my decision to join Penguin as chairman and editor, I had arranged for Lindeman to come to England as a lecturer to British troops under the auspices of the War Office, not only in the demobilization educational programs in England but in the occupying army's educational schemes in Germany.

I had known him since his very early days as a contributing editor of the *New Republic* when Herbert Croly was editor, and I subsequently saw a great deal of him at Survey Associates when Lindeman was professor of social philosophy at Columbia University.

He had grown up on the prairie and did not learn to read proficiently until he was twenty-one. He remained a slow though perceptive reader, yet was able quickly to digest trends in education, emphases in curricula and to rediscover dormant books that had new potential in modern mass distribution. He visited me in Maryland from time to time and took an enormous interest in the changing patterns of rural culture as light industry produced the nuclei for satellite towns circling Baltimore. He was active in all the major organizations dealing with education, libraries and welfare. He was thoroughly compatible with, although thoroughly different in temperament from, Judge Jerome Frank, who sat with him and me monthly or more frequently for five or six years until Frank moved to Connecticut and was unable to attend regular meetings. As a federal judge, Frank was bound by the conditions of his position but, off the record, was frequently indiscreet and prophetically in advance of the Supreme Court decisions dealing with alleged subversion or obscenity in the first five years after World War II.

I was deriving a great deal of moral support as well as constantly favorable mention of our books in *Publisher's Weekly,* the main organ of the book trade. I had first become really well acquainted with Fred Melcher of *Publisher's*

Weekly at the moment of his greatest triumph, a visit to England at the end of the war immediately following a great celebration dinner in New York at which Elmer Davis presided. Fred's visit to England had allayed the fears which the British publishers were already beginning to have about the competition of American books in the export market. He was a true believer in the community of interests of everyone involved in writing and publishing in the English language. He was toasted on one grand occasion by John Masefield, the poet laureate, who was capable of descending from lyrical heights to the language of a sort of cheerful Rotarian.

On this occasion, Fred mentioned how moved he was earlier in the war by the awful tragedy of the bombing and burning of Paternoster Row, the great London book center where most of the publishing warehouses were located. Fred was apparently unaware of the fact that most of the books that were destroyed were covered by war damage insurance and that it was the most beneficial act to English publishing that Hitler, unaware of the circumstances, could have contrived. Out-of-date and unsellable merchandise had been liquidated, leaving the publishers with their insurance money to resume postwar operation with profitable books and the initiation of new projects. In the middle of Fred's tearful commentary on the evil Nazi book destroyers, a prominent publisher sitting next to me kicked me on the shins and suggested that I remove my smile and join in the weeping. Fred Melcher, despite his naïveté on this occasion, was one of the best-informed book men that I have ever known. His memory was almost as infallible as the files of the Bowker Company which he headed. His knowledge of the book trade was matched by his acquaintance with libraries and librarians. His advice to me until his death in 1963 was constant and always good.

When he was in London and I was in charge of his itinerary, I suggested that Allen Lane take him for a drive around the countryside near the Penguin offices and by all means to Stoke Poges, where "An Elegy Written in a Country Churchyard" had been composed by Thomas Gray. Fred told me that he was so overwhelmed by this gesture that he almost decided to buy a burial plot at Stoke Poges in which to consign his remains upon his death. Fred was easily touched by the tragedies and triumphs of writers and always elated by the success of publishing enterprises which grew in stature and prosperity. He was always saddened by declines and failures in the publishing business and relieved when weak enterprises were rescued by strong concerns rather than obliterated by bankruptcy.

When I once confided to Fred that we were not doing as well financially as we appeared, he recounted the number of idealists who had succeeded by adhering to a policy rather than by pandering to the lowest common denominator of taste. Fred was convinced that I was right to put emphasis on scholarly nonfiction and genuine literature as well as upon ephemeral although useful best sellers.

As a civil libertarian he did not mind the fact that some of the best of modern literature was realistic in the coverage of sexual behavior or even of cruelty, so long as the purpose of the author was to illuminate the human condition. He gave me courage. He seemed to appreciate more than most of the people whom I consulted the difference in taste between British and American readers, and he explained with many examples the fallacy of thinking that best sellers necessarily transplant themselves across the Atlantic automatically in either direction.

My only editorial aides during the first few years after the war, apart from advisors such as Lindeman, were Arabel J. Porter and Donald Demarest. Demarest was a scholar with incredibly fine taste reinforced by a British education. He wrote some of the finest editorial letters I have ever read. He was restive to enlarge the scope of his activities and soon assumed responsibility for press releases and publicity. Arabel J. Porter, still with the enterprise, had been educated at Swarthmore and had worked for a few years with Elliott Macrae, of E. P. Dutton on the Everyman's Library series. I affectionately called her my "Bohemian Quakeress." Her affiliation with the Society of Friends, of which she was a heritage member, had not curbed her appetite for worldly writing and radical literary experimentation. She has never compromised her taste. She always had incredible patience with boring or laborious personalities and with the necessary drudgery of editorial detail, but never lost her enthusiastic talent for discovery and advocacy of excellence.

Although Arabel never quite managed to handle the tough and savage side of competition and negotiation, her exemplary spirit reflected our inner grace more perfectly than any of my own conduct or rhetoric. She remains unspoiled by success, a rare example of the best attributes of literary editorship. In due course, I named her the presiding genius for *New World Writing* when that literary periodical was created, not only because of her great talent but also to divert attention from myself as a patron of the Bohemian set and an indirect potential poacher on the private preserves of the traditional publishers who were our principal source of supply for paperbound reprint material.

Arabel Porter is blessed with an instinctive radar for the spotting of promising talent at an early phase, ranging from the early days of later visible writers, such as Norman Mailer and James Jones, to more subtle writers, such as Truman Capote, Flannery O'Connor, Louis Auchincloss and Thomas Merton. In twenty years of intimate acquaintance I have never seen Arabel really angry, except occasionally at herself in brief bursts of chagrin that she had overlooked a promising author. She always seemed to sense when her capacity for firm bargaining was challenged and knew exactly when to turn to me for help.

Despite the jolly atmosphere which I sought to inspire, I was really troubled by our financial situation and the lack of sufficient capital without additional credit from the printer; and the printer in turn, quite naturally, was cautious and prudent, not knowing for certain, so long as Lane had not been directly involved, who actually was representing the company. We had a working understanding, supported by occasional memoranda from Morris Ernst, that Enoch and I were assured of approximately two-thirds of the earnings shares while Lane would retain two-thirds of the voting shares, with many qualifications on every detail. Even this was very hampering.

So in March of 1947 I went to London to talk with Allen Lane prior to his planned trip to New York in April. The prospect of a reunion delighted Allen Lane, and he suggested that it would be nice if I brought with me some dogwood saplings to plant at Priory Farm as a memorial grove to his brother John, who once had written from America in the springtime a lyrical letter about the dogwood blossoms up the Hudson River Valley.

I planned my trip for a long weekend stopover in Ireland, to visit friends in the West Meath country near Crooked Wood Lake, where even in modern times the swans are called Lear's Daughters. This district, not far from the old garrison town of Mullengar, which boasts the largest lunatic asylum in Ireland, was enchanting but dangerous fox hunting country. I envisaged myself hiring a horse from Paddy Pickersgill and going out on a Saturday before proceeding to London on Sunday afternoon. Wadley and Smythe, the florists, were to deliver to me just before I went to La Guardia Airport, the dogwood seedlings. Instead they delivered a clump of fifteen-foot trees with about sixty pounds of frozen earth enclosed in burlap. With fond thoughts of Priory Farm, I decided to assume the overweight on my personal account.

I landed at Shannon to transfer to Dublin Airport. The agricultural quarantine officials threatened to confiscate the dogwood trees, but finally agreed to let me proceed if I would leave them at the Dublin Airport and not expose them to soil or natural vegetation in Ireland. By the time I reached Dublin the great blizzard of 1947 had descended upon the British Isles with raging snowstorms and deep frost, so there was no hope of hunting or any other outdoor activities. I spent two nights with my friends in their underheated cottage and then discovered that all planes to London were canceled, so that I had to take the Dun Laoghaire Holyhead Ferry and the train to London, dragging the trees with me, since the blizzard had obliterated any trace of porters.

The blessed staff of the Dorchester Hotel in London did not find it at all out of the ordinary for me to arrive with a dozen fifteen-foot trees as part of my baggage. Since the ground was too deeply frozen to plant them at Priory Farm, I had them dropped at Silverbeck.

Allen Lane and I commenced our talks about the future. I stayed in England a week discussing the relationships between the London and American companies, but nothing practical was arrived at except that the New York company had to pay a $2,500 bill owed to Penguin Books Ltd. to clear the exchange restrictions record at the Board of Trade and the Bank of England.

Allen wanted to defer all talks until his arrival in New York. I warned him to come prepared with the legal papers. I foresaw an unpleasant showdown, but meanwhile we had a number of gay evenings with intermittent discussions of editorial matters with the Penguin staff in England. All I had achieved was a continuation of our wartime rapport, and warmhearted hopes for the pending visit of Allen and his wife, Lettice, in New York.

Soon afterward they arrived and installed themselves most hospitably in a suite in the Elysée Hotel in East Fifty-fourth Street, just one floor above the Monkey Bar. After Allen had concluded his fruitless talks with the Crowell-Collier people, who had invited him to New York and paid his expenses, he agreed to go with Enoch and me to Chicago to confirm his responsibility for the Penguin Books, Inc. account at the W. F. Hall Company. To our astonishment Allen, who had discussed the situation on the trip out on the Twentieth Century Limited, changed his mind and stated that he really could not stand back of the obligations of the New York branch.

He came back with me to Maryland, which we reached by changing trains at Harrisburg to York and driving from York to Keysville. It was a tense weekend despite the show of interest in the farm. I put Allen on an earlier train than I had planned to take him back to New York from Baltimore, with the understanding that I would drop in at the Elysée the next evening for cocktails and a final talk.

When I arrived the hotel suite was filled with strangers who had nothing to do with Penguin Books, Inc. I said that I would return later after dinner. This was the real end of our association, the coda of the symphony. I frankly told Allen that I did not see how we could work together, given his suspicious attitude toward the enterprise, his unwillingness to support our credit and, above all, his expressed hope that I was *his* personal representative vis-à-vis Enoch. I made it clear that I had learned how to work with Enoch and intended to do my best to carry out reponsibly our undertakings with publishers from whom I had licensed rights, with distributors and with our printers. When I left the Elysée, I called up Enoch and reported to him the outcome of my evening with Lane. He was surprised but not displeased. He had anticipated a break and simply asserted that he no longer regarded me as Lane's stooge.

The next morning I telephoned Morris Ernst, and Morris and Harriet Pilpel agreed to try to work out some solution. After Lane's departure for home, Morris and I had several very private talks in which we agreed that an orderly separation from Penguin Books Ltd. and the acquisition of all their American assets, perhaps with a change of corporate name and imprint, would be the only way out.

I had known Morris for many years as counsel—with Arthur Garfield Hays—for the American Civil Liberties Union. He had also volunteered from time to time for Survey Associates. During the New Deal he had achieved singular visibility as a confidant of FDR and the White House circle. His efforts not only to be in the know but to be known to be in the know led him frequently to such nighttime resorts as the Stork Club and "21" Club, to pick up the gossip, and also impelled him to use the comfortable drawing room of his house in Greenwich Village as an intermittent salon frequented by writers, economists, artists, parsons and celebrities. One could forgive him his boyish enthusiasm because of the genuine goodness of his heart and the simple zeal which characterized his presentation of the most abstract points of law, philosophy or political science.

He had started life running a furniture store, but by the 1930's he was the kind of legal personality in New York that Clarence Darrow had been in Chicago and elsewhere during the three preceding decades. During World War II he had twice visited London as a sort of emissary of the Writers' War Board to *Trans-Atlantic Magazine* and managed to visit all sorts of old friends, such as Sir Harold Hartley and Lord Beaverbrook, in the course of his peregrinations. I had introduced him to Allen Lane at that time. He had been fortunate to recruit as a confidante and aide Mrs. Harriet

Pilpel, a charming woman who shared Morris' adherence to Article 1 of the Bill of Rights as basic American gospel, and who also shared his fascination with the problems and personalities of the communications industry, especially book publishers and authors.

He was (or is) a paradox—a modest exhibitionist, a common-sense logician, a warmhearted curmudgeon. He regularly converted enmities to friendships and viewed opponents and clients alike as if they were characters in a novel of which he was the omnipotent author. He has written many excellent books, and all of them reveal the wisdom and compassion that he has learned by the ordeal of looking after a deaf-mute daughter and the enforced loneliness of summers in a remote part of New England. Morris had always regarded me as something of a protégé because at Survey Associates I had paid strict attention to his tutelage on the laws of libel, the nature of censorship and the Brandeis anti-bigness doctrine which to a considerable extent he espoused more fully than I.

It was therefore not difficult for me to get along with Morris Ernst as counsel for Penguin Books, Inc. and also for Allen Lane, who still controlled our company. At first it was not so easy to accommodate myself to the rigid advice, particularly pertaining to literary contracts, for in those earlier days Harriet Pilpel could not forsee that the nature of our business would change and that contracts should contain flexible clauses that would make it possible to avoid renegotion as changes came about. For example, her draft of our contracts bluntly referred to 25-cent books, that being the price then established in the mass paperback field, with no escalator clause for royalties should the price be raised. As time ran on, I came to have a tremendous admiration for Harriet Pilpel's legal knowledge and capacity to learn the rapid lessons of change in a dynamic and revolutionary enterprise.

Enoch consulted his personal attorney, Rudolf Littauer, but I relied upon the goodwill of Morris Ernst in the formulation of the pattern for severance negotiations in London.

Littauer, Enoch and I flew to England in October. Our American company paid Morris Ernst's way and fee but not the fee of Allen Lane's British solicitor, William Crocker.

England had not visibly recovered from the fiscal, fuel and food emergency which had been so apparent to me in February and March. To add to the grim aspect of our first meeting in Morris Ernst's hotel suite, Allen Lane appeared with a patch over one eye from a slight bump the week before. "The Nelson touch," I said impishly upon greeting him, but nothing could restore the mood of personal rapport. Allen was grim as any member of the Royal Family seeing the Union Jack come down on a liberated colony. Morris Ernst and Rudolf Littauer conducted most of the conversation on a formula for orderly separation upon which we had previously agreed, and Sir William Crocker concurred.

Allen was aware of a number of auspicious, best-selling titles which I had signed up during the previous year and which were scheduled for autumn release, including some which might indeed turn the tide toward more abundant working capital in due course for the New York enterprise which we were acquiring. He knew that only several months earlier we had raised the price of our Pelican, later Mentor, titles from twenty-five cents to thirty-five cents with a hint of higher prices when bigger projects came along. I had been meticulous in sending a copy of my memorandum to publishers to Allen Lane so that he would be aware of the move which, in view of higher costs, would give a better margin to us and also a more tempting proposal to publishers and authors.

No reference was made to the unpleasant confrontation at the Elysée Hotel in New York six months earlier. The negotiations lasted nearly a week. Billy Williams and Eunice Frost sat sadly in the sidelines. Littauer and Enoch, with whom I shared a suite at the Savoy, were so obsessed with continuous repetition of each day's developments and repetitions of the next day's strategy that I decided to spend my evenings with London friends. The first night I went to a concert at Covent Garden with Sylvester and Pauline Gates.

A frightening conclusion to the evening's pleasure ensued as we went from the concert hall to Sylvester's automobile to return home. A group of four footpads set upon us, bruising Pauline's face and arms and giving me a mild black eye. We went to the Bow Street Station to complain, then took Pauline to St. George's Hospital for a quick inspection and, finding no serious damage, went our way. The next day I appeared at the negotiations with a black eye as if in some grim and monstrous attempt to ape Allen's eye patch. The next night, to avoid the tension of the rehash between Enoch and Littauer, I dined late and went to the 400 Club with the Earl and Countess of Portsmouth, who were masters of the gentle art of relaxation.

The outcome of the negotiations was complete severance; payment of a sum of money to Penguin Books Ltd.; agreement to change our corporate name and imprints, to avoid any confusion with the former parent company; permission to use the Penguin and Pelican imprints jointly with our new imprint, for a brief period; an agreement by Penguin Books Ltd. not to enter English titles for sale in the mass market in the United States for a stated period; and certain other conditions easily acceptable all around.

Allen Lane was regretfully relieved, certainly not elated, to be total master of his own greatly reduced domain without any actual dilution of his equity or enhancement of his prospects. We were pleased to be on our own, even though it meant a tremendous public-relations effort, legal and financial problems to solve, and the selection of a new corporate name and new imprints by the end of January (actually much earlier, since we had to prepare new releases which necessarily had to bear the new imprints by February 1). Signet, indicating authoritative seal of quality, was finally struck upon by Enoch. I, who had grown up in the traditions of the old *Mentor Magazine,* now defunct, first proposed Mentor, the wise counselor and friend.

We had to check these imprints through the maze of legal research. In the case of Mentor, we had to purchase the right to use it from the owner of the old Mentor files, who had taken them over from the Crowell-Collier Company entirely for the valuable collection of photographs.

The corporate name was compositely arrived at: The New American Library of World Literature, Inc., shortened only recently to the New American Library, Inc. We especially wanted to display an expressed interest in international literature. Over an autumn weekend at Hollow Rock Farm, I prepared the press releases, communications to publishers and general statements on the change of name, imprint and ownership.

Enoch and I firmly retained 42½ percent each, absolutely, and gave an option of 7½ percent each to Littauer and the O'Shaughnessy Trust. New bylaws and resolutions confirmed *absolute parity of ownership and control* between Enoch and myself. I was empowered with full responsibility for planning, formulation, development and implementation of our editorial policies. I was so confident of my ability to mobilize literary and scholarly resources for rapid growth that I opposed any outside financing except printer's credit to get us over the immediate hurdles. Hall's credit on the day of our separation from Penguin Books Ltd. amounted approximately to $500,000. It was the best investment in support of a publisher that any printer had ever, to my knowledge, made. Within three years, despite the constant need for greater working capital, we were on a fully current basis; and within twelve years, when the New American Library of World Literature, Inc. was merged into The Times Mirror Company, the price paid at the modest rate of 13½ times earnings was roughly $13,500,000 in a pooling of interest deal through an exchange of shares (which exceeded $40,000,000 by 1967). There was delivered to Times Mirror, in 1960, the world's foremost publisher in the inexpensive field, with the finest list of best sellers, of classics, of school, college and university titles thus far to appear in the world of widely distributed books, plus the beginnings of a hardcover program.

Soon after we became independent, I gave up my farm, my leisure, my sports and many clubs to put in a total effort to demonstrate that NAL—as we came to call it—was not a beneficiary of outside financial support but could gain more from the capital in my busy mind and the stamina of my rugged constitution. True, the art of publishing with a dedicated purpose was Lane's concept; to it I happily and steadfastly adhered, diversifying as new needs appeared for new and different types of books.

Only once in the decade following separation from Penguin were we in a real financial squeeze again, and that was when, during the glut of paperbound books in 1953, the company heeded too well and not too wisely the advice of our new marketing executive to meet the glut by putting out more books, as the comic publishers did, to hold our place in display even if sixty percent of the merchandise was returned. This episode taught me the unforgettable lesson that an editor cannot and for practical reasons, if for no other, dare not abdicate any of his forward responsibilities to salesmen who are mainly concerned with today and yesterday.

Chapter VIII

A DEMONSTRATION OF FAITH
IN MAN'S HIGHEST DREAMS

Historically, there is thought to be a difference in the ideas which predominate over successive epochs, and there are data for marking the genius of the Classic, of the Romantic, and now of the Reflective or Philosophical age. With the views I have intimated of the oneness or the identity of the mind through all individuals, I do not much dwell on these differences. In fact, I believe each individual passes through all three. The boy is a Greek; the youth, romantic; the adult, reflective. I deny not, however, that a revolution in the leading idea may be distinctly enough traced.

Our age is bewailed as the age of Introversion. . . .

. . . If there is any period one would desire to be born in—is it not the age of Revolution; when the old and the new stand side by side, and admit of being compared; when the energies of all men are searched by fear and by hope; when the historic glories of the old, can be compensated by the rich possibilities of the new era? This time, like all times, is a very good one, if we but know what to do with it.

—from: *The American Scholar* 1837
by Ralph Waldo Emerson

BY OUR TREATY IN LONDON we had emancipated ourselves from British control, but for several years we were very rigidly scrutinized by our printers, who fortunately abstained from editorial intrusion even when they recommended severe budgetary control of personnel, of display rack costs and of any buildup of paper inventory until the time of the Korean War, when it seemed desirable to be protected against shortages, salary freezes, and other possible governmental controls.

It was during this period that I reached the appallingly sad decision that I could not continue as an active farmer and at the same time put in an all-out seven-day week, at the work of editorial formulation, planning, implementation and negotiations. I discussed my professional plight with my wife. She and I agreed on a divorce. She would take over Hollow Rock Farm, to which she had become greatly attached. It was a cruel wrench to move my center of gravity wholly to New York. I managed to find a pleasant suite of large rooms in the old Langdon Hotel, now the site of the Corning Glass Building, at Fifty-sixth Street and Fifth Avenue. I maintained a close link with friends in Maryland, with Louis Bromfield and Friends of the Land and with the conservation movement generally. But I threw 99 percent of my energy into New American Library.

It soon became apparent that this personal and seemingly perpetual sacrifice of pastimes and pleasures for complete dedication to the enterprise was undoubtedly the principal factor that led to our massive and qualitative growth. On many occasions I wondered whether the result was worth the travail. But as time ran on I realized that nothing could have halted the process of compulsive work to make New American Library a success not only financially, but as a constructive force in the life of the times.

It did not deter me to face, occasionally, the fitful bursts of censorship that threatened the distribution of authors such as Caldwell, Faulkner, Farrell and Moravia. I took the witness stand in local and federal courts from Philadelphia to Boston and from Youngstown, Ohio, to Cleveland. I worked manfully to persuade the American Book Publishing Council—the book trade organization—to support the cause of freedom to read, regardless of the price or method of distribution of books, and to prevent the establishment of a double standard—one for the rich, another for the poor, i.e., one for the $5.00 book in the nation's twelve hundred book shops, another for the 25-cent book in over a hundred thousand retail outlets.

In 1948 and 1949 we turned the corner with a strong Mentor program and with Signet best sellers which ranged from Richard Wright, William Faulkner, James Joyce and Truman Capote to the early work of Gore Vidal; Mentor Books by Edith Hamilton, Margaret Mead, Arthur M. Schlesinger, Jr., Alfred North Whitehead, J. W. N. Sullivan, John Dewey, Julian Huxley, Susanne K. Langer and the translations of W. H. D. Rouse.

An interesting example of how great events far away influenced decisions at the time is the case of Ludwig Lewisohn's tolerance when suddenly mellowed by the satisfaction he derived from the formation of the state of Israel. As a comparatively young man he had written a semi-autobiographical novel under the title *The Case of Mr. Crump,* which Harper had planned to publish and then suppressed because of family pressures and fear of costly libel suits. Soon after the formation of Farrar, Straus and Young, Roger Straus, head of the firm, contrived a way to present the novel by negotiating with those who might have made trouble. I read it in galley proofs and determined that we should reprint it. I encountered vehement opposition from Enoch who, when pressed, said that the unpleasant book really annoyed him because of the misleading title, which sounded as if it might be a mystery or even a book dealing with the political Boss Crump of Memphis. I said,

"I think I can secure permission to change the title."

Ludwig Lewisohn demurred. Roger thought that in due

course Lewisohn would consent and suggested that I work up some possible title changes to recommend for the reprint. It so happened that at the time I was working with the Population Reference Bureau on a book dealing with the challenge of world population increase. In this book, later published as *Human Breeding and Survival,* I ran across the phrase "the tyranny of sex" and proposed it to the authors. They thought it was a bit too flamboyant a title, even though it was their own phrase. But I thought it was not a bad title for *The Case of Mr. Crump,* which dealt with the jealous tyranny of the wife of a talented man who derived great inspiration from his devoted younger sweetheart.

When I telephoned Roger to try the title on him, he said he wouldn't pass it along. Ludwig Lewisohn was in his office, apparently in a very benevolent mood, and he would ask him to call upon me. Soon the elegant and stylish man of letters appeared, wearing a broad-brimmed Spanish-type hat and carrying a gold-headed walking stick. He was so elated as he entered the door that I suspected that he might be indulging in some sort of stimulating drug. Instead, Ludwig, whom I later came to know better, sat down at my desk, hat in hand, and benignly said,

"Ask me anything you like. Israel is a certainty. I shall grant any favor you want today!"

I shyly volunteered that, to insure the greatest possible sales in reprint, we would like to rename his book *The Tyranny of Sex.* He regarded me archly and said,

"Today, before I change my mind, it is okay."

I promptly drew up a brief written consent which he signed, and the matter was neatly closed. Enoch was not pleased by a maneuver which brought under license a book for which he had expressed great personal distaste. A little later that season Enoch and I were driving out to Greenwich for a regular conference with the Fawcett people, who were our distributors; all the way up the Hutchinson Parkway, Enoch ranted on and on about Lewisohn's obnoxious theme. I said,

"Never mind, I shall put the best possible face upon it."

To my surprise, when we reached the Fawcett office, I hadn't a chance to mention the book. Enoch with a grimace of malevolent guile announced that *he* had a long-suppressed book by a great man of letters and that it contained every aspect of sex and violence from the beginning to the very end. He didn't mention that he had up to that moment been against the book or that at the end the protagonist, Dr. Crump, beat his wife's brains out with a poker. The book was a tremendous success, selling over a million copies. I learned later from Maurice Ragsdale of *Reader's Digest* that he had lobbied for it for condensation, but that DeWitt Wallace was too squeamish to permit it even in a digested version.

Nearly every day at this period some new and exciting possibility arose. I managed to license Faulkner's *Sanctuary* from Bennett Cerf of Random House, *Short Stories* of Thomas Wolfe from Whitney Darrow of Scribner's and *Young Lonigan*, first of the Studs Lonigan series by James T. Farrell, from James Henle of Vanguard. When I wanted to negotiate with Random House on other Faulkner titles to follow *Sanctuary*, not even a file copy could be found. I, personally, paid fourteen dollars for a rare secondhand copy of *The Wild Palms* which we used as a setting copy, and which I still retain as a marvelous literary trophy of the time when Faulkner was widely discussed, but very little read.

I had been fortunate enough to find in the dusty stacks at Nelson's Parkside Works in Edinburgh, Scotland, available titles which included translations of Homer by W. H. D. Rouse. The Rouse *Odyssey* had, oddly enough, been brought out in the United States before the war in an obscure Modern

Age edition which received no attention and achieved no sales. Luckily, when Penguin reverted their E. V. Rieu translation of Homer after our separation, Henry Z. Walck, then director of the Oxford University Press in New York, refused to license T. E. Lawrence's rendition: *The Story of Odysseus*. This was lucky for us. The Lawrence prose translation of Homer is floridly nineteenth century in tone, with no comparison in appeal with the very similar translations by E. V. Rieu and W. H. D. Rouse. Rouse had antedated Rieu by some years, but the war had come along and Nelson had not actively sold Rouse's translation in their hardcover editions nor had they endeavored to sell reprint rights.

The discovery of Rouse's modern and vigorous scholarship as a translator was an extraordinary delight as well as a profitable one. When I learned that W. H. D. Rouse, venerable headmaster of the Perse School in Cambridge, England, had recently died, I got in touch with his family and took over directly his translation of Plato, almost completed before his death. I employed a classical friend to edit the manuscript, which was annotated in Greek and English in Rouse's fine, scholarly hand.

When we published *The Great Dialogues of Plato*, even *Time* magazine recognized that the widely used translation by Benjamin Jowett was made obsolete overnight. Rouse's rendition of Plato became the most popular Plato text in schools and in colleges, at home and abroad, and still maintains its acknowledged place as the best.

I was determined to find the best scholars and authors for our emerging educational list. We very early prevailed on Norton to license to us Edith Hamilton's classical essays, *The Greek Way* and *The Roman Way*, then I followed with her *Mythology*, which I licensed from Little, Brown. *Mythology* has averaged nearly a half million copies annually ever since. By masterful persuasion I managed to license from

Macmillan, Alfred North Whitehead's *Aims of Education*
and other Whitehead titles. Largely because of my friendship with Margaret Mead, William Morrow's president,
Thayer Hobson, permitted me to reprint her South Seas
trilogy and all her other titles.

The Mentor list had begun to grow and to be recognized
as a genuine contribution to educational literature. Nevertheless, to my horror, one day Roscoe Fawcett telephoned to
say that he would like to have a private luncheon with me.
The burden of his talk was that in the popular newsstand
market, the Mentor volumes were too special for massive
general distribution. He recommended that we drop the
whole Mentor program. I had to resort to almost devious
arguments to avert such a catastrophe, which at the time, according to Roscoe, had the support of Enoch. Roscoe said
we should rest Mentor for five years, then enter the market
when distribution circumstances had changed.

I pointed out with some justification, but certainly not as
my basic argument, that the Mentor list was essential as part
of the character and prestige of our company and an indispensable exhibit when our more daring fiction—by Faulkner,
Farrell and Caldwell—were attacked by the censors. I pointed
out to Roscoe that if his local distributors would undertake
special displays of Mentor Books, reference books and certain
educational Signet titles, and locate such displays in educational areas, the vast new untapped market might surprise
them. Indeed, I asserted that magazine wholesalers of paperbound books were as yet hardly acquainted with the potential of the market if they would really endeavor to go all
out with the college bookstores and even high school outlets.

The consequence of this debate, in which I was happily
the winner and Roscoe an appreciative loser, was our leadership in the publishing revolution by making quality inex-

pensive books available for students and for aspiring general readers with a yearning for self-education.

There was at that time in the Fawcett distributing organization no one qualified to deal with scholarly books of quality. Fawcett wanted sexy sizzlers. So did Enoch. Nearly every day he inquired if I had discovered a new "hot" book. It was my task to deliver sizzlers and fast turnover along with the stable literary fare which was developing into a recurring back list. Like most marketers, the Fawcett people were really distributors who judged everything retrospectively and currently according to what was good yesterday and today, with no serious thought of the changing trends of tomorrow.

One day at Greenwich, Allan Adams, then circulation director, vehemently advised me to skip mysteries for a while since they seemed to be piling up on the market, including the Pocket Books reprints of Erle Stanley Gardner's Perry Mason books. My reaction was to state that I had just read a humdinger of a mystery. "Forget it," said Enoch in a typical preference for distribution rather than informed editorial advice. The book was *I the Jury* by Mickey Spillane. I predicted it would turn the tide. It had just been published by Dutton with practically no hardcover sales; indeed they later told me that they took on the first Spillane manuscript on the basis of a very perfunctory reading by a sub-editor, largely as a favor to Jack McKenna, the man who had brought the manuscript to them for consideration. It seems that during the war when wood, metal and plastics were restricted to the zero point for toys, Jack McKenna had brought to Dutton a substantial quantity of cardboard from his lithography plant. This had been manufactured into three-dimensional books for children—depicting villages, farms, factories and military themes. They were profitable not only in bookshops but in toy departments and variety stores. So Dutton owed McKenna a favor and took on *I the Jury*.

The book had been thrown at me in a fit of annoyance by Donald Demarest, who was too disgusted to finish it. I promptly read it and decided we must have it. When I returned to the city on the Monday noon after our morning visit with Fawcett—I refused to remain for lunch with the group—I called Dutton from a booth in Grand Central. John Edmondson, then vice-president and treasurer, who dealt with subsidiary rights, said, "Two thousand dollars will take it." I said, "Who in the devil ever heard of Mickey Spillane? What about five hundred dollars?" He said, "Fifteen hundred." I said, "Seven hundred fifty." He said, "You have the book." It was a book without a friend except myself until Roscoe Fawcett read it several months later. I had been absolutely right. Spillane became a best seller, then a cult; and he still retains a great deal of his original appeal in spite of a gap of nine years between the first group of titles and his later books.

With the exception of John P. Edmondson, and possibly Nicholas Wreden who was then with Dutton, I don't believe anyone in the upper hierarchy at that conventional and righteous house had ever read a word of Spillane. Mickey was not exactly the type of character to appeal, at first glance, to Elliott Macrae, president of the house who, like his father before him, was a dedicated and elegant man.

They soon tended to pass Mickey's manuscripts on to me to serve as working editor, since the sales of his books seemed destined to be primarily in cheap paperbound form. The first time Mickey appeared, he was without a coat or tie to wear to lunch. I did not want to offend him by suggesting that we go to one of his Third Avenue haunts but boldly escorted him around the corner to a restaurant frequented by advertising men. There he was frowned upon as not suitably garbed, but he managed to charm the headwaiter into permitting him to borrow a necktie and jacket from the cloakroom and to follow me into the dining room. He was a fierce egoist, a genuine member of Jehovah's Witnesses and he made it clear that he was a writer, not an author. He was interested in money, religion and automobiles.

Despite his calculated uncouthness he was handsome, attractive and much better educated than he appeared to be at first. I drew out of him, without much difficulty, that he had served in the Air Force and had been educated, with a B.A. degree, from Manhattan College in Kansas. He confided that he dedicated a certain amount of his time to Jehovah's Witnesses, selling *The Watchtower* on street corners and assisting at the mass baptism rites at their colossal gatherings—"Especially when there are some pretty dames to dip."

He lived with his wife and several children outside of Newburgh, sixty miles up the Hudson River, and invited me to visit him there. He said he was fed up with writing horror comic dialogue in Jack McKenna's enterprise and that he planned to write three or four books a year. I drove up to his place soon afterward and found that he lived in practically a one-room, cement-block cottage which he had erected himself and which was primitive in its conveniences. What little money he had made up to then he had spent on automobiles and firearms, and together we must have squandered five or ten dollars worth of pistol ammunition before he would settle down to talk. He had dreams of large volume literary production, not only by himself but by an assortment of apprentices who would learn to write by active participation in Mickey's backwoods studio.

Our volley of shots at a variety of tin can targets soon attracted three or four mysterious characters from the vicinity, and they joined in the discusssion of Mickey's potential as a writer. My own dreams of glory almost matched Mickey's as I became persuaded that, stimulated by the admiration of his disciples, he would achieve an output of three or four books a year which, selling by the millions, would enrich us all.

The first books came along according to plan. Then Mickey slowed down. After producing a total of seven, he did not write another book for eight or nine years. The films had bought several of his first titles. John Edmondson had managed his funds on a sustained trust basis, so that the daily greed for wealth was not the motivating force which Mickey himself had imagined it would be. He delighted in doing brief articles on automobile racing and in taking the applause at stock-car races and rallies. He particularly enjoyed visiting chain stores and wholesalers and autographing books. This stimulated publicity and sales to a fantastic level.

By 1952, when we launched *New World Writing*, the literary semiannual writing publication, Mickey was a world celebrity. He had expressed contempt for literary critics who tended to ignore his work and also argued savagely against the social critics who paid an uncomfortable amount of negative attention to his Mike Hammer stories. He was soon tagged by Max Lerner as the exponent of sex and sadism. It became apparent that he was eventually going to be a vulnerable target for censors if something were not done about it.

First of all I publicized the fact that Mickey Spillane was required reading at William and Mary College in a course on existentialism. This did not divert the critics of his rationalization of direct action vengeance, even though the savagery of Mike Hammer reflected a sort of crude chivalry. It was Charles Rolo, then the literary editor of the *Atlantic Monthly* (who, along with Leonard Russell in London, had discovered the unique quality of Raymond Chandler as a hard-boiled writer) who turned the tide. I asked Charles if he would undertake an article comparing the work of Europe's best-selling crime writer of that period, Georges Simenon, and America's runaway thriller writer, Mickey Spillane.

After accepting the assignment, Charles was puzzled for a theme. Finally one night when I was in bed he telephoned to say that, eureka, he had struck it. Could he see me at once? He appeared within a few minutes, and I sat in my library in pajamas and robe, overwhelmed by his primary thesis, later developed into his article "Murder for the Millions" in *New World Writing*. I planted the article for simultaneous appearance in *Town and Country* with an illustration of Spillane and Simenon together to indicate that both writers were genuinely chic. Charles's interpretation was fundamentally persuasive. Simenon represented the fatalistic European Catholic with a genuine and compassionate understanding of human frailty. In contrast, Spillane, a much more elementary man, was an Old Testament writer inspired by his faith as a member of Jehovah's Witnesses, hence an exponent of an eye-for-an-eye and a tooth-for-a-tooth as exemplified by his best-selling title of the moment, *Vengeance Is Mine*.

Charles Rolo succeeded in getting across to the intellectual world the resemblance of Spillane's themes to folklore and to the fairy tales of the Brothers Grimm. His cruel justice served as a catharsis, and dispelled aggressive tendencies by vicarious means. To polish off the campaign against Mickey's Catholic critics, I put special emphasis on the plot of another of Spillane's titles, *One Lonely Night*, which dealt with Mike Hammer's bloody annihilation of a sinister and godless Communist conspiracy in New York. I have since wondered about the ethics of my strategy, but never about the efficacy. Spillane had not tarnished our publishing character.

One evening when Erskine Caldwell was in New York, I gave a cocktail party for him and Spillane, as well as for Kathleen Winsor and other writers who were under attack by the

Catholics. I invited a handful of literary Catholic priests, since it was the Jansenist Catholics who were the most active instigators of censorship of widely available paperbound books. The priests and Mickey soon disappeared from the group, and I apprehensively followed to see what sort of row might be developing. I found Mickey engaged in theological debate, thrusting copies of Jehovah's Witnesses literature into the hands of the clergy and defying them to produce Biblical justification of purgatory. After that there was no sustained religious or social criticism of Mickey Spillane or his work.

My main concern was to persuade publishers who licensed material to us that Mickey was a legitimate author who was published in hardcover by Dutton right along with *Winnie-the-Pooh* and *Everyman's Library;* therefore, we were equally responsible and eclectic in providing a vehicle for a boldly original writer with whose philosophy we were not enamored but whose social purpose was described as useful as a catharsis, the point so brilliantly developed by Charles Rolo.

It was not easy to leap from Mickey's primitivism to the scholarly and genuinely intellectual world without a good deal of cheerful explanation, but never apology or any disdain for Mickey's genuine talent. At this stage of our growth in the late 1940's I had to strive manfully to develop a publishing list that was not wholly dependent upon the obvious untapped resources of the past such as Faulkner, Caldwell, Farrell and Thomas Wolfe.

I think that one of my happiest recollections of that period was the discovery through Arabel Porter of the early writing of Truman Capote and the ultimate negotiation of his first novel for reprint from Bennett Cerf of Random House. Truman was then a prodigy, no doubt of it, in talent as well as in appearance. To me he always seemed to be kind of a

miniature Alexander Woollcott with the same gift of intimate vision and unexpected aptness and wisdom which later
came to characterize all of his books, culminating in *In Cold
Blood*. But he was, from the beginning, a giant in imagination, intellect and artistic integrity.

Eventually it became apparent that prices of paperbound
books would have to rise beyond the established twenty-five-
cent price or we would be driven to abridgement in order to
hold the quarter level of prices. After a great deal of discussion we had decided upon a twofold approach—first, to raise
the price of Mentor Books to thirty-five cents and conceivably
fifty cents; second, to toy with a few abridgements until the
time seemed right to sell fiction through the magazine distribution machinery at a higher price than a quarter.

I turned to skilled abridgers, Alice Ten Eyck and Donald
Porter Geddes, to tackle the problem of certain books too
long to reprint in their original form. I did this very reluctantly and as a temporary expedient. Earlier in the year
(1947) I had written to Kurt Enoch, from London, about
Allen Lane's approach to long Penguin books in England, a
price of two shillings and a large imprint of two Penguins or
two Pelicans to make it clear that it was a *double value,* not
just a markup in price. This, however, coincided with the
looming separation of our operation from Penguin Books,
Ltd., so that the ultimate breakthrough of American accept-
ability of longer books at a higher price was delayed for
several years.

When Whitney Darrow of Scribner's decided that he was
not prepared to license paperbound titles by F. Scott Fitzgerald or by Ernest Hemingway, I did my best to emphasize
their contemporaries—James T. Farrell, controlled by Vanguard Press; Erskine Caldwell, controlled by Duell Sloan &
Pearce and Little, Brown; William Faulkner, controlled by
Random House; and James Joyce, controlled by Viking.

Caldwell and I, as well as James T. Farrell, were born the same year, 1903. Indeed, Erskine Caldwell and I had shared somewhat similar experiences in our early life. At least we each came from the rustic upland South, from comparatively simple and pious backgrounds, and we both had studied for a while at the University of Pennsylvania. It meant a great deal to me to become Erskine Caldwell's reprint publisher—and eventually his primary publisher—as our professional friendship ripened into a close personal association. I have always felt, and acknowledged, that perhaps our vast sales of Erskine Caldwell's books had an adverse effect upon his critical acceptance from 1946 onward. The reverse snobbism of literary critics, who were aware of his best-sellerdom in the drugstores and on the newsstands, was understandable.

I had an enormous admiration for his natural, artful genius, related to that of Dickens, Mark Twain or Balzac. He scarcely ever uses an adjective, and his writing is devoid of such ambiguities as the subjunctive mood. Having danced around the Maypole in my youth, I recognized that Caldwell's work derives a great deal from folktales and ballads, as his style derives a great deal from Chaucerian and Elizabethan English—simple, sincere, direct, sardonic, earthy and dramatic in its conceptual approach to life. This lyrical and concise genius, in my opinion, might eventually decline for a while in appeal but can never suffer oblivion. When many of today's fads and literary pets are forgotten, Erskine Caldwell's work will be read and remembered, loved and treasured. His folk art, refined and beautified by artistry into classic American literature, is what accounted for his sales in the years after World War II, when he was discovered by G.I.'s in the Armed Forces Editions and by millions of readers in our own reprints of his books.

Caldwell had frequently visited me in Maryland when he was east from Tucson, where he then lived, and he met his present wife, Virginia Fletcher, who is a Marylander, at Hollow Rock Farm. Tall, Scottish in complexion, with boyish oatmeal freckles and a crew haircut, Caldwell had undergone poverty and hardship in his striving to become an author. He had become an internationally celebrated journalist before and during the war, sometimes in partnership with his wife at that time, Margaret Bourke-White, the photographer. He was not afraid of the revolution in book publishing even if it indirectly diminished his reviews. He has always been interested in three points of view: his own, that of his publishers and that of his readers. He knows that the ups and downs of appreciation will eventually mean that critics of the sort who applauded him when his first work appeared in Paris *transition* and New Orleans *Double Dealer* will again be on the critical bandwagon when the pendulum swings.

I first met William Faulkner in Hollywood before the war, but at that time he was so shy that no sense of association developed. Subsequently, I met him through Bennett Cerf and Robert Haas of Random House. Once I had a most delightful visit with him in Oxford, Mississippi, soon after his nomination for the Nobel Prize. He was a small and rather courtly gentleman, unmistakably southern and to me somehow reminiscent of Puss-in-Boots. That is, he was a miniature and self-made cavalier, having assumed some of the aristocratic attributes of his literary Tennessee ancestors. He was obsessed with privacy, modern in viewpoint toward Negroes but not inclined to be a conspicuous personal integrationist. He had an almost quixotic view of his own role as an errant knight of the Red Clay Road. He pretended not to read novels at all, including his own after they were written. He was a very able farmer and horseman, but liked to invent trimmings to his experiences, such as telling me that he had trained a mule to jump barbed-wire fences in the moonlight.

The family name was Falkner, but he had inserted the "u" in his own surname. When asked why, his only response was that he liked it that way. His genuinely urbane phase followed the Nobel Prize in 1949, when he made a particularly brilliant response at Stockholm. Afterward, in well-fitted tweeds as an author in residence at the University of Virginia, he seemed to have achieved full development of the rich and mature personality which had been concealed by decades of hard times and, sometimes, too much to drink. I don't know how he could have got through some of the years of his greatest creativity without the friendship of Saxe Cummings, his editor at Random House. He used Saxe's office, and after Saxe's death, Harry Maule's office as a private camping ground in New York. He was totally unimpressed by the high volume of our reprint sales even though he liked the revenue. He seemed to enjoy a bit of strutting on the streets of Oxford, Mississippi, when the courthouse square was rehabilitated and the Confederate monument straightened up as part of the filming of his novel, *Intruder in the Dust*. Like Caldwell, whom he greatly admired, he was not wholly reconciled to city life.

In contrast, James T. Farrell was and is a city man, a South-Chicago man, very Irish in voice, stance and manner, except completely devoid of the magic lyricism which distinguishes most Irish and Irish-American authors. Farrell, like Theodore Dreiser, never became a polished stylist, but his intellect led him to infuse into his work a great deal of social philosophy and social criticism. His greatest handicap as a major American author is that he has never been able to escape from an obsessive concern with the South Side of Chicago in a day and age that coincides with his young manhood. Although he has traveled widely and mingled with great thinkers and eminent world figures in politics and literature, the people in his stories and novels remain largely himself and his circle from puberty to young manhood, abounding in nostalgic recollection of his immigrant ancestors. Like Thomas Wolfe, he is a compulsive writer in great volume and, frequently, repetitious. Whatever his fate in the history of American letters, James T. Farrell must be considered a tremendous influence upon American writers of his generation, who were deeply involved in the economic and ideological forces of the great Depression. *Studs Lonigan* will stand for generations as an American classic of extraordinary significance because of its melancholy candor and compassion.

When we moved our office in 1950 to 501 Madison Avenue, at Fifty-second Street, we were in the heart of the ultra-sophisticated sector of New York—near most of the better publishers and within a five-minute stroll to New York's major magazines, broadcasting companies and best restaurants. A hundred yards down the street the city's most cheerful publishing group, led by Bennett Cerf, were making literary history. Alfred and Blanche Knopf were tenants in the same building as we and nearly every day one had the pleasure of encountering Alfred and Blanche in the elevator or in a nearby restaurant. For years Alfred's former butler was headwaiter of the Oak Room of the St. Regis Hotel. During the fifteen-year period at 501, I became much more intimately acquainted with Alfred and Blanche than I had ever been before. Although Alfred disliked cocktail parties, he occasionally came to our apartment, and from time to time on a Saturday or Sunday we drove out to Purchase to visit the Knopfs for lunch. Alfred's private cuisine and wine cellar reflected his extremely good taste, which for nearly fifty years he had exemplified through the publication of the finest books in the United States on food and wine. Blanche maintained a smart little apartment at Fifty-fifth Street just west of Fifth Avenue, a remarkable miniature salon which exhibited her discriminating taste in people and in artistic and literary talent until shortly before her death in 1966.

My colleagues and I felt ourselves practically a part of the Knopf family, personally and professionally, and I was in constant association with Knopf's top executives, especially William Koshland and Joseph Lesser. All of our NAL editors associated with the Knopf editorial staff in a spirit of dedication to a common cause—good books. Some of our best authors in reprint were derived from the Knopf list: Thomas Mann and D. H. Lawrence, for example. But we never could prevail upon Alfred to permit a reprint edition of any of the books by Camus or H. L. Mencken.

The Knopfs had only one heir, Alfred Knopf, Jr., called Pat by the family and all of his friends. Pat, chafing under the parental reins, went off to found Atheneum in association with Michael Bessie of Harper and Hiram Hayden of Random House. Thus there is still a Knopf carrying on the original faith of the family in a compact and closely held publishing enterprise.

Gradually, as it became apparent that our publishing enterprise was not a panderer to obvious taste and that my associate editors were not mere purchasing agents or procurement executives for a remote manager, authors increasingly came to us as sensitive publishers who were genuinely interested in books.

One remarkable man was the late Alain Locke, Professor of Philosophy at Howard University and a third-generation Negro college graduate, whom I had not seen for ten years when he had been in the councils of Survey Associates. He wanted to write a definitive account of the Negro in American culture. A grant from the Rockefeller Foundation to Howard University enabled him to undertake it. He was not well and never completed the task, but his notes and first draft of the major chapters were in good enough form for the volume to be completed, after his death, by Margaret Just Butcher. The book was placed with Alfred A. Knopf for hardcover publication prior to our Mentor edition.

When I licensed a number of books by Negroes or about Negroes, for reprint, I used the circumstances to develop rapport between NAL and the Negro leadership of the 1940's. I had for many years given generously to the appeals of the Urban League and the N.A.A.C.P., so I was not considered a mere opportunist. We not only attracted attention in the Negro press but stimulated the distribution of books in predominantly Negro neighborhoods such as Harlem, South Chicago, Atlanta and Baltimore, where previously the magazine wholesalers had insisted that self-service book racks would be doomed by excessive pilferage. Our experience demonstrated the very opposite. Aspiring young Negroes were a substantial and grateful audience, pleased by the fact that they did not have to buy their literature "downtown." In this effort, Walter White of the N.A.A.C.P. and Mrs. James Weldon Johnson were especially helpful, lending their influence and presence whenever requested.

Eduard C. Lindeman, as a social philosopher and a Unitarian, had always evinced a gentle resistance to our venturing in the direction of any special interest in Roman Catholic apologetics, classical or modern, so I felt a slight sense of guilt when I signed up my first Catholic authors without his knowledge. I had been keen to revive interest in the sainted Catholic philosophers, but didn't dare embark on a major scheme to embrace their work until I met Anne Fremantle. An extraordinary scholar and philosopher, she was sent to me by Saxe Cummings of Random House when she submitted to him a project which he was certain Random House would not undertake. It was a proposal to prepare a book of generous excerpts with connective interpretive comment on the medieval Catholic philosophers. I told her at our first meeting that I would hesitate to undertake such a project unless it might form part of a wider ranging series on Western philosophy.

"Why don't you write to Isaiah Berlin?" she asked me.

I had to admit that it really hadn't occurred to me to tax the genius of the leading English philosopher at All Souls, Oxford, despite the fact that he was a friend. I straightaway wrote Isaiah and, with certain misgivings, he agreed to edit a series of volumes for me. The result was the Mentor Philosophers, six volumes which almost immediately replaced several expensive college textbooks in orientation courses on Western philosophy. Anne's book, not quite under the editorship of Isaiah Berlin—(The Medieval Philosophers) *The Age of Belief*—has continually outsold all the rest, the greatest competitor being that of Morton White—(Twentieth Century Philosophers) *The Age of Analysis*.

Anne Fremantle, certainly one of the most formidably intellectual women whom I have ever met, had achieved distinction at Oxford and during the war had taken out American citizenship when she was working in Washington. Her charm and beauty added to her influence as a prominent Catholic and gave her an outstanding position in our group of friends and authors. Almost single-handedly she was responsible for the incredible reception of Mohammed Marmaduke Pickthall's rendition of the Koran into English as part of our attempt to include the leading religious philosophers of Asia in our list—Confucius, Lao-tzu, Buddha, Mohammed and others. As a child, Anne Jackson, as she was then, had come to know Pickthall, who was a Moslem convert, and temporarily she was nearly a convert herself. She reviewed *The Meaning of the Glorious Koran* in *The New York Times*, and the book immediately attracted tremendous attention and vast sales, sometimes selling fifty copies a day to commuters at the Doubleday Bookshop in Grand Central Terminal.

I like to think that the timing of the book had a great deal to do with it, too, at the period of Moslem ferment from Morocco to the Phillippines, when very little was known in the United States of the Koran as a motivating and unifying force in modern times. The Pickthall rendition had been commissioned by the Nizam of Hyderabad-Deccan and approved by Al-Azhar, the Moslem center at Cairo. It was first published in London by Allen and Unwin, who had taken it over from Alfred A. Knopf's English office of that period, and only a few copies had ever been imported to the U.S.A. Sir Stanley Unwin licensed the book to us after I explained to him that we had the blessing of the Nizam and of Al-Azhar. I scheduled the book to coincide with an Islamic colloquy at Princeton and the simultaneous dedication of the new mosque in Washington. All these developments would have given some slight impetus to the attention which the book received, even without Anne Fremantle's review in *The New York Times*.

I had taken care to have the book cover designed by a Moslem—a Pakistani art student in New York—and to warn all of our staff that we should never refer to it as a translation, but to adhere to Mohammed Marmaduke Pickthall's stipulation that it always be referred to as The Meaning of the Glorious Koran. As a result we had the only inexpensive Koran that was permitted in English in the Arab countries, in West Pakistan and in the Moslem areas of India.

It is remarkable still to notice the awe in which Anne Fremantle's scholarship is held, not only by educated Catholics but in the widest ecumenical, theological and philosophical circles as well as at many American universities and at the United Nations, where she occasionally functions as an advisor.

Increasingly, I turned to British scholars and translators for the Mentor and classics programs. They were not so firmly committed to publishers as most Americans, they usually wrote in better style, and they were less grasping than most American academic writers. They understood without any special coaching that NAL was striving toward a more comprehensive sort of nonfiction in the Mentor series than some of the more esoterically specialized Pelicans published in England. In the course of procuring British and occasionally Continental talent, I worked with the major English and European publishers whenever possible. In those days, before the softcover industry had developed in Britain, Penguin dominated the field, and the newcomers such as Pan and Panther were not inclined to contract for the more literary titles that, for one reason and another, Penguin had not signed up.

Many English publishers were cooperative but none more so than Sir Stanley Unwin, chairman of George Allen and Unwin and the dean of British publishers, and W. A. R. Collins of William Collins Sons and Company. Both of them are outstanding amateur tennis players as well as magnificent publishers.

Billy Collins added a vast new dimension to British publishing when he decided to branch out from the Bibles, dictionaries and greeting cards which had created the prosperous house of Collins—with the works in Glasgow supervised by his brother Ian and the planning, editorial and marketing under Billy's direct supervision in London. Undisturbed by the bombing which had destroyed the premises in London, the Collins firm moved into several connecting mansions in St. James's Place and soon succeeded in becoming one of the finest and most profitable publishing enterprises in the world. A Davis Cup tennis candidate in his youth and a man who regularly rides to hounds, Billy is a lean and solid six-footer plus, with the stamina of a migratory bird. He has visited his authors personally, and also his salesmen, on every continent; and he frequently is the discoverer of spectacular subjects in natural history such as Elsa, the lioness in Kenya. He is a courageous publisher of iconoclastic memoirs and of such frank authors as James Jones (although I believe he had the composition of *From Here to Eternity* undertaken in Holland to avoid the hazards of British censorship statutes if it had been set in type in Glasgow). He is keen about new talent, almost to the point of greed, but has remained a complete gentleman even when other people's authors have come to him and he might have been charged with raiding.

Sir Stanley Unwin willingly granted us British selling rights on his older titles by such outstanding authors as Julian Huxley and Bertrand Russell. He is a great gentleman, despite being a hard negotiator. He was always pleased when I called him "my favorite socialist" because he remained a dedicated and grasping capitalist at heart.

During this period I wanted to abandon the practice of abridging certain books which, published complete, could not have been produced at less than a 50-cent price. Donald Demarest refused to have anything to do with certain slightly condensed books that Enoch insisted should not carry an abridgement notice on the cover, but be labeled simply "special edition." I went along with Enoch only to have to appear as the principal witness when in due course the Federal Trade Commission cracked down on such practices as being in violation of the Robinson Patman Act requiring adequate and fair labeling. This humiliating experience was persuasive in the matter of raising prices beyond the 25-cent and 35-cent level in the mass market.

One of my wisest advisors and truest friends in this period of my publishing career was Edward M. Crane, president of Van Nostrand. Ted Crane had come to London for the Allied

Ministers of Education meetings which were instrumental in the formation of UNESCO in 1945, and while there he frequently used my office or apartment. His mission at that time had been the organization of USIBA—the United States International Book Association—a cooperative venture of all participating publishers at the end of the war to form an export organization. USIBA initially was a great success but because publishers fell into two groups, those who were export-minded and those who were not, it split up. Those that were export-minded formed their own groups for selling abroad and those who thought of it as purely a public relations activity used the American Book Publishers Council for that purpose. What Ted did was to excite the imagination of people who thought we should be active in the foreign market and in this he was highly successful even though USIBA as an organization did not continue. He was a charming scholar, sportsman and citizen, whom I never failed to visit when I went to New Jersey to see some of my family and grandchildren, who lived nearby. When he died in 1962 his wife cabled me in Marrakech, Morocco, that it was one of the few places they had hoped to visit together in the coming season. Through the years I had run into him in London, at the Frankfurt Book Fair, and in Madrid, and he never failed to tell me all he knew of educational trends around the world. He had been at Princeton with John Gilbert Winant and had moved his offices to Princeton, close to the University which he loved, soon after the war.

Chapter IX

A HOUSE BECOMES AN
INSTITUTION

━━━━◦⟨∞⟩◦━━━━

Genius is made strong to rear
The monuments of man beneath the dome
Of a new Heaven . . .
> —from: *Tribute to America*
> by Percy Bysshe Shelley

SOON AFTER WE RETURNED from London and the successful
consummation of the acquisition of the American Penguin
company, I was shocked by news of the suicide of John Gilbert Winant. The last time I saw him was in his New York
apartment only a week before he went to his house in Con-
cord, New Hampshire, and ended his own life. He had completed *Letter from Grosvenor Square*. A prepublication copy
was brought to my office by Julian McKee of Houghton
Mifflin the day before Winant's suicide.

"One of the deeper reasons for wanting to write [the
book]," said the Ambassador in the first chapter, "is the growing disillusionment of today, which not only dims and
obscures the present, but is trying to cloud the past." Those
words were penned in London in 1945. How much more true
they seemed when read in 1947.

In a small sense Gil Winant was too good a man for his

own good. He was sometimes too generous of his time and money, and occasionally too tolerant of people who abused his gift of friendship. He was human in his small faults.

If, for reasons which no one should now speculate upon, that faith had begun to falter; if a feeling of weary ineptitude had triumphed over the will, if the disillusionment referred to in *Letter from Grosvenor Square* had grown too great to bear, who was there in the world to begrudge him his decision? I could only be grateful that, in addition to the living monument of his good works, he had left behind him his written "account of a stewardship—a study of an enduring friendship of men and of nations." It was begun as "a letter from Grosvenor Square" to his friend Geoffrey Strong Smith, and completed in America just a few months before his death.

I was swamped with letters and phone calls from England by friends seeking a clue to the reason why. All I could do was write my review of the book for *Survey Graphic* and send copies to all of the old friends who were puzzled as well as shocked. I did not then reveal my own feeling that, beset by disappointment in every aspect of his personal life and professional career, Winant had become aware of the small influence of all his high ideals and good work on the massively cruel tide of history. He almost took the responsibility upon himself that there was no corridor to Berlin, even though everyone knew that the European Advisory Commission was not the actual architect of the victory and of the disposition of the occupying forces. He could, and probably should, have gone forward to an elder statesman's career such as that of Averell Harriman, but he decided, with consummate courage, to write an end to his chapter in history.

Winant was the first of my intimate friends who had survived the war to go. I would have felt a great deal more bereft if it had not turned out that President Truman brought a genuinely constructive and courageous quality into American life—with the Marshall Plan, the Berlin Airlift and all of the moves which he made to fulfill the mission of his office from the moment of his inauguration, including the decision to espouse the United Nations and to use the atom bomb. Truman was capable of being abrasive to friends as well as opponents, but fundamentally he believed in the destiny of Americans, in their duties no less than in their rights.

I was happy to win a number of small wagers on his re-election in 1948, against formidable odds, from a dozen Marylanders as well as from such well-informed New Yorkers as Bruce Gimbel and Julius Ochs Adler, general manager of *The New York Times*. In a personal way his courage was an inspiration which I frequently referred to at the time. To my friends who thought it quixotic to try to buck the brutal competition with our young and tender enterprise, I judiciously referred to the stalwart example of the President. To a much lesser degree, I faced similar obstacles and said so, pointing out the difficulties of vicious competition and at the same time remaining benignly confident of a destiny that was harnessed to the stars.

My most disturbing challenge was the resolve to give up Hollow Rock Farm, as part of a series of developments in connection with my divorce, and to retain, at the same time, a continued interest, by proxy if necessary, in the cultural and economic progress of my native Carroll County.

Although no longer a resident there, I continued to support local causes and to keep in touch with those who were among my older friends. Instead of visiting Hollow Rock, I stayed with my friend Charles Rogers, at Timber Ridge Farm, when I visited Maryland.

At this period it became increasingly important to keep closely in touch with the colleges and universities, to watch curricular developments and to get acquainted with the new academic talent that was replacing that of the past. I went frequently as far as the West Coast to get to know firsthand the scholars and writers, and the new figures in the film industry and in the burgeoning electronic and research organizations that were beginning to attract easterners to the dynamic West Coast.

In the course of visiting nearby campuses to recruit editorial assistants, I encountered at Princeton a brilliant young man of the class of '47, actually graduated with honors in 1949 because of his two-year interlude in the Army during which he was wounded at the Battle of the Bulge: Truman Talley. He was on the staff of the Princeton *Tiger*, and had majored in English and economics. I had met his mother several years earlier at dinner at the apartment of Frederick Rinehart, son of Mary Roberts Rinehart and a partner in the family firm with his brother, Stanley Rinehart, Jr. Mrs. Talley had been married to the founder and director of 20th-Century Fox Movietone News, who had died in 1942. In due course, the year following my divorce, Helen Talley and I were married. Meanwhile, six months before our marriage, I had inducted Truman Talley into NAL as a trainee and had met his younger sister, Helen, now Mrs. Amory L. Haskell, Jr.

Although it is not the purpose of this book to dwell on intimate family details, it should be noted that I took great pride and pleasure in the role of stepfather and was eventually best man for Truman Talley, when he married Madelon DeVoe, and I gave away Helen Talley, my stepdaughter, when she was married to Amory L. Haskell, Jr. My new family was wholly dedicated to the furtherance of my activities as a publisher, which included the career of Truman Talley at NAL as well. In a four-page article in *Newsweek,* written by Robert Cantwell, there appeared a better description than I could give of the congenial circumstances

of my new incarnation as a surprisingly happy publisher in
the city.

> Weybright is a sociable individual whose daily round often
> includes three or four literary cocktail parties (sic!) and who
> collects at his apartment best-selling novelists, visiting Eng-
> lish editors, Greek translators, advance-guard poets, science-
> fiction experts, reviewers, publishers, and agents. He has re-
> cently remarried, his second wife the widow of the editor of
> Fox Movietone News; and his literary gatherings, with his
> handsome stepdaughter and stepson mingling with the poets,
> suggest a pleasant combination of art and enterprise.

My wife, a gracious and sparkling hostess, took delight in
entertaining authors and publishers and in traveling in the
United States and abroad in search of new authors for the
NAL list. By the end of 1950, when NAL was so magnificently solvent that we feared the Korean War taxation would
eat into our earned reserves, we frequently had to accelerate
investment in growth, in long-term reference projects, in
original books that might not be completed for publication
for several years, and in higher advances where necessary to
secure major reprint properties.

In the inflationary 1960's, it is seldom remembered that it
was not until 1950 that the 50-cent price was launched by
New American Library on a mass produced and distributed
book, with substantial advances against royalties in order to
secure the rights. In one week, after we had made our plans,
I signed up the first four 50-cent titles in February, endeavoring to provide a range of fiction that would break the price
barrier based on the length of the books and at the same time
represent a big value to impulse buyers at the newsstands.
They were *Forever Amber* by Kathleen Winsor (Macmillan)
with an advance of $30,000; *The Naked and the Dead* by
Norman Mailer (Rinehart) with an advance of $30,000; *The
Young Lions* by Irwin Shaw (Random House) with an ad-

vance of $25,000; and *Knock On Any Door* by Willard Motley (Appleton) with an advance of $25,000.

I swore to secrecy everyone from whom I had licensed these big books so that when we launched them in the autumn, we could do it with an audacious and not simultaneously imitated surprise selling campaign. To our delight, they all became paperbound best sellers. Some of our competitors, under the illusion that any long book could be priced at fifty cents, soon tended to depress the market with imitative but lesser titles, but nothing could now prevent flexible pricing of widely distributed inexpensive books. Within two years we launched Ayn Rand's best seller, *The Fountainhead*, licensed from Bobbs-Merrill at a 75-cent price, and in 1952 signed up with a stipulated 75-cent reprint price *From Here to Eternity* by James Jones through competitive negotiation (and a $102,000 advance) with Whitney Darrow of Charles Scribner's Sons.

All of these items confirmed the fact that the so-called mass market was no longer a standard-price matter in the manner of magazines, but that big books were marketable at higher prices.

There was, unfortunately, an ominous atmosphere to the increasingly competitive nature of our industry. Some of our friends in the traditional hardcover publishing field slyly encouraged censorship of books which were considered innocuous when priced at five dollars and restricted to sale in conventional bookshops. It became obvious that eventually, although not in the immediate future, the paperbound publisher would have to command greater control over fiction source material as well as nonfiction, a field in which I had been a too obviously successful pioneer to evade some imitative competition. I first of all attempted to commission more original Mentor books so that we would have them with selling rights throughout the world as the educational export operations increased with the liberation of currency exchange around the world, either directly or with the assistance of the United States Government. Moreover, in the period ahead we might well find it useful to have more direct relations with authors of fiction as well.

It occurred to me that NAL had an obligation to discover and deliver authors on behalf of others as well as entirely for ourselves. After a good deal of reflection, I determined that the best next move at NAL would be the initiation of a literary publication—a "little magazine"—in book form.

This was how *New World Writing* was begun.

Arabel Porter was named coordinating editor, and all of the other editors, including me and several juniors, pitched in to help with as much amateur enthusiasm as if we were struggling in an attic or a cellar. We did, indeed, publish the first volume in the following spring, as anticipated, with a list of contributors that included Christopher Isherwood, Alain Locke, Louis Auchincloss, Tennessee Williams, Flannery O'Connor, Thomas Merton, Rolfe Humphries, Shelby Foote, James Laughlin, Gore Vidal, Wright Morris, Howard Moss, Giuseppe Berto, William Gaddis, Robie Macauley, Charles J. Rolo, Jean-Baptiste Rossi and Oliver Evans.

The intention of *New World Writing* was to provide a friendly medium through which new, promising, genuine and vigorous talent might be communicated to a wide and receptive audience, and also to provide an instrument for serious letters and criticism. It had no prejudiced link to any special school, group, cult or movement—academic, literary or political—in the field of criticism. Our publishing experience, and our close association with people who wrote, edited and published books, constantly demonstrated that today's new writing becomes tomorrow's "good reading for the millions." Therefore, we wanted *New World Writing* to attract and interest the significant writers of the future.

The intention of *New World Writing* was well fulfilled. In a remarkable fashion it achieved an international audience and critical recognition throughout the world. After seven years, all of them financially profitable, it had served its purpose and inspired a score of independent "little magazines." We reluctantly decided that our "torchbearing" period should not be continued forever, that we might tend to become ingrown, and we welcomed an overture from Lippincott in Philadelphia to take it over, which they did for a considerable period, giving us an option on new authors.

Naturally enough, *New World Writing* led us into more intimate acquaintance with major and aspiring authors at home and abroad. To an extent which we had not anticipated, *New World Writing* led authors of their own volition to recommend that, the price being right, NAL be the favored reprinter selected by their hardcover publishers.

Even such a capricious writer as Norman Mailer was pleased that we, who had reprinted *The Naked and the Dead* and *The Barbary Shore,* published him in *New World Writing,* a circumstance which gave us the inside track on his later controversial book, *The Deer Park.*

I had met Norman Mailer at a number of literary gatherings during the 1948 season when his first book was published. I told him then that in due course we hoped to publish it unabridged, if we could negotiate the rights with Stanley Rinehart, and that we were not frightened by censorship. Our main concern was with the ability of the magazine wholesalers to market in large quantities books which must bear a cover price of fifty cents or more.

At that time Norman seemed to be less concerned with money than with his status as the first major American novelist to emerge out of the war. He lived simply and associated with the avant-garde of the period, most of whom were radical but not Communist, simply disrespectful of

I

tradition and traditionalists. He has obviously suffered from some social ostracism as a Jew at Harvard, which left scars on his personality that were deeper than any cruelties endured in active service in the war. It was apparent that drink and possibly drugs as well were involved in his insatiable quest for every sort of experience, physical and mental. He was disdainful of most of his contemporaries with the exception of Gore Vidal, whose grace and wit and incredible sense of learning—although he had never gone beyond prep school—baffled Norman as too sophisticated for anyone not a Jew. Gore, with a precocious reputation as a novelist, formidable gifts as a critic, and promising qualities as a dramatist, demonstrated the sort of prowess as a young man in society that irritated the uncouth when Gore was in a patronizing mood, slyly mentioning without ostentation the names of the rich and the famous whom he genuinely knew well in Washington, New York and London.

Gore was so handsome and charming that he did not need to run after influential friends; they sought him out. If it were not for his strength of character, they might well have blanketed his talent in the exhaustion of lunches, dinners and parties every day of the week. It was not long after Gore began to earn substantial money as a writer that he bought a large mansion a hundred miles up the Hudson River, remote from interruption except for the nearby faculty of Bard College or the landed aristocracy in the great houses nearby. A grandson of the blind Senator Gore, as a boy Gore had served as a page in the U.S. Senate. His father had been the first head of the Civil Aeronautics Agency of the United States Government, and his mother was active in the social life of Washington, New York and Long Island. His cousin by marriage, Louis Auchincloss, lawyer and distinguished novelist, moved with ease in the upper reaches of society in the 1940's. There always existed, and still does, a bit of one-upmanship between Gore and Louis, a friendly patrician rivalry over their reviews and book earnings, not to mention their film sales.

Gore Vidal had participated most generously in recruiting talent for the first volume of *New World Writing*, which he had urged me to initiate, and his creative interest never flagged. I have always been convinced that *New World Writing* was an effective instrument in the struggle against censorship which beset the paperbound book industry through the early 1950's—curiously, although indirectly, stimulated by the election of General Eisenhower as President. President Eisenhower, converted by responsibility, was baptized and became a church member on the morning that he took the oath of office. His influence was one of condonement of the censors, whether attacking alleged sedition or obscenity. Except for one speech at Dartmouth College, he did not take a positive role in the genuine challenge to intellectual freedom on the right to read at the critical stage of repressive challenge, symbolized by Senator Joseph McCarthy, during his administration.

A notable weekend conference on May 2 and 3, 1953, representing a joint conclave arranged by the American Library Association and the American Book Publishers Council, produced a seven-point series of propositions so important that they deserve inclusion in any account of those troubled times.

I was only one of the thirty-seven individuals present at a conference representing a conclave arranged by the ALA and ABPC, which issued the famous "Freedom to Read" statement at that time.

I was not there simply as a defender of my right to publish, but rather to help establish in the public conscience the need for defense of the reader's freedom and integrity and free choice of literature. This historic conference was bound to have an indirect influence upon the logic of the courts, including the Supreme Court of the United States, and upon legislators.

Only a few months before the conference a House of Representatives committee on current pornographic materials had invited me to testify, but when I appeared they suddenly announced that the hearings were concluded and refused to enter my statement in the record. As a result we reprinted ten thousand copies of my statement "The Complete and Unabridged Statement to the Gathings Committee by The New American Library of World Literature, Inc.," which I quickly sent to congressmen, senators, educators and selected members of the bar and of the clergy. It echoed a number of speeches which I had made during the period in New England, New York and Chicago, and happily enabled a minority of the Gathings Committee to make a dissenting report on the question of the necessity for supporting Federal legislation that would, if passed, have served to ban from circulation the works of Moravia, James T. Farrell, Georges Simenon, Erskine Caldwell, Mickey Spillane and dozens of other outstanding novelists of the United States, Great Britain, France, Italy and Germany.

I was greatly aided in my campaign against the censors by Theodore Waller of the American Book Publishers Council, later for a time an editorial vice-president of NAL, and by Dan Lacy, director of the American Book Publishers Council, and his able staff, which included the council's attorney, Horace Manges.

Despite the imaginative and substantial support of the ABPC, there were many cases of censorship which we had to fight on our own, with only the moral support of our industry. For example, in the spring of 1953 I addressed a conference on College Composition and Communication (an affiliate of the National Council of Teachers of English).

They had boldly named me and Professor T. A. Barnhart of State Teachers College in St. Cloud, Minnesota, under the chairmanship of Karl Dykema of Youngstown College, Youngstown, Ohio, to attack the precensorship which the chief of police in Youngstown had initiated with respect to all paperbound books. Many books at the retailers or in the stockroom of the wholesaler had been confiscated.

Although I was speaking on behalf of NAL, I took it upon myself to represent all of my competitors in our paperbound industry. I emphasized in particular the inconsistent discrimination against paperbound books which was growing under an assault by censors in a dozen major cities, large and small. Our industry was fighting for its life.

It is refreshing, looking back, to note how the atmosphere of 1953 has been cleansed by an alert community of publishers, educators, scholars, librarians, lawyers, clergy and good citizens, hundreds of whom concurred in my Chicago remarks.

None of us at that time was defending hard-core pornography or outright sedition. But we were defending the right to write, publish and read legitimate literature and legitimate radical expressions of thought. This is a battle which is never fully won, but which came to be the basic constructive doctrine of the United States Supreme Court in a number of cases deemed worthy to serve as precedents.

I am prouder of my role in this struggle than I am of my individual accomplishments in sponsoring good books. It served to put me into an enduring alliance with busy and dedicated men and women and to give a liberating sense of fulfillment of loyalty to the fundamental wisdom of Thomas Jefferson when he wrote the Bill of Rights, especially Article I thereof.

A lot of censorship, of course, is extralegal, representing the prejudices of booksellers and magazine wholesalers, who are often less courageous than they might be in facing local pressure, especially the pressure of Catholic organizations such as the NODL (National Organization for Decency in Literature).

Some publishers and some authors inevitably take advantage of Supreme Court decisions and attempt to publish obviously lewd and lascivious books and cheap smut for the sake of sales through titillation. The only way to discourage them is to educate teachers and parents to elevate the taste of the young, who then will inevitably avoid their tawdry wares, and to encourage better taste on the part of the adult reading public.

After having been instrumental in combating censorship and in building a list of books that sold by the millions on the newsstands and in schools and colleges, I was primarily concerned with our relationships to the literary profession and the publishing industry at home and abroad. I was a literary Nimrod in quest of the fascinating new writers who, often obscure and unknown in the period immediately after the war, were worthy of wider attention. One writer in this category who interested me particularly was Dylan Thomas, perhaps the greatest lyric poet to appear after the death of William Butler Yeats. I met him, oddly enough, through Oscar Williams, the poet and anthologist, who brought him to my office to submit the first chapter of *Adventures in the Skin Trade*. Oscar was the last man on earth whom I imagined would seek my company for any purpose, since in 1946 I had physically thrown him out of my office when he refused to deliver to me a manuscript packet until I presented to him the check due upon delivery of *Modern American Poets*.

When he insisted upon the check before he handed me the packet, I told him that I had no way of knowing what was in the packet—sandwiches or wastepaper—and that I would certainly give him a check as soon as I had an opportunity to open it. When he stubbornly refused to reveal the contents, I had taken him by the scruff of the neck and escorted him to the elevator and given him a shove. He had forgiven all of this indignity when, as time ran on, he came to admire the program which I had developed and especially my interest in poets. He appeared one day with Dylan Thomas, and while the two of them sat on the sofa in my office, I read a portion of *Adventures in the Skin Trade* which Dylan had nearly completed. I immediately accepted it not only for *New World Writing* but for later publication in book form, providing that New Directions, Dylan's regular publisher, would consent. James Laughlin of New Directions was elated by the concurrence of my judgment with his, and we had the honor of introducing Dylan's first prose writing to American readers on a really large scale.

A year or more later when Dylan appeared in the United States, we gave a large cocktail party for him at the apartment. This occasion has been somewhat inaccurately described in John Malcolm Brinnin's *Dylan Thomas in America,* published by Little, Brown in 1953. Brinnin was apparently jealous of Oscar Williams' association with Dylan Thomas, and he wrote in his memoir that Dylan arrived after the party had actually broken up. This is in error— Dylan came almost on time and with great effort from an appearance at Sweetbriar College in Lynchburg, Virginia, and did not depart until long after the occasion was actually breaking up around nine o'clock, when he left with Arabel Porter, Brinnin and Howard Moss of *The New Yorker.* I saw Dylan a number of times after this and was always struck by the cherubic innocence and natural goodness which he invariably exhibited in my presence at home and in the office. He was eventually and easily seduced into drunkenness and irregular habits, but in all of our meetings he was as sublimely innocent and lyrical as an angel graven on an old-fashioned tombstone. I was never exposed to the morose or abusive side of his personality, so frequently described after his death. On the contrary, on a number of occasions when he and Oscar Williams and I met together, Dylan was as pristinely nice, even naïve, as a precocious Welsh Druid.

After Dylan's death, I saw a great deal more of Oscar Williams, who functioned as general editor of notable poetry collections for NAL. With great generosity, Oscar had long since forgiven me my first rude reaction to his perverse maneuvers when we met. I had known Oscar slightly years earlier when he was a junior employee of the old Butterick Company, but I came to have a high regard not only for his poetic taste and editorial skill but for his integrity as a special poetry anthologist. I used to visit him occasionally in his loft studio overlooking the Battery and sit on the roof patio outside his atelier watching the ocean liners come and go. I came to appreciate his quality as a person and to admire his forgiveness of my reaction to his technical stubbornness in 1946. His principal fault, if it can be described as such, was a fanatic dedication to his wife's ability as a poet long after her death, and his insistence that her verse should be included in any anthology which he compiled. She was, of course, talented, but I do not believe that Jean Derwood will survive in the annals of American literature, despite Oscar's attempts to memorialize her through the years of his editorship of many volumes of contemporary poetry.

My theory of operations, often at variance with the more obvious tactics of Enoch, was that so long as we were reprinters, the best reprint books would be derived from the best publishers. If and when the time came that we could commission original fiction books on our own, it was obvious that the best books would come from the best authors, whether or not they were known or famous at the time of our first expressions of interest. I consequently paid a great deal of attention to the resource list of publishers such as Little, Brown. In our early days, Little, Brown would have nothing to do with us because of the prejudice of Alfred McIntyre, president of the company, against any concern which had had anything to do with Allen Lane. This prejudice on the part of the estimable Alfred McIntyre was overcome by Arthur Thornhill—later president and then chairman of Little, Brown—while he was still representing Little, Brown in their New York office.

He had started out at Little, Brown as an office boy, then went on the road as a book salesman, and became better acquainted with the book buyers of the nation than anyone I have ever known, with the possible exception of Stanley Rinehart in his early days with George A. Doran and later with Doubleday-Doran. Arthur eventually headed the New York office of Little, Brown and somewhat to his own surprise was called to Boston and nominated to succeed Alfred McIntyre as president of the company. Although he has never made any pretense at being an editor, he has a nose for good books that will sell and, above all, a natural concern with the welfare of Little, Brown authors and also the authors of the Atlantic Press for whose books Little, Brown manufactures, promotes and sells, including subsidiary rights. The great attribute of Arthur Thornhill, quite apart from his knowledge and charm, is his absolute integrity. Although he was on the board of Bantam Books, our competitors, he never failed to place an author with NAL for reprint if in his opinion the author was better suited to our qualitative list. He managed to keep everything on an even keel at Little, Brown through critical editorial turnover that would have paralyzed an ordinary publishing house.

As time ran on Arthur became not only a good friend but a professional colleague and an unusual confidant. He is the

1*

only man whom I ever interrupted on a weekend to seek reprint rights. One Friday afternoon I had received an advance copy of J. D. Salinger's *Catcher in the Rye*. I read it that evening and went into a cold sweat lest the reprint rights should be seized by a competitor if I waited until Monday morning. I tracked Arthur down on the telephone, made a deal, and discovered later that we had beaten the field, most of whom did not receive their advance copies until the Monday or Tuesday following. Although *Catcher in the Rye* was not enormously successful in hardcover, we managed to sell millions of copies.

My routine in the early 1950's was wholly dedicated to NAL. I had not had a vacation for more than a decade and had no interest in holidays. My family cooperated to the hilt by providing me with a thermos of hot coffee available at 4 A.M. so that I could spend four hours reading before breakfast, then proceed to my office to undertake the day's office work. In twenty years of book publishing after the war, I never read a book in the office, undertaking all of the appraisal and analysis in my own home and on my own time. In addition, with the cooperation of my family, I converted my apartment into a rendezvous that nearly every day included guests for lunch, for dinner, for the evening or for the weekend.

Victor Gollancz was one of at least three-score English publishers whom I came to know as well as I knew the leaders in American book publishing. His taste was often obnoxious to me, because of his uncritical leftish tendencies, but his enthusiasm reflected the kind of adherence to his individual criteria that had made famous, on the home front, such outstanding publishers as Alfred and Blanche Knopf.

The one English publisher who grew and grew and grew into importance as a man to watch in the 1950's was George Weidenfeld. When I first met George Weidenfeld, he was an

occasional visitor at the apartment of Israel Sieff in Chesterfield Gardens in London and was working on a series of
annuals for distribution by Marks and Spencer, the multiple-
shop organization of which Israel was a founder and in due
course chairman, and whose niece, Jane, was soon to
become George Weidenfeld's first wife. At first acquaintance
I could hardly have predicted that George, in partnership
with Nigel Nicolson, would within a decade become one of
the most important, creative and successful publishers in England. In a very short time the reviews of his books matched
the attention given to works published by Oxford, Longmans,
Nelson and Collins, and the sales kept pace with the critical
recognition. Unlike most London publishers, George was
from the beginning enamored with Continental scholarship
as well as diligent in his attention to the postwar writers and
scholars of the United States. He soon became, to me, a publisher to cultivate not only as a source of important books but
as a friend, and within a few years we were involved in social
as well as professional engagements in London, Paris, Frankfurt and New York. The ordinary English publisher is a great
respecter of weekends and ill at ease in the linguistically con-
fusing gathering places from Madrid to Vienna. As a result,
George soon established a liaison, quickly converted into successful books, with the outstanding talent of Spain, Italy,
Austria, France and Scandinavia. His voracious appetite for
stimulating society soon brought to his flat in Belgravia not
only dons and Pimlico poets but dukes and duchesses, bankers and journalists. He was so utterly charming that when
his first marriage went on the rocks, he retained the affection-
ate loyalty of Israel Sieff and Lord Marks, who have never
failed to respond to his invitation to small and intimate, or
impressively large and glamorous, parties. By happy chance
after a decade of bachelorhood, recently, at the age of forty-
six, George was married to Sandra Payson Meyer, a beautiful

and gracious New Yorker whose mother is devoted to her art collection, her racing stable and her extraordinary Mets baseball team, and whose uncle, John Hay Whitney, a distinguished sportsman, financier and publisher, was Ambassador to the Court of St. James's during the Eisenhower Administration.

Within five years of the founding of his own publishing house, he had recruited the ablest scholars and many of the finest writers of Europe, Britain and America to his list. Unlike Gollancz, George Weidenfeld built an organization with trusted lieutenants and advisors, so that he could become mobile enough to spend a great deal of time away from the office and entrust urgent minor decisions and follow-through to a senior staff. George Weidenfeld is urbane, creative, a veritable dynamo of energetic taste.

George and I collaborated from the outset of our acquaintance on dozens of publishing projects, all of them distinguished and successful and some of them destined to produce profitable revenue for ourselves and our authors for a generation, especially the new scholars in the fields of art, history and the social sciences.

In the 1950's, George mastered a knowledge of university curricula in the United States, in Great Britain and on the Continent which enabled him to inspire and commission books that were acceptable in institutions of higher learning all the way from Munich to Seattle. I have never known any entrepreneur in publishing quite so perceptive and genuinely interested in good books in such a wide area of scholarly disciplines. Oxford, Longmans, and Nelson in England found him a fantastic competitor not only for authors but for the discriminating review space in the *Times Literary Supplement*, the *New Statesman and Nation* and the *Spectator*, as well as in the highbrow critical pages of the *Sunday Times*, the *Observer* and, as soon as it was established, the *Sunday*

Telegraph. He very wisely refused to dilute the Weidenfeld and Nicolson list with ephemeral books, and bought the firm of Arthur Barker, Ltd., which published Mickey Spillane in England, as a "semidetached cottage" that could control such material for the pleasure and revenue of deploying it for high prices to British reprinters.

I was especially pleased to be involved on a number of collaborative projects with George Weidenfeld because of our increasing export sales of serious books, not mere ephemeral entertainment or books so elementary that they might never be discovered by newly educated students who were usually not fully at home with the English language until they were well along in higher or even university level courses.

In 1945 I had been an alternate delegate to the Preparatory Commission for UNESCO which met in London, and I had, during that time, become acquainted with many educators from the British Commonwealth and Colonial areas who were mainly English speaking. I had collected a great deal of material on overseas education in the social sciences and English-language literature, not only from UNESCO sources but from schools of education in England. This material, when studied in relation to American education as reflected in a large cross section of college and university catalogues, enabled me to discuss with easy competence long-term projects with George Weidenfeld.

Without the development of recurring educational sales, which did not represent the hazards of total dependence upon big fiction titles, NAL could not have grown into the profitable institution which it became in less than a decade after we went on to a current basis without any long-term credit of any sort in 1950.

The only interruption of the profitable course of NAL came in the early 1950's when, facing a glut of books on the newsstand market, the magazine wholesalers accelerated the returns of unsold merchandise in order to reduce their bills. Even best sellers were sometimes sent back in unopened cartons. Our situation was imperiled not so much by the lack of appeal of the books which we had distributed, and which if they had remained on display would have continued to sell, as by the decision of our distributors, Fawcett Publications, to take advantage of the experience they had gained in handling our products to launch their own paperbound books, sharing over a million dollars worth of rack furniture which we had placed throughout the country and putting their own books on the racks which we had financed, often making space for their own wares by authorizing the return of our Signet and Mentor Books.

This imitative operation was an unparalleled reverse of the understanding which we had with them, but to have criticized it would have exposed us to antitrust action under the Federal restraint-of-trade statutes. We had recruited a distribution executive from Independent News Company, Jack Adams, who asserted that the only solution was to force more and more merchandise on the market. The end result was a large deficit which threatened to obliterate the book value of the company. Jack Adams, sales vice-president, who triumphed over my arguments, was not at the time a book man and was not really acquainted with books and their unique audience for at least the first five years of his tenure with NAL. He blamed the plight of the company on the Fawcetts, who were actually his cousins.

Our export sales in the early 1950's were partly dependent upon the American Government's helpful intervention in expediting foreign exchange where local funds were unavailable for dollar conversion; but, eventually, the principles of the conference of Allied Ministers of Education, which had created UNESCO, prevailed so that the free flow of idea and information among the peoples of the world became normal.

UNESCO's goals came to be accepted everywhere except in Communist countries. They were parallel to the aims of a good commercial publisher. New American Library had a substantial educational list—the most substantial such list in the inexpensive paperbound form in the English-speaking world. This circumstance enabled us to hedge against the uncertainties of the so-called newsstand markets in the United States and Canada. In addition, before we moved our distribution from Fawcett to Independent News Company, Enoch had created a field staff of our own to police the domestic displays and to stimulate distributors into more effective distribution of the right books in the right places for the natural audiences that we knew existed.

I was the beneficiary of extraordinary editorial talent. After several years of apprenticeship and tutelage, Truman Talley developed into a rapid and perceptive reader and a superb negotiator for publication rights. By his own efforts, he won the total cooperation of the editorial staff, which had hitherto been slightly despondent when I was absent. He was made an editorial vice-president with authority commensurate with his responsibility. However, Enoch insisted on simultaneously making vice-presidents of Peter Gruenthal (his son-in-law) and Milton Rosenblitt, chief accountant. Unlike any other member of the staff, Truman Talley had a knowledge of source material and of the market which covered a range as wide as my own—from thrillers to classics, from science fiction to philosophy and from slighter entertaining fiction to more universally important novels of top quality. He worked closely with the Committee on College Reading which produced our perennially best-selling reference volume, *Good Reading*, first under the chairmanship of Atwood Townsend and later under the chairmanship of Sherwood Weber. Truman Talley assumed responsibility for the development of books of reference as well as fiction, and was especially diplomatic in the placement of original books with hardcover publishers or university presses prior to our issuance of them in paperbound form. He became actively involved with the American PEN Center, functioning on a number of committees, and within a few years after his marriage in 1951 developed his apartment into a gathering place especially for younger critics, poets, novelists, scholars and booksellers. He recruited a number of associate editors who have since gone off to function as editors-in-chief elsewhere—not because NAL did not provide sufficient opportunity, but because of an increasing apprehension amongst the creative employees that Enoch fundamentally disdained, if he did not actually dislike, editors.

On one occasion, while I was in London, Enoch put forward an edict that under no circumstances should editors have access to cost and sales figures. Upon my return I announced to the editors that this was nonsense, that I could not depend upon a recommendation to publish a book that was not based upon a practical financial projection of its prospects. I provided the editors with cost figures on paperbound books projected to six decimal points on books of various lengths and various quantities ranging from fifty thousand to a million; with a formula for calculating the profit with allowance for all costs on copies sold, and allowing for estimated returns of unsold books; and with a special calculation based upon experience on the sales of returned Mentor books that, if returned in mint condition, could easily be resold from our warehouse in the future as they became adopted by schools and colleges.

Chapter X

THE STRENUOUS LIFE

————·◦∞◦·————

I wish to preach, not the doctrine of ignoble ease, but the doctrine of the strenuous life.

—Theodore Roosevelt

ONE OF THE PLEASANT although demanding aspects of life in the fifties was that with a seasoned, young but mature editorial staff working under Truman Talley's operational direction, I could make my annual visits to London, Paris, Frankfurt and Edinburgh a bit longer and better organized and increasingly productive. By the summer of 1951 I was so confident that we could lead a global approach to publication of inexpensive books, with emphasis on education, that I recommended the establishment of a modest office in London under the shelter of a friendly publisher to deal with British distribution and to assist in the procurement of British material, scholarly and otherwise. This proposal was voted down, and as a result we soon placed our distribution in the United Kingdom in the hands of Frederick Muller Ltd. and continued to sell directly throughout the rest of the British market.

Some eight or nine years later, as Pan Books became a substantial enterprise, the chairman and managing director flew to New York in the middle of a blizzard to plead with us to buy Pan Books for a figure in the $2,000,000 range. Pan at that time was owned by Heinemann, Hodder and Stoughton, Macmillan and Collins, the Bott Trust and several of the directors. Billy Collins was willing to sell the Collins interest, but his brother, Ian Collins, demurred on grounds of resistance to American intrusion in British publishing. Then Maurice Macmillan, M.P., the son of Harold Macmillan, agreed with Ian Collins—and Macmillan and Collins purchased the other interests and became the proprietors of Pan Books. It would have been easy enough to have organized, with practically no investment, a British subsidiary in the early 1950's, but by 1960 imaginative entrepreneurs in the paperback field in England had grown in the style of the more successful American companies, with the exceptions of Ace Books owned by the Locker interests and 4-Square Books owned by Godfrey Phillips Ltd., a tobacco company which was developing itself into a general holding company.

In the summer of 1960, when it became obvious that Pan Books Ltd. were not available as an acquisition by NAL, I learned that Godfrey Phillips were acquiring Ace Books. I went to Commercial Street in East London, where the home office of Godfrey Phillips Ltd. was located, and expressed interest in knowing whether they would be interested in selling out all or 51 percent of their interests if, upon analysis, it appeared a good investment on our part. Since the saga of 4-Square Books really belongs further along in this account of my times, I shall at this point refrain from further comment except to say that the ultimate acquisition of 4-Square Books as a publishing enterprise deserves a great deal more research and more space than I could devote to it in a lifetime.

The growth of NAL, after the setback of 1953, was well-planned and upward in turnover, in profits and in the recognition which we received from educators, librarians and booksellers at home and abroad, including increasingly fine relations with authors, agents and, above all, the major hardcover publishers who licensed reprint material to us. After serving as chairman or as a member of a number of committees of the American Book Publishers Council, I was elected to the board—the first publisher so elected who was exclusively concerned with softcover books, without any hardcover affiliation whatsoever. I was also named a founding trustee of Franklin Publications (subsequently Franklin Book Programs), concerned with reinforcement of foreign language publishing overseas, especially in areas which lacked a substantial book publishing industry. Franklin had been envisaged by some of the founders as an adjunct to American propaganda abroad, but Datus Smith, former director of the Princeton University Press who became Franklin's president, soon established a policy that Franklin would never become a propaganda organization. It developed as the friendly advisor and occasional short-term creditor of book enterprises which now operate under local management in most of the Arab countries, in parts of India, Indonesia, Malaysia, Africa and South America.

Datus Smith prevailed on American publishers to grant translation rights on a generous basis, since the money received was really a modest windfall that would never otherwise have materialized at all. I was pleased to find that from the very beginning books controlled by NAL were so well adapted to foreign translation that a large number of our titles were utilized.

I had established a contract office that was quick to refer translation requests directly to me for immediate decision. I soon discovered that many writers were more delighted with a collection of their works in an impressive variety of foreign languages than if they had received a vast sum of money. I made it clear that I would not haggle over money for rights in those non-European countries which had very little money to spend on rights or on translations; but that I would haggle to the hilt with publishers in countries with a prosperous book industry—Great Britain, France, West Germany and Italy—with concessions for more modest payments from countries with a comparatively small native-language population such as Holland, Denmark, Finland, Turkey, Norway and, in some cases, Sweden, Portugal and Spain.

The annual journey to the Frankfurt Book Fair was especially useful in the purchase as well as the sale of rights of translations and often for the opportunities provided for close inspection of the books issued by publishers in other countries. I soon learned to recognize the difference in book designs in countries outside the tradition of Western Europe, such as Hungary, Czechoslovakia and Poland.

I was most ably assisted at Frankfurt by Jacques David, my Paris agent, who was a versatile linguist, and also by an increasing number of friends who were familiar not only with European langages but with Russian, Japanese, Chinese, Arabic, Urdu, Hindi and Korean. I established local representatives for the sale of rights, first under the direction of Walter Wriggins and then under an even more aggressive home office executive, Dorothy Sherreff, whose contractual decisions were handled by me, personally, until years later, when NAL was fortunate enough to secure the services of Michael Cohn. After graduation from the University of Pennsylvania and the Harvard Law School, Cohn had been trained by Philip Wittenburg, an extraordinarily able lawyer in the field of literary law, conveying of rights, copyright and scrutiny for possible invasion of privacy or libel.

As my small but able supporting staff in editorial, contractual and production processing became more self-reliant in the handling of every detail except important policies and final decisions, I found myself able to devote more time not only to editorial reconnaissance but to the assistance of the marketing staff by covering major meetings of booksellers, librarians, magazine wholesalers and college-bookstore groups.

One blazing hot day when I was going the rounds of Hollywood and Beverly Hills, developing promotional liaison with film producers, I was introduced by Al Manuel—then an agent, now a producer at Paramount—to Ted Loeff, who had done a spectacular performance in the advance promotion of the long-delayed United Artists release of the film based upon Erskine Caldwell's *God's Little Acre*. At first, I found Ted a typical, and almost obnoxious, Hollywood press agent. He knew everything and everybody, rose from the table and walked across a restaurant to chat with stars and starlets, producers, directors or script writers. As my visit came to the hour of my scheduled departure, I extended my stay for a week, in the course of which I became much better acquainted with Ted Loeff. He was a swarthy Hungarian, prone to tell tasteless Jewish stories. I wondered why so many of his friends seemed to love and admire him, despite his often disheveled appearance and habit of mumbling to himself. Then, fortunately, I discovered that underneath all of his acquired Hollywood characteristics he was a widely read scholar, a compulsive book collector, an author under a dozen different pseudonyms and a remarkable literary critic and observer of literary trends, regardless of whether or not they were linked with his film connections.

Loeff proposed that he become my scout in California, not only among recognizable established writers with demonstrated popular appeal but among the avant-garde and university circles. I was understandably hesitant, but finally worked out a simple formula—a modest overriding royalty to go to him on material which he discovered or developed, providing that under no circumstances would he poach on other publishers' authors or make a commitment without my written approval. He agreed but, first of all, he insisted upon sponsoring a project, an original softcover book based upon the news story by a Pulitzer prizewinner that was being produced as the film *I Want to Live!* The picture was the first produced by Walter Wanger after his release from prison for shooting a friend of his wife's in a Los Angeles parking lot, and it dealt with the case of a girl, played by Susan Hayward, who because of an unsavory reputation was convicted of a murder on less than adequate proof and went to the gas chamber for the execution of the death sentence. When it turned out that Montgomery's manuscript was literal journalism, hastily written as a film treatment, Loeff acquired the publication rights of a rewritten version on his own account. He assigned a well-known author—Irving Shulman—to start from scratch and write the book under the pseudonym Tabor Rawson. It turned out to be a phenomenal success as an original paperbound book, not only because of its topicality and the climate of opinion concerning capital punishment, but because Shulman had made a stinging and almost Zolaesque tour de force of his manuscript.

It was turned down in England by Victor Gollancz, who was then in the vanguard of the anti-capital punishment crusade, because he found the detailed account of the capital punishment of a frowsy and somewhat faded beauty distasteful. Clarence Paget of Pan Books, whom I took to a preview of the film, rejected it on the same grounds for British publication. However, the promotional enterprise of Frederick Muller Ltd., our distributing organization under the direction of James Reynolds (now with George Weidenfeld as head of the Arthur Barker concern), sold some seventy thousand copies of our American edition in the United Kingdom alone, while we marketed it in the rest of the British Commonwealth.

This experience convinced me that Ted Loeff was not only a good literary scout but something of an original character as a book entrepreneur. Eventually he set up an office and a corporation, Literary Projects, Inc., which delivered to NAL, under contract with West Coast authors, a number of extraordinary books, many of them in the best-seller category. Although as time ran on Ted Loeff became ill and his overhead devoured his enterprise, he gave NAL an editorial foothold in California which the company never had enjoyed before. One day, not long after the success of *I Want to Live!* he telephoned me at 9:00 A.M. (6:00 A.M. in Beverly Hills) collect, as was his frequent habit, to ask if I wanted to publish Irving Wallace's extensive screen treatment expanded into a book on Barnum, the showman. He told me that the treatment had already been bought by the movies—which I confirmed was true—for a panoramic film in the fashion of *Around the World in 80 Days,* to draw on short appearances by a number of famous stars as part of Barnum's fabulous exhibit of showmanship. Since there had been no book on Barnum since several popular volumes in the 1920's, I said okay so long as we did not conflict with Alfred Knopf, who had published two books of collected articles by Wallace, and also so long as we did not short-circuit Wallace's agent, Paul R. Reynolds. Later in the day Ted put Irving Wallace, whom I had never met, on the phone, and he confirmed all that Ted had said. He said that he would clear the matter with Alfred Knopf and would stipulate Paul Reynolds as agent. I sent along the contract.

When the manuscript came in, production of the film was not imminent, so I asked Alfred Knopf if he would like to undertake it in hardcover, making his contract with New American Library. Since Alfred had taken several books from us for prior hardcover publication, I regarded the matter as routine. But when *Fabulous Showman* became a Literary Guild selection, Alfred expressed great annoyance that he had taken his own author from a reprinter. We patched up

our differences on this point, the book was a success and I had
assumed that Irving Wallace was not in any sense an NAL
author except for this special project deriving from his film
treatment.

On my next trip to California, I did not have Irving Wallace in mind. I had not yet met him personally. When I
checked into the Beverly Hills Hotel, there was a message
that "Mr. Wallis" had called. I immediately called Hal Wallis, the producer at Paramount, and although he had not
telephoned me, he invited me to visit him on the lot as was
my perennial custom. I was still puzzled while unpacking
when Irving Wallace—the real caller—telephoned, not only
clarifying the mistake in the spelling of his name in the
message which had awaited me, but insisting upon an early
appointment the next morning along with Ted Loeff. I
immediately canceled my plan to visit Santa Barbara on my
first day West. The next morning Irving Wallace appeared
and expressed an urgent desire to talk business. "I want
twenty-five thousand dollars," he said. I replied that for that
matter, I could use twenty-five thousand dollars myself. He
then said, "I have two unwritten books, and for twenty-five
thousand dollars you can have them, so long as you place the
hardcover rights in good hands!" I asked what they were.
"One," he said, "I call *The Chapman Report*. It will be a
novel dealing with a sex survey directed by a Dr. Chapman
in a California community, and what it reveals of the ladies,
of the members of the survey team and of life in general. The
other," he continued, "is a nonfiction book which I call
The Twenty-seventh Wife, an account of Brigham Young's
last bride." By this time Ted Loeff arrived and I promptly
said to both of them that I would do the books. As Irving has
published in one of his numerous interviews:

> I showed him nothing on paper. Instead, sitting there in
> his hotel suite, I told him my ideas for *The Chapman Report*

in five minutes and my conception of *The Twenty-seventh Wife* in five minutes, and he nodded and stood up, and said, "We accept both books. We'll pay you for the paperback rights in advance!"

We agreed that we would place the prior hardcover rights to them through Paul Reynolds, and that I would have to have a warranty that there was no lien by, or option to, Alfred Knopf or any other publisher. Irving Wallace agreed. I telephoned Walter Wriggins, my office contract man in New York, and asked him to prepare contracts at once to send to Paul Reynolds, the agent, for forwarding to the author for execution. I warned Wriggins not to discuss the matter at all until my return as I didn't want anyone to think I had made a reckless commitment with a nonnovelist for two books within twenty-four hours of my arrival in Beverly Hills.

The Chapman Report made a fortune and an international reputation for Irving Wallace. He had demonstrated that he had great gifts and imagination as a novelist seriously interested in social and psychological themes. As Irving told me recently, despite his large earnings as a journalist and film writer,

"That twenty-five thousand dollars got me out of movies for good."

I naturally felt that I had made a good bargain, too. "You were courageous and astute, and if ever you want my letters and journal notes on that meeting, you may have them," Wallace said.

Paul Reynolds placed the hardcover rights with Simon and Schuster. Because of the threat of litigation against Wallace by another publisher who had subsequently taken on a minor novel which Wallace had written earlier, and also because of a hint of legal action by the Kinsey Institute, which feared that the book would impair their continuing claim for Federal funds for sexual research, I took the advice of Littauer's law firm to convey the hardcover rights back to Wallace so that he could contract with Simon and Schuster directly. This pattern was established for further books on which, in the first instance, New American Library acquired rights in all languages; *The Prize*, dealing with a group of individuals brought together by the propinquity of the Nobel Prize awards, and *The Three Sirens*, a novel dealing with a female anthropologist, not too unlike Margaret Mead, endeavoring to find useful behavioral patterns for modern urban dwellers in the tribal rites and customs of a South Pacific society not yet entirely altered by exposure to Western civilization.

I later discovered that the abdication from control of Irving Wallace's hardcover rights gave Simon and Schuster a unique relationship which, while it did not diminish our friendship, certainly led Irving to feel that Simon and Schuster were his real publishers. I was fondly described on an autographed photograph as "mine Earl of Southhampton," but in the final showdown on financial terms in the winter of 1963, when Irving thought we should have made some retroactive adjustment in his royalty rate, and I stood alone in favor of such a financial gesture, NAL lost Irving Wallace.

I could hardly go against the adamant attitude of Enoch and Adams that we shouldn't give an inch to an insistent author. Despite this, Irving still expressed the hope that NAL would work out reprint arrangements with Simon and Schuster on a satisfactory basis. On reflection, I'm convinced that Irving Wallace was justified in asking for a retroactive adjustment and that his professional alienation from NAL was a catastrophic management mistake. However, by 1963 NAL had been merged into the Times Mirror Company, and a devastating set of rules prepared by McKinsey and Company, management consultants, had been promulgated by the Times Mirror Company, making it almost impossible for an editorial operation to function efficiently because of the transfer of ultimate power on major decisions to the president, and through him ultimately to Los Angeles. More amplification of this will appear later in this narrative, but it has a bearing on the odds against which the editors performed after the Times Mirror acquisition.

To return now to Ted Loeff and his work on behalf of NAL in California: In the early period of our relationship, when he was buoyantly creative and in comparatively good health, he discovered and developed a score of authors. Not any of them quite equaled the extraordinary performance of Irving Wallace, but they did provide a respectable supply of interesting and profitable books which strengthened our schedule and consequent profits.

After a few years, Ted's health declined. At the same time he could not resist the temptation to saddle his office with expensive staff and space that could never be covered by his retainer and overriding royalties on work which we accepted upon his recommendation. It is a sad commentary on modern life that long after we ended our association, and Ted Loeff died in straitened circumstances, no corporate beneficiaries of his one-time brilliance sprang to the aid of his widow. A handful of old friends, including Irving Wallace and me, made personal contributions. This was a long time after Ted's period of greatness. Indeed, his end, after long periods of hospitalization, came in April, 1966, on the day that I returned from London after a trip around the world. I received a telephone call from Irving Wallace with the news of Ted Loeff's death. I cite this now to make it clear that Irving Wallace never was disloyal to Ted, who had brought us together, or to me, whom he realized and acknowledged had been a modest instrument in providing a vehicle with which his meteoric career as a novelist, with a world audience in practically every major language except Russian and Mandarin, could be launched.

During the 1950's my life was enlivened not only by a sense of financial success but by the constant realization that NAL had an obligation to its authors that transcended money. We demonstrated, almost daily, that quite apart from corporate budgets, it was a pleasure as well as a duty to give an author moral support and encouragement. One example which comes to mind is Paul Roche, the translator and poet. In London I had chanced upon a charming little volume of modern fables and got in touch with Paul Roche, the author, to inquire whether a group of these charming short pieces would be available for *New World Writing*. I was agreeably surprised when he consented, and even more pleasantly startled when one day he appeared at my office in New York for the first time. It was our first encounter. Tall, handsome, with a mop of flaxen hair, his voice was vibrant with the love of poetry in Greek and Latin as well as in English. Although British, he was married to a girl from Saginaw, Michigan, and at my suggestion he brought his wife, Clarissa, and children to the States for several years. He taught at Smith College and lectured to college audiences around the country. He delighted in reading his poetry and his magnificent translation of the *Antigone* of Sophocles, which we published.

One day I invited twenty-five people to come to my office at lunchtime for a light repast of sandwiches and coffee to hear Paul Roche read his *Antigone*. It was such a stirring event that I later invited him to our apartment to read to more than seventy-five literary friends and scholars. Frequently thereafter he read to groups in our apartment as well as at such established centers as the Y.M.H.A. in New York, at the home of Senator and Mrs. Jacob Javits and the Parish House of the Madison Avenue Presbyterian Church just a few blocks away, where Dr. and Mrs. David Read, formerly at Edinburgh, were and are remarkable patrons of poetry and the arts.

I and all of my editorial staff learned that we should make every effort to introduce visiting authors, poets and scholars when they were in New York to their opposite numbers no less eagerly than when introducing solvent visiting publishers from England and Europe. Most of these activities were undertaken voluntarily and totally off the expense account, as part of the gratifying, even though sometimes laborious, role of a good publisher. I carefully briefed my staff that personal concern for authors on special occasions should not be permitted to lead to sloppy familiarity and continuous intimate association. This was clearly understood by all of them. We endeavored to make our letters of acceptance of manuscripts brief and clear, so that our authors would not brood over positive decisions that could be interpreted as having been made for the wrong reasons.

"Let authors be confident of your wizardry in understanding and appreciating their work," was my admonition. "On the other hand," I said, "never be abrupt or terse when rejecting a manuscript. The psychology of a writer who works in solitude is one of extreme sensitivity, and any author whose work is unsuitable for us deserves a statement why not and, if possible, what other publisher might be interested."

I encouraged our editors to participate in cultural and community life at every level of appropriate interest, and not simply remain content with a little perfunctory help to good causes and to the financial appeals of obvious institutions. Rather, I wanted them to avoid the mediocre middle of the road and to stand for something that would give them the satisfaction of a challenge faced and of hope fulfilled. When our editors came to our apartment for dinner or an evening soiree, they appeared in black tie and evening dress and mixed not only with literary people but with bankers, diplomats, businessmen, museum curators, educators, film stars and sportsmen. Obviously, not all occasions called for the formal touch. The point is that I wanted them to feel well-rounded and socially mobile. In a dramatic sense, most of them achieved a wonderful sense of the great status of their calling.

A spectacular occasion to which all of the editors and top executives of NAL were invited to our apartment in 1955 was the publication date party of *Buffalo Bill and the Wild West,* written by Henry Blackman Sell and me during Sunday mornings, or afternoons, over a period of nearly two years.

The project had grown out of idle banter at the Butterick Company thirty years earlier, when Henry Sell had confided to me that he was a collateral descendant of Colonel William F. Cody. Although there were extant a number of books on Buffalo Bill, including the dime novels ghosted for him early in his career, there had not been a genuinely popular adult book that conveyed the spirit of the man who, as a showman, had established the Western theme as a perennial romantic saga throughout the world.

Most moderns are inclined to think that Buffalo Bill was something of an old faker, which was not the case. Through the years on trips to Cody, Wyoming, to Denver and other Cody areas, I had collected a considerable number of books and pictures dealing with Buffalo Bill's relationship to Western Americana. One day when Henry Sell, then the editor of *Town and Country,* sent a photographer to my office to take a picture for a series dealing with prominent figures in the communications industry in Madison Avenue—ranging from William Paley of CBS and Bennett Cerf of Random House and Alfred Knopf to me—I jokingly said that Henry's sense of showmanship and interest in Madison Avenue seemed to be derived from his Uncle Bill. "Bill who?" asked the photographer. "The one and only Buffalo Bill," I replied. "He was a greater showman than anyone on Madison Avenue today."

This persiflage, when related to Henry, led him to suggest that we actually write a book.

I explained that I was working sixteen hours a day and couldn't think of such a thing. He agreed to finance the research that would be necessary and to make available his family archives, and I was finally persuaded to join in the fun.

We then employed an able teacher who had written a number of books, Horace Coon, and he went to all of the principal archives—the Coe Collection at Yale, the Cody Museum and Library, the Denver Public Library—and we also employed foreign researchers, at Henry's expense, to delve into the strange attraction which Buffalo Bill had for Europeans and especially for Queen Victoria, and how, for instance, he catapulted the Queen out of mourning (twenty-five years after the death of Prince Albert) to view his Wild West Show at a command performance at Windsor Castle. Horace Coon had a graphic eye and produced extraordinary illustrative material as well as copious notes organized in the schematic pattern which we had evolved. The result was a book published by the Oxford University Press in New York and by Hamish Hamilton in London.

It was more than a book—it was a pleasant project for us both to emerge from serious concerns and work together in my study at the apartment every Sunday for two years. When first copies were available, Henry persuaded Marshall Field and Company of Chicago to fly all the principal writers and critics of Chicago to Cody, Wyoming, for a vast autographing party. Henry and I went west by air to Minneapolis and by night train to Billings, Montana, where we hired a Hertz car and arrived in Cody just in time to meet the United Airlines plane which had been chartered for the Chicago-Cody expedition. The whirl of activities in Cody would have been the envy of Buffalo Bill himself.

The people in Cody who had known Buffalo Bill—and there were many—understood the real Horatio Alger story of his life and appreciated our approach to the theme of a boy, self-made, who became Mr. Everyman in the wilderness; a preatomic superman, endowed with the Great Spirit of the Indians, who by the age of twenty-six was a member of the Union Club in New York, then went back to fight in the Indian Wars and ultimately became an important leader in the creation of the soil-reclamation service and in the introduction of machinery in the West.

Some modern scholars had fallen into the error of describing him as a converted "noble savage," exemplifying romance against the machine. However, we had independently given the modern world a picture of Buffalo Bill as romantic because of his precocious association with the machine—first, he welcomed the coming of the telegraph which obliterated his first job with the Pony Express; then, he employed the repeating rifle to provide local provisions for the railway builders; and eventually he founded cities, built hotels and introduced irrigation to the Great Plains in Wyoming. If he had lived longer, he would have been a film star with sophisticated modern investments, but as it was he provided the pattern of folk ingredients upon which Western movies and television have subsisted ever since.

Upon our return to New York my wife and I gave a huge party for everyone involved in the book at Oxford University Press, for my colleagues at NAL and for scores of friends and critics. In the back of my mind was not an attempt to aggrandize myself as an author, but to make it clear to the censors of the period that the editor-in-chief of NAL had a decent and innocent interest in America's romantic contemporary of Theodore Roosevelt, Dan Beard and Baden-Powell, who were his friends and who regarded Colonel Cody as a wholesome example to the young.

I have discovered that in many parts of the country I am not known at all as a publisher, but as an authoritative historian of the Old West. I still regard my friends in Cody as the warmest-hearted group of people I have ever met, and I can easily understand how their goodness of heart and respect for the founder of their city led William Robertson Coe to contribute millions of dollars to their local institution, and Cornelius Vanderbilt Whitney to give a half million dollars to build the Whitney Museum of Western Art at Cody, overlooking the great equestrian statue which his mother, Gertrude Vanderbilt Whitney, did in a classic example of American sculpture, unmatched even by Remington a generation before. There is a tendency in the West for old-timers to look down their noses at New York publishers whom they consider ignorant, with a few understandable exceptions, of their tradition and beautifully indigenous culture. There is no such attitude toward NAL, from the Rio Grande to the Bad Lands, as a direct result of *Buffalo Bill and the Wild West.*

Even the late Lucius Beebe drove nine hundred miles from Virginia City, Nevada, to Cody for the occasion, wearing a morning coat and a Stetson hat and startling the natives by feeding precious antelope chops to his St. Bernard dog, T-Bone Towser. He washed his own dinner down with generously shared magnums of champagne. During the interminable toasts at the dinner which was given with Governor Milward Simpson introducing the guests and establishing Richard Frost in the chair, Henry Sell coined a phrase when saluting Lucius Beebe which seems more suitable than anything that has been written in Beebe's recent obituaries. Henry raised his glass with a flourish and, looking at Luscious Lucius, said, "Ladies and gentlemen, I give you the rich man's W. C. Fields!"

A less fashionable but undoubtedly a more constructive

K

book project grew at about this time out of my long-estab-
lished association with key officials in the United States Department of Agriculture. The editor of the yearbook of the
department, a volume of surpassing quality, was Alfred Stefferud, who used to visit me at Hollow Rock Farm. We had
often speculated on how any institution could have such a
fine influence on modern young people in the cities as the
Extension Service appeared to have had on the country youth
of my generation. Once, at Hollow Rock, he pointed to a
framed award from the Extension Service to me as a member
of the Boys' Corn Club, as the early 4-H Program was sometimes described.

"Surely," he said, "your outlook on life and your adult
ideals were influenced by the dedication of your early 4-H
activities no less than by your family, your schooling or your
later experience."

I was reminded of Stefferud at a conference on rural reading which inevitably led the Committee on Book Promotion
of the American Book Publishers' Council to attempt something more effective than the stimulation of reading by
young people in rural communities alone. The Committee,
under the chairmanship of Cass Canfield of Harper during
the period when Harold Guinzburg was president of the
ABPC, suggested that a nonprofit book to be used by teachers
and librarians would be useful ammunition in such a campaign. When I volunteered to bring the book out under the
imprint of NAL, the Committee was unanimously in favor of
it. They asked me to select a general editor for the project,
and I selected Alfred Stefferud. He recruited the ablest literary and educational talent of the country to provide the
various chapters, which most of them did for nothing, including the illustrator, Robert Osborn, who produced a hundred
drawings for a nominal fee. When the manuscript reached
my desk it was so splendid and appealing that I suggested we

place the hardcover edition on a nonprofit basis with an equally appropriate publisher. Houghton Mifflin, whom I nominated, were pleased to cooperate. The result—which was a sort of gospel for and inspirational forerunner of the National Book Committee—was a spectacular best seller.

It was only then that Enoch wondered how I had been such a fool as to embark on a nonprofit project without consulting him. I reminded him that the opportunity had arisen at a committee meeting, where an instant decision was essential. Others would have been just as keen to undertake such a book. I finally persuaded him that although the book was nonprofit, the benefit to our character and recognition by teachers and librarians would be inestimable. This, happily, proved to be the case. The book is still in demand by missionaries for the cause of books. It ranks with the expensive series of advertisements by the International Paper Company, "Send Me a Man Who Reads," as outstanding institutional promotion not connected with immediate profits. The *Wonderful World of Books*, simply as a dedicated gesture, paved the way for a vast growth in the acceptance of NAL's books in high schools as well as in colleges.

The Committee on Book Promotion of the ABPC spent a great deal of energy and money publicizing the book, directing all inquiries to NAL for bulk paperbound copies and to Houghton Mifflin for hardcover copies. I, like many others, have found it through the years a marvelous source of inspiration, especially when asked to speak to schools and library audiences. Stefferud had injected into the book a great deal of the spirit of education which for scores of years has been characteristic of the work of the Extension Service of the United States Department of Agriculture.

The book world had come to recognize the ideals of NAL not only for the taste and skill of our publishing program, but for the vista which we gave to new readers of the horizon of the future. Noted authors who were tied to other publishers increasingly suggested to their friends and to their protégés that NAL, unlike other paperbound publishers of the 1950's, was really interested in authors and readers and had a purpose.

Among the dozens of authors sent to us by eminent men of letters, one who stands out is Victor Wolfgang von Hagen, who came to see me at the suggestion of Van Wyck Brooks. Von Hagen had written a number of books, mainly in the field of his greatest interest—Latin American history and pre-Colombian history. When von Hagen seemed to be at loose ends about what to do next, I recommended that, if he really wanted to be widely read, he could undertake three books for us over a period of time. They became three near classics: *The Realm of the Incas, The World of the Maya,* and *The Aztec: Man and Tribe.* These books, like original Pelicans in England, were written without any thought of an expensive hardcover edition, but subsequently they were drawn together into one volume magnificently produced by the World Publishing Company.

Von Hagen is Germanic, and resembles an athletic Heidelberg scholar more than the south St. Louis man that he actually is. He has written many extraordinary books since he came to NAL. He is currently living in Rome and working on a vast study of the old Roman Roads in North Africa, the Middle East and the Iberian Peninsula. Although he is a man of considerable temper and in the past has delighted in a certain amount of litigation, we never had a quarrel that wasn't ended with forgiveness and expressions of mutual esteem.

The saddest of our differences was the result of a ghastly accident. While living and doing research in Lima, Peru, he asked me to airfreight five hundred copies of *The Realm of the Incas.* I cabled him that they were on the way, and he promptly stimulated an enormous conclave of scholars and diplomats at which each would receive a copy. At the occasion, before the assembled guests at the American Embassy in Lima, when Victor opened the package containing the presentation copies, they were not *The Realm of the Incas,* but five hundred copies of Walt Whitman's *Leaves of Grass.* It took six months, punctuated with acrimonious correspondence, to persuade him that no one at NAL had made the error, but that it was an error made in the Chicago warehouse which handled our storage and dispatching.

Warehousing was not my personal responsibility, although I was frequently troubled by wrong shipments even when they were handled by other members of the firm. One of the weirdest mistakes was an airfreight shipment some years later to Ian Fleming in London. It was supposed to be a "dump bin" display carton containing five hundred copies of Ian's James Bond novels, but when it was opened in London, it proved to be a huge carton of "Mad" books. Ian cabled he was sending them to the nearest insane asylum, where they would undoubtedly understand them better than he possibly could.

In the mid-1950's when interest in the Dead Sea Scrolls, stimulated by Edmund Wilson's book, was at its peak, I was in a quandary how we might cope with the subject, since it looked hopeless to secure reprint rights from Oxford on Wilson's book. Bearing manna from heaven to a publisher in the desert, Marie Rodell, the enterprising agent, came to my office to inquire whether we could distribute an offset collection of sermons by A. Powell Davies, rector of All Souls Unitarian Church in Washington, which he had reproduced because of local demand. The subject: "The Meaning of the Dead Sea Scrolls." While Marie waited in the office I read the brief scholarly offset manuscript and immediately suggested that it would be hopeless to distribute it in Dr. Davies' improvised format, but that we would be delighted to distribute it if he could add additional material to give it more adequate coverage and publish it in standard softcover format. The result was a best seller and an enduring volume, written with style. It was based upon impeccable scholarship. Dr. Davies subsequently wrote other books which we published, including a life of St. Paul which was placed with Farrar, Straus under the title *The First Christian*.

It is often impossible for a publisher to predict where his next books may come from. In the summer of 1957 Stanley Horwitz of Sydney, Australia, visited me in my office and said he would like to submit a series of thrillers by Carter Brown. He explained that Carter Brown was a pseudonym owned by his company for monthly books written by a young Englishman named Alan Yates. Although Yates had never been to America at that time, he read American magazines and newspapers so assiduously that his books were in American lingo, with American characters. They were a sensational success in Australia. The first manuscript arrived while I was abroad in the early autumn and somehow found its way unopened to the windowsill in Marc Jaffe's office, where it gathered dust for some months. When Stanley cabled, I tracked down the manuscript, read it in the evening and immediately replied we would be happy to undertake it, and I suggested modest terms. This, however, was not what Stanley Horwitz had in mind. He insisted that although it was all right to accept one or two Carter Brown mysteries, what he wanted was for us to guarantee to take at least ten books a year by Carter Brown and, as time ran on, to reissue older titles and perhaps reduce the commitment to six or seven new books a year so long as ten were published annually by NAL.

This was the beginning of a series by Carter Brown that now numbers nearly a hundred, and the end is not in sight.

Alan Yates did visit America with his charming wife and his precocious children, and continued his output without interruption. The cleverness of Stanley Horwitz as a successful promoter was manifest. Carter Brown books are now issued by dozens of publishers in various languages throughout the world. The arrangement, although always profitable at NAL, is hazardous in one respect: If NAL or any other publisher fails to continue to issue new titles and reissue old ones as stipulated, the deal is off and the rights of all of the books in print revert to Horwitz, who is then at liberty to place them elsewhere. He is a man of such genuine integrity, however, that when from time to time I found a book lacking the usual verve, and said so, I was permitted to reject it or to suggest revisions without facing the contractual termination penalty. This is as near as I ever came, I suppose, to publishing dime novels at a quarter. But I have no apologies, for they are good entertainment, antic and jocose even when the conversation in the books sometimes sounds out of P. G. Wodehouse by a crossbreed of Variety-Time-Esquire-Playboy-Winchell.

In June, 1958, when Carter Brown (Alan Yates) arrived in New York, NAL made a tremendous promotional effort, announcing that we envisaged total sales of thirty million copies of the Carter Brown thrillers, a figure which of course has long since been surpassed. I invited a number of distinguished literary guests to our apartment to a reception for Mr. and Mrs. Yates, including Stanley Horwitz and, because the books originated in Australia, Sir Josiah Francis, Australian Consul General, and Lady Francis, along with a group of professors from Yale University. My wife and I made the occasion a combined one, celebrating also NAL's gift of *New World Writing* files to Yale University's Library. This occasion marked the end of a busy half year during which I had served as chairman of the National Book Awards

Committee earlier in the year and planned to visit Africa in August.

In August 1958, when I made my editorial and distribution trip around the English-language areas of Africa, I found a carbon copy of a Carter Brown manuscript sent, simultaneously with a New York copy, to me while traveling, at Lagos in Nigeria and again, three weeks later, at Nairobi in Kenya.

The purpose of my African trip was twofold: To discover a better entry than we had hitherto enjoyed to the educational and recreational markets and, if possible, to pick up the work of unpublished authors who, because of their remote situation, might not have been successful in finding a publisher. Although I did not go to Africa until August of 1958, I commenced my planning throughout the previous winter. I was greatly assisted by Emory R. Ross and his staff at the African-American Institute who gave me priceless information on local institutions and conditions as well as more than a hundred letters of introduction. I had met, over the previous decade, a great many Africans and African specialists, ranging from such visitors as Kwame Nkrumah of Ghana, Tom Mboya of Kenya and a great many others at the Graduate Institute of International Affairs of The Johns Hopkins in Washington, among United Nations personnel and delegates. I was well acquainted with such outstanding African spokesmen as Dan Chapman, Alan Paton and Nadine Gordimer.

My first stop was Monrovia, in Liberia. My wife and I met nearly everyone in that extraordinary capital city and, although we avoided diplomatic circles, we were invited on the spot to look in on the formal debut party of President Tubman's daughter at the Mesaruba Hotel. I called on every sort of potential distributor and on the schools and colleges. Just as I had despaired of finding an author on my first stop in Africa, I was approached by the proprietor of

Les Ambassadeurs, a pleasant little hotel overlooking the Atlantic, with a Dutch manager, a French chef and a jaunty French barmaid. The proprietor was Dr. John B. West, an American Negro with a medical degree from Harvard; certainly one of the most remarkable men I have ever encountered. Prior to the war the United States Public Health Service had lent him to the Government of Abyssinia, but when America entered the war he was called back to the African West Coast by the Medical Corps which wanted to utilize his enormous knowledge of tropical medicine in the areas where the Air Force was operating on the routes across Africa. After the war, he practiced medicine in Monrovia, developed a flourishing pharmaceutical business, a furniture factory and his small but comparatively deluxe hotel. He came out of his office off the lobby in his white medical garb, a stethoscope dangling at his chest, and said:

"I understand you are the publisher of Mickey Spillane." I was nonplussed but admitted that this was indeed the fact. He confided that he was at work on a thriller, based on a New York setting where he had been on the staff of the Medical Examiner in his younger days and had become familiar with the official scrutiny of criminals and their victims. He had incorporated this background into his thriller which, he said, had a white hero by the name of Rocky Steele. With some hesitation and skepticism, I volunteered to read the manuscript within the next hour. It wasn't bad; indeed it was strikingly good, a typical hard-boiled thriller, rich in character and action. I took it on the spot. I airmailed the manuscript back to the office, asking that a contract be sent to the author. It was the first of six hard-hitting thrillers which he wrote for NAL. His literary career was cut off by a fatal automobile accident at Kumasi in Ghana, where he and his charming Dutch wife, a trained nurse, were enjoying a motoring holiday.

K*

Before that, however, John West visited us several times in New York, when on business projects of his own. He had, I gathered, provided John Gunther with a lot of background material when he was working on *Inside Africa*. I later learned that his medical career had indeed been a brilliant one. In 1958 John West provided us with additional letters as we proceeded along our route in West Africa.

In Ghana, which had been independent for only a year and which had just begun to reflect the messianic "African personality" of Nkrumah, I visited all of the major book-selling and book warehouse concerns, the extraordinary university at Ashimoto and the National Library. Through the good offices of James Moxon, an Englishman who had taken out Ghanian citizenship, I met most of the educators and writers in the Accra region. After three days my wife and I felt that we must reciprocate some of the generous hospitality which we had received, including a luncheon by the Chief Justice Sir Aku Korsah, who during the absence of Lord Listowel was functioning as Governor General. We gave a cocktail party at the roof garden of the Ambassador Hotel.

In Ghana I found a splendid collection of poetry—*Voices of Ghana*—for *New World Writing*, and a seriously fanciful essay by Dr. Samuel Kofi Otoo of the Fanti fishing tribe, an accomplished scholar in the field of African tribal languages. He gave us a dissertation on the tribal significance of the elaborate and expensive Kinte robes and presented my wife with a beautiful example of the most elegant Kinte cloth.

My greatest literary discovery in Ghana, through the suggestion of James Moxon, was a novel by the headmaster of the local high school in Accra: *The African* by William Conton. This charming, poignant and well-written little novel was placed with Little, Brown for prior hardcover publishing in the United States, and with Heinemann in London. William Conton has since returned to Sierra Leone, his homeland, as a teacher, and has written a number of text-books. He occasionally visits the United States on the invitation of special educational seminars and has become as much a member of our family as any close relative. I took him with me to Carnegie Hall to the African Freedom meeting in April 1959, which I suspect was the occasion which launched Soapy Williams, ex-Governor of Michigan, as the African expert in the Department of State. It would be an endless saga to recount the experience of first visiting such a varied and potentially important region.

Nigeria was awaiting freedom and teeming with intellectual and artistic movements. Leopoldville and Brazzaville on the Congo were predominantly French speaking and thus only punctuation stops on the trip to South Africa.

Our books were comparatively well distributed in South Africa, so I limited my visits there to the universities and schools, and I never felt more liberated in my life than when we took the plane out of that beautiful but obviously damned country.

In Bulawayo an African member of the legislature could only reach us at our hotel by describing himself as my servant. This incredibly modern city with its skyscrapers, and Salisbury, in turn, were uneasy and ominous. The book businesses were prosperous and their credit was good, but few of them were catering to educated Africans except through the mails. The USIA man, hearing that we were in Salisbury, invited us to a small gathering at his house, and only after the European guests had departed did a handful of courageous African intellectuals appear.

Not so Nairobi, where it was possible to entertain Africans and to be entertained by them as well as by my old friend Lord Portsmouth, who farms in the highlands near Kitale, raising coffee, tea, livestock and a splendid dairy herd. He had not left Kenya during the Mau Mau emergency, even though many of the Africans on his plantation were members of the Kikuyu tribe. Lord Portsmouth has mastered Swahili and uses that language universally in his travels in the north, through the Rift Valley, and also in Nairobi and in Mombasa, where he spends occasional holidays by the sea. Nairobi is an excellent center for the distribution of books. When I was taking my first order from the Educational Supply Association (ESA), which had changed its name from the Church Missionary Society (CMS) because too much modern literature was too spicy for a religious distributor, the manager said that I should make up the order myself, picking some good books for the Africans, including some homosexual poetry for the Asians and ephemeral rubbish for the Europeans. He was half-joking. He realized that many of the British Europeans ordered their better books by mail from London and that what was sold to the Europeans in paperbound form was mainly adventure novels and thrillers. When I mentioned this criterion to Tom Mboya, whom I had previously met in New York, this promising and well-educated young African objected. In his opinion Africans had as much right to read Mickey Spillane as the Europeans did. He suggested that we make available every sort of book for which we had selling rights in East Africa to all readers, without assuming that Africans were only interested in books of an educational nature.

I later discovered that Kenya abounds in native language best sellers, fiction of thirty or forty pages, printed in tribal tongues on newsprint, and often selling fifty to a hundred thousand copies each.

It was in Nairobi that I first felt the looming impact of Boris Pasternak's *Dr. Zhivago*. The local press began to carry articles about the book long before it would be available to them in the Collins-Harvill edition from London. I had only discovered before leaving New York that although *Dr.*

Zhivago was to be published by Pantheon in New York, the reprint rights were tightly controlled by Collins through their arrangement with Feltrenelli in Italy, who had managed to get the manuscript out of the Soviet Union. I cabled Billy Collins to make a date in London and became so obsessed with the prospect of the reprint rights of *Dr. Zhivago,* which I had not yet read, that I persuaded my wife that we must cut our African trip short with the exception of a one-day stop in Khartoum in the Sudan. At the Khartoum Bookshop the proprietor ordered at least one copy of every available book on our list and insisted that I include books on flower arranging and abstract Mentor books as well as simpler titles.

Our whole journey around Africa, except for a night in Cairo, had been completed in thirty days. When I reread the reports of my journey and its consequences, I am convinced that it was the most impressive publishing tour of my career, but that I should have allowed twice as much time to the search for new writers, especially in Nigeria and Kenya, which at that time were comparatively neglected by English language publishers except the great textbook houses of England and Scotland—Longmans, Nelson, and Oxford. It is not uncommon for the pooled orders of the educational departments of some of these countries to amount to a half-million dollars annually.

The majority of Africans felt more at home in sterling than in dollars—even where, as in East Africa, they had a rudimentary decimal system for the local shilling. Everywhere they were depressed, including the tremendous organization of Unilever, by the red tape and forms which had to be filled out to order anything from the United States. Only in Liberia was the American dollar used as the local currency, and even there the procedure of ordering foreign merchandise was complicated by bureaucratic routines.

On this one visit I came to appreciate and love African

people of many tribes, and especially to admire their almost universal cleanliness, kindness and hospitality. The disappearance of tribal discipline through modern urbanization will undoubtedly bring about great changes in conduct, especially among the young. Except in South Africa and Rhodesia, one could not fail to appreciate the educational urge and sense of progress which, no matter how extravagantly wasteful and sometimes violent, was reflecting, in Harold Macmillan's phrase, "the wind of change." In Rhodesia as in South Africa, where the white minority is entrenched, one often heard Cecil Rhodes' old phrase "equal rights to all civilized men," which really meant that there was no desire to bring modern civilization and education to the African except to the point where he was literate enough to be an able worker for his white employer.

I had practically overlooked in my itinerary beyond Cairo—which I had sent direct to the Lancaster Hotel in Paris—that it was not possible for me to proceed directly to London after a night in Paris. I had committed myself months before to serve as an American representative and, as it turned out, as vice-chairman of a UNESCO conference on the importance of more interchange between Western and Oriental publishers. I had been named to this assignment by Luther Evans, director general of UNESCO, as well as by his successor, René Maheu, because of the considerable contribution that NAL had made in publishing widely distributed books in the West of the religious, philosophical and political literature of the Middle East and the Orient. Since I was representing the entire American publishing industry, I leaned over backward not to exploit in any narrow sense my own enterprise. I discovered, however, that I was something of a hero to the top officials of UNESCO because I had committed our company to publish, when available, the comprehensive global history under preparation by a special commission of

UNESCO: the *History of the Scientific and Cultural Development of Mankind.*

My commitment was in the form of a reprint license with Little, Brown of Boston, who had signed up world rights in the English language for this formidable project. Little, Brown were becoming impatient concerning the completion of the six-volume project, and I made many inquiries on their behalf as well as our own. As it later turned out, within two years Little, Brown abandoned all hope of delivery of the long-delayed volumes and terminated their contract under the deadline clause. This, in turn, left NAL in a somewhat dangling position.

By 1960 the Little, Brown termination was effective. Dismayed by the prospect of no English language hardcover publication of the *History of the Scientific and Cultural Development of Mankind,* UNESCO and the Commission made an oral agreement with the publishers of Julian Huxley, who as director general of UNESCO had initiated the project. So it appeared that the project would go to Allen and Unwin in London and Harper in New York. To protect NAL's interests in the project, Arthur Thornhill of Little, Brown dispatched Randy Williams to Paris to make certain that in the transfer of rights, NAL would not be left in the cold or in any way at a disadvantage. I wrote to René Maheu in 1960 and announced that I was coming directly to Paris to protect NAL's rights to the paperbound edition. He replied that it was impossible to assemble all parties involved in such approval in the middle of the August holidays. I insisted, by telephone and cable, and to his surprise as well as to my own, the qualified executives of UNESCO and of the special commission dealing with the *World History* project were present, along with Randy Williams of Little, Brown.

To my great satisfaction, I secured a worldwide paperbound contract for English publication, for the period of copyright of the project, which successfully established NAL as a direct licensee from Allen and Unwin, thereby enabling me to stipulate that Harper could not publish the book in paperbound or in any limp edition—such as Modern Library —rights which were established firmly to NAL. In this tough and prolonged negotiation I had reason to be grateful not only to Little, Brown and Randy Williams but to Sir Stanley Unwin and his nephew, Philip Unwin, who in due course signed and affirmed NAL's rights. Recounting of this 1960 development in sequence to my 1958 visit to UNESCO departs from the chronological logic of a narrative such as this, but it represents the standing which NAL had in Paris, and in Boston as well as in New York in the 1950's and the period immediately thereafter.

I shall always have reason to be grateful to the Ritz Hotel in Paris for making available to me, at the peak of their tourist season in 1960, one of their most splendid suites for a cocktail party for the UNESCO executives, scholars and advisors as well as for a number of NAL authors who happened to be in Paris at that time: Ludwig Bemelmans, Irving Wallace, James Jones and principal critics and reviewers of the English-language press in Paris. The transaction had been concluded on a Friday evening, followed by the little party in celebration of it, but Philip Unwin had unavoidably to be in London that same evening and, therefore, was not available to sign the paperbound contract on the following day. We therefore flew immediately to London, and the contract which I had drafted was signed first thing Monday morning by Sir Stanley Unwin himself.

To return to 1958: After the East-West Conference we sped to London, and I kept the appointment which I had made by cable from Nairobi with Billy Collins, the principal item of discussion being *Dr. Zhivago*. Billy was in the throes of all the problems arising out of an international best seller which he derived from Feltrenelli and which he had placed on very special terms with Pantheon in New York. He made it clear that in due course NAL would be his favorite paperbound publisher in the U.S.A., but that he should have to weigh carefully all the proposals put to him by Pantheon, then under the joint chieftainship of Kyrill Schabert and Kurt Wolf, prior to their acquisition by Random House.

It took several years and a great deal of negotiation to secure the reprint rights from Pantheon, with the approval of Billy Collins, and an advance against royalties of $100,000. Eventually Billy Collins very graciously granted NAL inexpensive paperbound rights in Canada, a selling area which he exclusively controlled. He did it, he said, entirely because of his appreciation of and affection for me.

Our momentum was apparent to the entire literary profession and publishing industry in the late 1950's. We had modestly launched Ian Fleming in the popular market with *From Russia with Love*—an advance copy of which we had secured from Jonathan Cape in London in 1957.

Previously, Ian Fleming's James Bond novels had been a near-failure in their reprint editions in the United States. The first, *Casino Royale,* was published by Popular Library. Then Pocket Books did indifferently with *Live and Let Die* and *Moonraker* and *Diamonds Are Forever*. With my blessing, Truman Talley suggested to Macmillan that if Pocket Books would not offer a substantial sum for *From Russia with Love,* he would like to take it on for NAL and at the same time sign up the earlier titles as the licenses to Popular Library and Pocket Books expired.

It was apparent to Truman and me that Ian Fleming, whose books we had rejected as "too British" in 1953, had just indicated by 1957 that he could cross the barrier into a position of general recognition as a smart, readable, "different" writer of espionage thrillers.

I had met Ian Fleming casually in London years before he had written *Casino Royale,* and regarded him as a top journalist on the *Sunday Times* in the days before Lord Thomson bought that paper from Lord Kemsley. I had heard gossip about Ian during the war when, occasionally, I visited Donald McCullough at Nettlebed.

We usually walked across the village green to the large house which belonged to Peter Fleming—Ian's brother, who at that time was with Lord Mountbatten in Ceylon—to visit Mrs. Peter Fleming, whose children were playmates of the McCullough children. This slight and practically indirect association in the past had far-reaching consequences from 1958 onward.

When Ian stopped in New York once or twice a year on the way to Jamaica, where he spent the winter enjoying the sunshine and writing a James Bond novel each season, we became close friends. He was worried about Macmillan and determined that when their contract expired with *Dr.No,* he wanted to switch. He did not like options, but preferred three-book contracts.

The late Harold Guinzburg of Viking took on the next three: *Goldfinger, Thunderball,* and *The Spy Who Loved Me.* Their advance simultaneously was covered by our advance against the reprint rights. In addition to signing up the books promptly, in view of the increasing popularity of the James Bond novels, Truman Talley offered five thousand dollars in addition to the total twenty thousand dollar advance on the appearance, respectively, of a TV or film on each book.

Truman Talley, as usual, was right in his assumption of a rising tide of interest and by now (1966) the total Ian Fleming sales in Signet editions have gone beyond the 50 million mark. As an honorable gesture in 1961, Ian's agent (Phyllis Jackson of MCA, which soon after was detached from the agency business, whereupon Phyllis Jackson moved to Ashley Famous Agency) sent simultaneously to Tom Guinzburg of Viking and to me the first of Ian's next three books: *On Her Majesty's Secret Service.* I read it overnight and reported to Phyllis that I was delighted and wanted to sign up the soft-cover rights. She had not yet heard from Viking. She told me that Ian expected more keenness than that, and Phyllis mentioned that she had heard that we were entering the hard-cover business. I said that the rumor had some foundation, and if we got the book we would issue it first in hardcover and a year later in a Signet softcover edition.

She telephoned Ian.

He flew to New York the next day. While he was on the way, I prepared a three-book contract for hard and softcover for an advance of twenty-five thousand dollars each, to be paid respectively upon delivery. At this time we were a subsidiary of the Times Mirror Company, and Enoch said they were greatly concerned about a commitment to a hard-cover project without consulting them.

The die was cast. I would not renege. Everyone seemed happy except Mr. Robert Allan, Jr. of Times Mirror. I shall return to Ian Fleming as our first entry into the hardcover field later in this narrative, but it is very important to understand that Ian was a man who insisted upon an intimate and immediate relationship with his publisher and frequent communication in both directions.

Our list by the end of the fifties contained the work of a number of distinguished and popular writers, and also the beginnings of a science program, plans for a Mentor Executive Library and the development of a very impressive list of reference volumes—dictionaries and thesauri edited by Albert Morehead. We had demonstrated through the sale of *The Fountainhead* by Ayn Rand that we were ideally suited to imprint her books, so it was easy to arrange with Bennett

Cerf to reprint such lengthy books as Ayn Rand's *Atlas Shrugged*. Miss Rand, a determined individualist and the advocate of her Objectivist Philosophy, realized that although I was not in complete personal sympathy with her philosophy, I would tolerate no conscious or unconscious sabotage of her books by unsympathetic editors or by unfair critics. In the course of a few years we became so genuinely appreciative of each other's integrity that, with the friendly consent of Bennett Cerf, she moved to NAL as her primary publisher.

There is nothing quite so satisfying in any career, and especially in a career in publishing, as the role of a discoverer and prophet of the future which is ultimately rewarded by recognition as a combination of good taste and good judgment, reflected as well by substantial profit. Our small enterprise had grown in less than fifteen years into the leader in its field of softcover books, quantitatively and qualitatively. I continued my quest for the best books available from all sources with as much zest and sense of satisfaction as if I were just setting out to demonstrate that the true course of expansion lies in the direction of better and more diversified books to appeal to new readers throughout the world—for pleasure, for learning and for inspiration.

I had run the gauntlet and emerged with proof, widely acknowledged, that widespread cultivation of new and habitual readers of inexpensive books does not lead to vulgarization and the lowest common denominator of quality. In relation to the literary scene, there was scarcely a notable author, contemporary or classical, who was not listed in the current volumes of paperback books in print. The circumstances which resulted in the collapse of the paperbound industry in the 1890's did not exist, and we did not derive the profits at NAL from churning out opportunistic trash to maintain volume. On the contrary, our paperbacks gave new prestige and importance to books as compared with popular periodicals, and we had widened the availability of good books to older intellectual readers as well as to students.

The reading of books and the writing of books tended to become a universal sign of sophistication as they were among the small educated class in the nineteenth century. The effect of our revolutionary diffusion of learning and literature was bound to have an enduring and a constructive influence upon domestic education and culture and upon world understanding generally.

Chapter XI

FROM DREAM TO NIGHTMARE

————◦◦◦————

The turning points of lives are not the great moments. The real
crises are often concealed in occurrences so trivial in appearance
that they pass unobserved.

—from: *George Washington 1926*
by William E. Woodward

A WISE LITTLE MASTERPIECE, *The Hedgehog and the Fox,* by
Sir Isaiah Berlin, which we had reprinted, came frequently
to my mind in the dilemma of the NAL enterprise toward
the end of the 1950's. Sir Isaiah derived the title of his book
from the Greek poet Archilochus: "The fox knows many
things, but the hedgehog knows one big thing." Isaiah's thesis,
dealing with Tolstoy's tortured effort to reconcile his ambiva-
lent philosophy, had speculated upon Tolstoy's overwhelm-
ing desire to be a hedgehog, to command a unitary and
undeviating view of history and of life, while at the same
time struggling with his countervailing desire to be eclectic
and adaptable even if occasionally illogical and intuitive in
response to the myriad accidents, opportunities and unfathomable aspects of history and life.

Enoch was obviously a hedgehog, although he resembled
a lean fox; and I was a fox, although I undoubtedly resembled a rotund hedgehog.

In action, Enoch, an all-out hedgehog, believed himself

absolutely and uncompromisingly right in all arguments. He could illustrate his stubborn resistance to my foxy arguments with points ranging up to a hundred and tiresome subpoints from A to Z. His concept of publishing increasingly seemed to be that it was a book factory. He became intolerant of experimental literature, skeptical of new authors despite their possible future value, but willing to make any sort of financial offer for reprint rights on a proposition which some hardcover publisher had developed and advertised heavily with an atmosphere of ready-made best-sellerdom. He was, as a reprinter, more impressed by what he read in advertisements, even if specious, than by editorial evaluation, even when it was right.

In contrast, I was definitely a fox, in terms of Archilochus's neat description of two sorts of men, in terms of thought and outlook on life. Decisions must be practical and based upon sensible criteria for financial success; but, at the same time, they must reflect something of the inexplicable cunning of a horseman judging yearlings at the annual sales in Saratoga or Keenland. On the basis of no demonstrable logic based upon previous sales history, I had taken the plunge on Ian Fleming just as I had years earlier on Mickey Spillane. At a higher level of literature I had discerned the coming appeal of the urban writers, preponderantly Jewish, often perplexed, neurotic, or in their own language, "sick"—as the pendulum swung from the rustic novel, the war novel, the social novel, the philosophical novel and the novel of manners. I had also, against monolithic opposition, proceeded to build a list, on which we usually controlled world rights, of intellectual, philosophical, scientific, religious and historical Mentor or Signet books. My editors were totally in accord with my cheerful, exciting and glamorous pursuit of the best in every field—scholarship, classics, reference, and new approaches to science, philosophy and religion in the paperbound field.

It is needless to recite the hundreds of examples of the conflict between the hedgehog and the fox. Enoch in the late 1950's seemed to dwell constantly on the theme that he was no longer an obscure refugee but the president of a company earning nearly a million dollars a year. I was aware of the responsibility of financial success for more far-reaching reasons.

I suggested that we make a token public offering, that we merge into a public company, or that one of us buy out the other—anything to avoid the see-saw, with him and Littauer, his lawyer, on one end and me, alone, on the other. I brought up this question constantly at our board meetings throughout 1958 and 1959.

By good chance, throughout all of the years up to then, Enoch had been superficially polite to me, or sometimes outrageously obsequious when he wanted his way, but by 1959 he had become increasingly querulous and constantly critical of the editorial team at NAL. He stated repeatedly that all of the editorial staff were my "stooges"—a favorite word from the Allen Lane days applied to me. He stated that he regarded Truman Talley as a playboy. Talley was simply leading a civilized social life and was still, next to me, the hardest working man in the organization. I read about two thousand book-length works annually, he about eighteen hundred. We did not just read the ads and dust jackets. And we both did at least half of our work at home, on our own time, of evenings and weekends.

I pointed out on several occasions to Enoch that it was no act on the part of Talley and me that we were involved in the parties of our friends. I reminded him that in the social life of our family, he had always been welcome and invited to weddings, receptions and such events as naturally as any other colleagues; invitations which he frequently had declined.

After it was announced at a board meeting that Enoch intended to explore the matter of a token offering of NAL shares, I determined to seek another approach to the matter of going public. In the previous decade I had become personally and professionally intimate with top partners or executives of a great many of the first-class investment banking firms in New York. In appraising their possible usefulness to me and our enterprise, I naturally struck upon Blyth & Company as the ideal banker to handle such matters. Throughout the summer, I cultivated, in a more practical sense than earlier, Donald N. McDonnell, executive vice-president of Blyth & Company.

At that time we were tremendously preoccupied with the publication of the unabridged edition of *Lady Chatterly's Lover* by D. H. Lawrence, rights to which I had secured from Laurence Pollinger, literary executor of the Lawrence estate. Years earlier I had signed up the rights to the authorized abridged edition of Lawrence's book from Alfred Knopf.

The publication of the unabridged edition by Grove Press and others who took advantage of the technical public domain status of the work and had no contract or paid no royalties, gave us a strategic position in a highly competitive field.

In the midst of the first offering of Ford Motor Company shares, McDonnell took time out to advise me on matters and always asked just the right questions about the growth of New American Library. He was somewhat startled, on first meeting Enoch and his lawyer, to discover that these two Germanic men were indeed my associates and colleagues; but I gave him a very favorable account of their special talents in book production and corporate law respectively. In the weeks following their rather indifferent reaction to Donald's advice, I was tremendously preoccupied by basic publishing problems and the visit to New York of important London publishers, including George Weidenfeld and Jock and Diana Murray from London. I was also trying to recruit an executive who could function as a vice-president, reporting to me not simply as an editorial vice-president. Finally, I was fortunate enough by mid-November to enlist George McCorkle of Scribner's who rightly felt that he would have greater opportunity outside of a family-held company such as that of Charles Scribner's Sons.

Donald McDonnell, meanwhile, was putting his best thoughts to the solution I hoped might insure the dynamic qualitative corporate existence of NAL. In November of 1959 Donald informed me that he was going to San Francisco for Christmas, to visit his aging mother, and then on to Los Angeles where he expected to see Norman Chandler, head of The Times Mirror Company.

Enoch, his lawyer and I foregathered promptly, and Donald outlined the reasons why he believed that Times Mirror should be invited to explore NAL as a possible acquisition. The company was, he said, determined to diversify. From Times Mirror's long financial connection with Blyth Company—which had originated as a West Coast investment banking firm—he was well aware of the nature of The Times Mirror Company, its holdings and its hopes for the future in the field of communications, paper, printing and, at that time, television.

On January 19, 1960, I gave a large reception, at which Enoch was present, to introduce to our top staff the vice-president whom I had just recruited, George M. McCorkle, of Charles Scribner's Sons.

George McCorkle had been brought into NAL by me as a hedge against the possible retirement or serious illness after a number of disability absences by Enoch. I had insisted that George not be described as an editorial vice-president, that he function administratively without assignment to any specific area of operations. He had enjoyed a fine career at Charles Scribner's Sons and was forty years old.

In mid-January, as a result of the Blyth & Company overture after a visit to us by Robert M. Allan, Jr., of Times Mirror, we agreed to permit Times Mirror's auditors, Ernst and Ernst, to work in collaboration with our auditors, Haskins and Sells, and we further agreed to a quick survey of NAL's marketing by McKinsey and Company, management consultants. Although their assignment was primarily to evaluate NAL's marketing, they volunteered the opinion that the editorial operation was excellent and that I had provided management-in-depth for possible succession in Messrs. Mc-Corkle and Talley. They had not been briefed by me on this point, and certainly not by Enoch.

On Sunday morning of February 21, 1960, Donald Mc-Donnell and I flew to California and checked in at the Beverly Hills Hotel, where the Los Angeles office of Blyth & Company, in constant touch with The Times Mirror Company, had set up a briefing meeting for Monday morning, Washington's Birthday. An appointment had been fixed at The Times Mirror building early Tuesday morning. Enoch was still apprehensive that our talks would come to nothing and that he should inform his preferred banker to proceed with the secondary offering. We allayed his fears during the afternoon at Santa Anita Race Track where Donald had arranged a box through the absence of friends who, like so many southern Californians, felt it necessary to attend the Olympic ski preliminaries at Squaw Valley. Donald Mc-Donnell was certainly the persuasive impressario reinforcing the more formal report on Times Mirror which had been given to us in the morning by the Blyth experts. After a pleasant dinner we turned in early so as to go downtown promptly in the morning.

We were met by Bob Allan, then a vice-president of Times

Mirror, later President of Cyprus Mines, who piloted the negotiations. We first met briefly in the office of Norman Chandler. A tall, charming man, the eldest son of Harry Chandler who had married the daughter of General Harrison Gray Otis of the *Los Angeles Times,* Norman had carried the enterprise—and vast family holdings in real estate, investments, and insurance—to a position which could not have been achieved without his extraordinary character, grace, charm and handsome presence. He reminded me at once of a duke, or Cary Grant playing the part of a duke—quietly perceptive, a delegator of details. Donald McDonnell opened the conversation by introducing me, in more than fulsome terms, then by introducing Kurt Enoch and then by presenting Rudolf Littauer as the NAL general counsel. Donald then suggested a formula for the Times Mirror acquisition of NAL, complete with an establishment of value, and suggesting that the entire transaction should be through a pooling of interest by exchange of shares.

Times Mirror shares at that time were selling over the counter at 54, subsequently split three for one, or actually 18. It was suggested by Norman Chandler that after preliminary conferences with Bob Allan, we should inspect the Times Mirror properties in Los Angeles—the newspaper building and plant, the new Times Mirror Press building and plant and station KTTV, a television station which Times Mirror then owned, although it was later sold to Metromedia. We viewed the works at the newspapers which then included *The Evening Mirror,* and The Times Mirror Press, which handled vast printings of telephone books, catalogues, etc. on the West Coast. We were made privy to all of the relevant circumstances of the Chandler family and The Times Mirror Company, and after lunch the negotiations commenced. The outcome was comparatively simple—an agreement to agree, with a more formal agreement to follow in late March or early April if further investigation of NAL by Times Mirror and of Times Mirror by NAL resulted in accord.

The agreement to agree was signed, as a tentative understanding to be ratified in late March. I flew out prior to the discussions on the 25th of March to consult with authors and West Coast agents and to make arrangements to attend the Oscar Awards on April 4. The tentative agreement was ratified, and the closing was set for June 2.

The closing ceremonies in Los Angeles were pleasantly arranged in the proper sequence by the lawyers and officers of both companies concerned. Norman Chandler stated frequently, and included in his release to the press, that "As a distinct and separate member of the Times Mirror family of companies, NAL will retain its present management and personnel, the same policies and the same close affiliation with book publishers, authors, agents and magazine distributors." It was agreed that Enoch and I would alternate on the board of Times Mirror and in the draw for first time around, Enoch was named. This, at the time, did not genuinely trouble me. I was pleased to have my interest in the enterprise which we had created represented by an equal associate in ownership and management. Enoch was frequently absent during the summer, and in mid-August, as previously mentioned, I went to Paris to insure our claim on the world softcover rights of UNESCO's *The History of the Scientific and Cultural Development of Mankind*. In the course of this overseas journey, which included the Frankfurt Book Fair in Germany and a few busy weeks in London, I had made my overture to the Godfrey Phillips Ltd.

Upon my return from London, I found Enoch aloof and cool. Within a week when I invited him into my office to meet several authors who had appeared, he brusquely said, "Bring them to my office."

Despite a great many differences of opinion, we had

hitherto operated with an essential degree of formal com-
patability. Now all of a sudden, having been to California to
a board meeting and on another occasion to discuss a possible
acquisition which I had brought to his attention, all was
different. He had become a bitterly cantankerous opponent.
Within a month Truman Talley came to me and suggested
that he was going to leave. I prevailed on him to ride out
whatever storm might be brewing. He said that in more than
twelve years he had never had a word of encouragement from
Enoch for bringing in major literary talent that had eventually proved enormously profitable to the company. He felt
even more strongly about the increasing mechanization of
decision-making at NAL. The trend from dominance of
creators to rigid rule of controllers was clear. Enoch's German absolutism was in gear with top—or rather next to top—
management in Los Angeles. When I suggested to Enoch that
the blackout of the editors, and especially of Talley, under
the Times Mirror regime which he said he represented, was
bound to result in catastrophe, he shrugged and said:

"Why don't you take it up with California?"

It was little wonder, after this performance, that I was not
consulted except in the most perfunctory way on what eventually turned out to be the New English Library, publishing
4-Square Books, which derived their name from the pipe
tobacco manufactured by Godfrey Phillips Ltd. It later
turned out that the Lockers, father and son, who had sold
Ace Books to 4-Square, were not available for management
and that Godfrey Phillips Ltd. knew less than nothing of
the book business except for highly efficient warehousing,
dispatching and record keeping. Editorial—i.e. publishing
—judgment was effectively eclipsed by a cloud of figures,
mainly red.

After a series of inadequate managers and losses aggregat-
ing well beyond $1,000,000 by 1966, the Godfrey Phillips in-

terests were acquired by NAL so that the business is a wholly owned subsidiary, under a managing director who has made a series of contracts to publish Playboy trivia and Girodias pornography. However, in late 1960 and in the spring of 1961 when Enoch went to London to negotiate with Godfrey Phillips Ltd., I was as cooperative as I was permitted to be. I suggested that as an American-controlled company with 51 percent of the shares, the company should have as chairman of the holding company a friendly and competent English businessman.

I nominated Sir John Rodgers, Bart., M.P., deputy chairman of J. Walter Thompson, who had a great deal of experience in liaison with American business. Of great interest to me was that John Rodgers and I knew each other well and shared certain experiences in our lives which gave us a common viewpoint of the future in arts, letters, publishing and communications, generally. Despite his active role in the J. Walter Thompson advertising agency, he had been, with Brendan Bracken and others of my London friends, instrumental in bringing about the Independent Television Authority—giving the BBC the healthy competition of commercial broadcasting. Moreover, at the time of my overture, John was serving on the Committee of Management of the Society of Authors. John Rodgers, as a member of Parliament, who had served as Parliamentary Secretary to the Board of Trade in the Macmillan Government, was naturally associated with the business and banking leaders of Great Britain, as well as with the political, educational and cultural people of importance in postwar Britain. He agreed to serve.

John and I did our utmost to induce the New English Library to publish better books, but they seemed content to derive their prestige from imports from NAL—mainly Mentor Books, Signet Classics and, above all, the Signet Classics Shakespeare. This did not represent enough volume or profit to do more than keep the reputation of the New English Library from sinking clean, or unclean, out of sight. I arranged, with great effort, to get them American authors and succeeded in placing with NEL the works of Irving Wallace and, eventually, Harold Robbins's *The Carpetbaggers*. The year of *The Carpetbaggers* under their imprint gave NEL its only profitable year up to now (in early 1966).

I was especially busy in the summer of 1960 with visits to New York by Irving Wallace and an effort to secure a book by Leo Szilard who had written the Einstein letter to President Roosevelt urging the atom bomb project against Hitler. To add to the complications, I had had to make my urgent visit to Paris to salvage the UNESCO *History of the Scientific and Cultural Development of Mankind*.

From the very moment of the finalization of the merger with The Times Mirror Company, I found that, as chairman of the board, I was almost totally ignored by Enoch who conducted a continuous series of communications with Los Angeles in his new role as a sort of viceroy of the new domain. Even when he was abroad in the spring of 1961, and on behalf of NAL made the final settlement for 51 percent of 4-Square Books (New English Library), I was only nominally aware of the details of that incredible transaction.

Nevertheless, I felt very happy in the period immediately after the Times Mirror acquisition for a number of reasons which transcended the financial advantages; i.e., marketable securities which would protect my estate as well as the business in case of death or disability. I still treasure my memories of the early rapport with Mr. and Mrs. Norman Chandler and their immediate family and corporate associates. For example, at luncheon on the day of the closing, I asked Norman why the *Los Angeles Times* ran a statement on the editorial page that no payment will be made for poetry. Norman was astonished and said that no such slogan appeared in the paper, but when a copy was produced, there it was, and then he recalled that it had appeared ever since the days when religious and lyrical migrants from the Dust Bowl had swamped the paper with verse and doggerel. I asked whether he would print without even a thank-you a poem from Robert Frost, W. H. Auden, Carl Sandburg or Dylan Thomas. His reaction was to order the instant deletion of any no-payment affront to the poets whom I valued so highly.

There was a great deal of good-natured banter about the book-review policies and book-advertising rates of the *Los Angeles Times,* and it began to appear that the whole merger was, from my point of view, a happy marriage. I did not for a moment have any suspicion that the acquisition would soon enable Enoch to ally himself with the mechanistic sub-management group at The Times Mirror Company and, practically unknown to the Chandlers, employ the bureaucracy of big business to change the general editorial policy. However, in the merger agreement I had for the first time incorporated into our bylaws the establishment of an executive committee, with the chairman of the board as chairman, to handle many basic company matters that were not quite board level and other items which could be processed by such a committee to expedite forthcoming agendas for the board. I was empowered to sign any sort of corporate paper and signed the Federal Trade Commission compliance on Saturday evening, April 15, 1961. A month earlier I had already informed Robert M. Allan, Jr., of Times Mirror at a meeting in New York, that I was fed up with toadies and tyrants.

From the merger onward we had to argue to win nearly every constructive editorial decision; even to use better paper for Mentor and to publish NAL's Shakespeare series under the Signet imprint instead of under Mentor—which meant more universal distribution at home and abroad and that the large number of Shakespeare titles would not cramp the

L

creative development of the Mentor list. When, from August onward on my quarterly trips to Los Angeles for the next year, I referred to this intolerable obstruction, I was constantly reassured that Enoch had to have his day. He had been less than generous when Wagner College in Staten Island decided to present honorary L.H.D. degrees to three outstanding New York publishers, and it turned out that their choices were Cass Canfield, chairman of Harper's, Storer Lunt, chairman of Norton, and me as chairman of NAL.

In the autumn of 1961 I did, by good chance, take the precautionary measure of securing written approval from Enoch for the text of an article which I had written for *The Author,* the London organ of the Society of Authors, to dispel the widespread attacks upon the penetration of British publishing by American interests such as our own. The article was widely reprinted and quoted in the British press, and its influence almost ended the apprehension which the British had about the American juggernaut running over the book industry of Britain.

Of course, giving the management in Holborn home rule was, as it turned out, premature. That right had not actually been earned. NEL was a dependent colony, absorbing much of our energy and a great deal of our money to keep it going. My principle, however, was that we could not operate in detail a foreign branch any more than Allen Lane could have conducted an American branch in the early days of Penguin Books in New York. The problem was to find adequate management to set standards for prudent financial operation and to encourage much more qualitative editorial programs than NEL was conducting.

It soon became apparent that acquisition by The Times Mirror Company meant that the planning, i.e., editorial program, of NAL was delegated almost entirely to marketing executives under a scheme outlined by McKinsey and Company. Orwell's 1984 hit me in the midriff with a wallop from Jack Vance of McKinsey.

"You are a purchasing—a procurement—executive," Jack Vance said, "and you *must* be responsive to Marketing." Since it had been my talent to anticipate marketing by five years or more in my publishing program, I was shocked, but concealed my sense of outrage.

I carried on bravely but in confidence informed all concerned, including the new Times Mirror executive vice-president, Raymond D. McGranahan, that under the erosion of the understanding of 1960, I could not continue my function of editor-in-chief after the end of the five-year period which was stipulated in my agreement. I not only carried on bravely, but took on Ian Fleming as our first hardcover author, despite Times Mirror opposition, and signed up Richard Whalen's best-selling life of Joseph P. Kennedy, *The Founding Father*. I employed an able man—David Brown, recommended by Irving Wallace—to preside over the development of our modest hardcover projection. David Brown, whom I had known for twenty years, had after an editorial career been a brilliant story editor of 20th-Century Fox, had served on the studio's executive committee and had been instrumental in the success of his wife's book, *Sex and the Single Girl*. He was a scholar and author as well as an able and honest editor, with a useful promotional flair.

By the time of publication of Ian Fleming's first hardcover book under the NAL imprint on August 21, 1963, David and I had to fight manfully to win the struggle against everyone within the organization to price the book at $4.50 instead of the routine thriller price of $3.95. We called it a James Bond "novel." Our effort was grudgingly acknowledged as the book took off immediately—the first Ian Fleming best seller in America in hardcover form. All of a sudden everyone wanted to meet Ian Fleming, whom I had been seeing in New York and London several times a year. All of a sudden, too, everyone seemed pleased with the dynamic editorial program, hardcover and softcover, which reflected the kind of teamwork that often meant after-hours conferences to avoid the chilly hand of negative, faceless bureaucracy on every major editorial decision.

On the day before I planned to go to California for the quarterly board meeting of The Times Mirror Company in November, 1963, I had lunch with Erskine and Virginia Caldwell, at the Café Richelieu, across the street from our office. We were unaware of the assassination of President Kennedy until we returned to the office. It was the most melancholy day of my life and of those like myself who had come to appreciate the contribution which—except for the Bay of Pigs fiasco—President Kennedy had made to the fresh new course of the United States at home and abroad. He almost signified the inner values of NAL—including not only philosophy and poetry but the antic verve of his friend, Ian Fleming.

I postponed my California journey a day. With no other means of travel available except through a transfer at Dallas, Texas, which I would not have visited under any circumstances at that time, I took the direct flight to California that awful gloomy Sunday, November 24, my own professional problems completely forgotten in the mood generated by the President's assassination. Throughout Monday, the 25th, during the funeral broadcast, I sat transfixed by grief in my Beverly Hills Hotel suite as I watched the television broadcast, occasionally joined by morose friends such as Irving Wallace, Michael Blankfort and Irving Shulman. During the Times Mirror board meeting on the 27th, Otis Chandler was summoned to the telephone by a personal call from President Johnson who simply wanted to let him know how much he had appreciated the coverage of the previous five days in the *Los Angeles Times*. I had no opportunity in California to deal with the NAL matters which concerned me and which were temporarily obliterated by the death of President Kennedy.

From time to time in the following months I endeavored to become better acquainted with Raymond McGranahan, who was named to handle the liaison with all of the Times Mirror book subsidiaries. It was of little avail. He was a cold and insensitively impervious alumnus of the petroleum industry. I never succeeded in discovering any appreciation of the literary subtleties essential to the successful operation of a book publishing firm that was dependent upon the intangibles and trends of taste. He regarded my wide acquaintance with literary and scholarly talent as exhibitionism. In all of my career I have never met a man so disinterested in the verities of the aesthetic and articulate professions. He repeatedly reminded me that he knew an author—Norman Vincent Peale—whom he recommended that I go after. I said that Dr. Peale already had publishing arrangements, and I had already declined to reprint his books.

After becoming acquainted, in the spring of 1964, with John P. R. Budlong, nominated as Enoch's successor, who joined NAL as an executive vice-president, I gave him as clear a picture as possible of the softcover book industry of which he admittedly knew very little—and assured him of my full cooperation as his responsibilities would increase.

Budlong had worked for George Brett, Jr. at Macmillan and then had gone to McGraw-Hill. Despite the excellence of their technical and scientific publications, McGraw-Hill had never achieved a significant or distinguished position in their general publishing programs. I tried to explain to Budlong that the secret of NAL was development of a pioneering interest in the future rather than always attempting the obvious, and because of this, we often avoided unnecessary and expensive material for softcover publishing. He seemed to respond much more readily to the fiscal, production and warehousing problems of NAL, which had never been developed as scientifically or efficiently as our editorial operations. I explained to him that Jack Vance had interpreted the McKinsey report to mean that editors should be seen and not heard; nevertheless, eventually I was invited to speak at a joint sales meeting of NAL and World Publishing Company in Cleveland, a recent acquisition of Times Mirror. It was my belief, and still is, that members of the same group of companies can create greater profits by cooperation which does not violate the anti-trust laws than by a lot of petty striving for duplicating power and position in a congeries of disparate activities, and I said so. I had been saddled with the responsibility for the editorial and production handling of World's general books because most of the senior editorial staff at World had resigned after the Times Mirror acquisition. In order to fulfill their contracts with authors, the work was farmed out to NAL, which meant me, to assume the job. I had to do it, and did. I was not so happily situated and could not handily get a word through the Orwellian bureaucracy, established by McKinsey and Company's commissars, as did Otis Chandler, son of Mr. and Mrs. Norman Chandler, who was put in charge of the *Los Angeles Times*. He made the paper increasingly distinguished and profitable by winning his way without the interference of intermediaries on the spot.

I continued manfully to recruit authors, and working closely with David Brown and Truman Talley on hardcover and softcover projects, we were continuing our distinguished and profitable momentum. In May of 1964 I hired a bus to entertain the NAL board, including Raymond McGranahan and NAL's top executives, at a special luncheon at the Terrace Club on the edge of the World's Fair. I thought that with the new managing director of NEL, Gareth Powell, present, the occasion would be appreciated. It was not. Enoch regarded it as a presumption, obviously taking a cue from McGranahan, who must have imagined it was all on the expense account. It wasn't. It was a personal gesture by the chairman and editor-in-chief.

Chapter XII

THE BARD MUST SMILE

————◦◦◦————

What should we know
For better or worse,
Of the long ago,
Were it not for verse
—Oliver St. John Gogarty

LONG BEFORE ACQUISITION by the Times Mirror, I was determined to make our company the world's finest publisher of Shakespeare, with well-edited volumes of all of Shakespeare's work containing understandable and relevant historical background and retrospective commentary. I finally enlisted Sylvan Barnet of Tufts University who had been brought to my attention years earlier by Howard Mumford Jones. Barnet had edited a series of distinguished drama anthologies, in collaboration with Morton Berman and William Burto, for me. I went to Boston one weekend, and after a pleasant Friday afternoon with Arthur Thornhill of Little, Brown, I met Professor Barnet in Harvard Yard on Saturday morning. Over bowls of corn flakes and coffee we struck a tentative bargain, later confirmed, for an arrangement through which he would function as general editor and find the ideal special editors for each play, for the sonnets and for Shakespeare's other poetry.

The Signet Classics Shakespeare not only added greatly to

NAL's educational reach in high schools and colleges, but more than any other work which we had published—including *Why We Can't Wait*, by Martin Luther King, which received extraordinary praise on the eve of Dr. King's Nobel Prize—The Signet Classics Shakespeare imports added something of a respectable dimension to the New English Library. The year of the Shakespeare Quatercentenary, 1964, provided a vast opportunity for celebration of Shakespeare's genius and for widespread promotion of his plays and poems. A celebration of Shakespeare's birthday at Stratford on Avon, in the rain on April 23, was generously reported in the press throughout the world. At this point, Christopher Shaw, the promotion director of NEL, and Gareth Powell, the managing director, asked if I would lend my presence and my influence to an even more massive and auspicious celebration in England. I agreed to cooperate. Through a public relations agency they enlisted the cooperation of the Royal Shakespeare Society for a 400th Anniversary Midsummer Nights Dinner to be held at Hampton Court Palace in the great hall where Shakespeare's own company had played, where the King James version of the Bible had been collated in 1611, and which had not been used for a banquet for more than three hundred years.

In the beautiful Great Hall the guests in full dress—white tie, tiaras and medals—gathered after being received by Sir Fordham Flower and Lady Flower, on behalf of the Royal Shakespeare Theatre Company, and by my wife and me, on behalf of the only American publishing concern ever to bring Shakespeare's works to England amid such auspicious circumstances. Lord Cobbold substituted for the Earl of Avon—Anthony Eden—who was ill, in proposing the toast to Her Majesty the Queen and the Royal Family. Sir Fordham Flower proposed the toast to the guests to which Lord Mancroft, my very close friend and guest, responded with his

L*

usual wit and eloquence, and with appropriate *sotto voce* expressions of approval by his wife, Diana, sitting next to me. Mr. Peter Hall, on behalf of the directors of the Royal Shakespeare Theatre Company, gave the concluding toast "To Shakespeare; then and now." It was my pleasant honor to respond—possibly the greatest and most auspicious honor ever accorded an American publisher in England.

I had scribbled my remarks after attending the wedding of Jack Adams' daughter in Greenwich a fortnight before and had sent a Xerox copy of my handwritten speech to England, to make certain that my response was wholly appropriate and within the bounds of protocol. I was almost in tears of elation at the pageantry of the vaulted ceilings covering such a splendid and magnificent company, as I delivered my well-reported remarks.

The occasion was an impressive one, but the ten guinea admission of four hundred guests covered the expense of organizing the furniture and catering.

This occasion did more for the reputation and standing of the New English Library and of 4-Square Books than anything up to that time. The managing director and staff appeared in their formal splendor, mainly hired from Moss Bros., and most of them—except Christopher Shaw who had been at Eton—met for the first time a cross section of the Establishment, with white tie and medals, in or out of Publishing. It gave New English Library the cachet of New American Library, despite the shortcomings of their own list which had originated entirely for their own imprint at their offices in Barnard's Inn. To me, as chairman and editor-in-chief of New American Library, it meant a great deal more— it meant that I, who had frequently visited England and lived there during the war, had returned to receive an outstanding recognition of the career on which I had embarked when I left London in 1945.

It had become obvious that NEL was a hollow shell without adequate management. Eventually Enoch had taken on a managing director by the name of Maxwell Arnot who, although he had asked me to sign up *The Carpetbaggers* from Pocket Books, was otherwise not skilled in the development of publishing concerns and was eventually asked to resign. Enoch had then selected Gareth Powell who had been a protégé of Godfrey Phillips in the early days of 4-Square Books and who, after a spell at Panther Books, moved to Mayflower which was owned by the American Dell interests.

Almost simultaneously with the Midsummer Night's Dinner, NAL published *Why We Can't Wait* by Dr. Martin Luther King, Jr. The book had come to me by way of Joan Daves, Dr. King's agent, who had been particularly impressed by my swift decision, swift publication and later swift distribution of *The Meaning of the Dead Sea Scrolls*. I had first encountered the name of Martin Luther King in the pages of *The Christian Century*—of which ecumenical weekly he eventually became a distinguished contributing editor. I had followed Dr. King's courageous and inspiring career as a man of God and a man of all humanity, and I had long felt that it would be a service to the world to give wider currency to his dedicated expression, by word and deed, of the real significance of his mission in our troubled times. I, personally, had contributed money from the start to the Southern Christian Leadership Conference of which Dr. King was director; since then he had published several volumes of sermons which Harper had published through their religious department. I would never have gone poaching for his writings. It seems that Dr. King was dissatisfied with the small sale of his sermons and wanted to publish an amplification of his famous letter to the clergy, which he had written in jail, directly into paperback. I agreed on the spot to publish the book, provided that Miss Daves would get a release from Harper of any implied option that might exist. This she had carefully done.

When the manuscript reached us in early 1964, I felt that it should have a simultaneous or near-simultaneous publication in hardcover and asked Miss Daves to make arrangements with Harper, which she did. Harper published the book June 8, 1964, and we followed with our Signet edition a month later, with a first printing of 500,000 copies. I was asked to introduce Dr. King at his New York press conference. At that time when the world was celebrating the 400th anniversary of Shakespeare's birth and the 400th anniversary of John Calvin's death and the tenth anniversary of the Supreme Court Decision desegregating the schools, Dr. King more than any other man of our time since Gandhi reflected a man whose religious spirit, logic and style triumphed over narrow prejudices of a sort which have clouded history for centuries.

Why We Can't Wait, a title which I suggested and which was found immediately acceptable, was first conceived as a crash softcover book project before the march on Washington in 1963; it grew in scope and importance into a unique American classic, distilled in the crucible of head, heart and soul.

While in England at the Shakespeare Quatercentenary, I tried to persuade the New English Library to import a substantial quantity. It was not until I had a strong inference, later in the summer, that Dr. King would indeed receive the Nobel Peace Prize that they ordered more than a token shipment. I spurred NEL on and, to their credit, they arranged a luncheon with Lord Thomson of Fleet and outstanding members of Parliament and surrounded the book with the kind of sensational publicity which appealed to their promotional tastes. I did not mind that, so long as they were responsive to my urging.

Despite the exhilaration of recognition of my precious Shakespeare project, I was greatly depressed by the subsequent week which I spent in London observing the actual operation of the New English Library. I returned on July 3 and went immediately to the old Wyandanch Club at Smithtown, New York, just acquired by Robert Moses for an ultimate State Park and renamed, as a ten-year lessee, the Nessequogue Club. My host, Lester Brion, understood that I would have little time for sport. Instead of fishing and relaxing, I worked on the report of my fortnight in London. Immediately after the Independence Day holiday, I planned to make known to my family and intimate friends my planned resignation the following year as editor-in-chief of the New American Library at the earliest contractual date, June 1, 1965.

On the 18th of July my wife and I had a pleasant dinner at Le Pavillon with Donald N. McDonnell of Blyth & Company, during which I told him that I was finding my role in a Times Mirror subsidiary absolutely intolerable, as not only NAL, but World Publishing seemed to be run on the principle of absolute remote control. My early impression of Norman Chandler had been correct. He was a gracious duke, surrounded by mechanistic advisors, and in the manner of ancient dukes, he let the sheriffs and foresters fight it out on the periphery of the estates. He had, by way of Raymond McGranahan, made it utterly impossible for me to conduct a qualitative book publishing program. Donald was staggered by this description, not previously revealed to him, of the situation at NAL. I asked him to refrain from interfering since, if I could not make clear the true state of affairs, I did not think that he could carry any more weight than I alone; moreover, there was no reason why Blyth & Company should jeopardize their excellent financial connections with Times Mirror.

On the next day, Sunday, July 19—for the first time—I actually visited the New York World's Fair. My first visit to the Terrace Club, as host to a busload of NAL executives and guests, had not taken us inside the gates. My wife and I went early to the Fair. After viewing a number of exhibits, at twelve-thirty—a half hour before the legal Sabbath New York hour for cocktails—we decided to visit the Jockey Club Restaurant in the Spanish Pavilion and at one o'clock order a pitcher of sangrias, the Spanish beverage of red wine and lemonade. As we entered the restaurant we noted several restaurant captains whose faces looked familiar from the Jockey Club in Madrid. My wife decided to tidy up in the ladies' powder room. After she was gone for some ten minutes I began to wonder what could have happened.

Then a waiter approached, asking if my name were Weybright. I had the sudden thought that he had recognized us and had intercepted my wife for special hospitality. I followed him to discover that on the polished stone steps to the powder room, which lacked a railing, my wife had slipped and struck her spine and was obviously in great pain. We called a World's Fair ambulance which took us to the World's Fair Emergency Medical Center: There the personnel refused to examine her in any way. They insisted upon calling an ambulance to take her to the Flushing Hospital. I insisted that she should be taken to the Lenox Hill Hospital, which is only a hundred yards from our apartment in Manhattan. But before we could secure the right to make our exit from the fairgrounds, the staff of their Emergency Medical Center insisted that my wife, who was barely conscious, sign a waiver. Furthermore, they refused to give their names, under repeated questioning, while waiting for the ambulance to arrive, but they took copious information concerning our names and address. When I asked why, they insisted this procedure was followed upon Mr. Robert Moses' absolute orders. I began to appreciate the nature of Mr. Moses, which was later more fully revealed when many of the leading bankers of New York resigned from his financial advisory board because he would not provide them with information concerning the sorry financial affairs of the Fair.

It was obviously a tremendous relief to reach the friendly portals of the Lenox Hill Hospital and to discover from X-rays that the injury to my wife's back was serious but not too critical to respond to prolonged hospital treatment, actually nearly two months, with several weeks thereafter in a metal back brace. I did not mention this accident at the office, except to my wife's son, Truman Talley.

Within four days after the weekend, David Brown handed in his resignation. He soon returned to 20th-Century Fox as chief story editor. Within a week, Truman Talley came to my office and resigned from NAL without the knowledge of his wife, who was at East Hampton with their children, or of his mother, who was in the hospital.

Neither David Brown's resignation nor Truman Talley's resignation was in any fashion based upon disloyalty to the enterprise as each had known it, but based upon circumstances which would very soon have extinguished their careers at NAL if they had remained. Truman Talley, whose salary had been fixed by Ray McGranahan, based upon several perfunctory telephone calls made by McKinsey and Company to other publishers, insisted that nothing would persuade him to remain except a vote of confidence expressed by election to the board and promotion to executive vice-president—editorial.

When I returned to my office after a board meeting on August 4, 1964, after my own notice of intent to resign, the entire editorial staff was in tears. All of them said they wanted to resign, too. I urged them not to do anything so rash. Within a month Edward Doctorow, senior editor, resigned to go to the Dial Press as editor-in-chief. In the following months Edward Burlingame, senior editor, resigned to go to Walker and Company as editor-in-chief, and eventually Thomas J. Davis III resigned to go to Charles Scribner's Sons as a senior editor to handle history projects.

My only consolation was that by August 7—three days later —Raymond McGranahan had resigned as executive vice-president of the Times Mirror Company. The havoc which he had created in our organization was irreparable and made my recruitment of a successor and of two editorial vice-presidents, and others to replace members of the staff, appallingly difficult.

No public announcement of the decimation of the top editorial executive staff of one of the world's leading publishing houses was made—but the word spread like wildfire, and tended to depress the scores of individuals whom I interviewed as candidates to succeed myself, David Brown and Truman Talley. I personally absorbed responsibility for putting the World Publishing Company's books through the press because of the almost 100 percent resignation of World's editorial staff. It was obvious to most of the men I interviewed that something had gone wrong at NAL. I cannot decide whether it was to my credit that I abstained from even a hint of the difficulties we had all been facing in the critical heart of the enterprise. Within the next three months I interviewed, often with a preceding "feeler" from intimate professional friends, more than one hundred individuals. Fortunately, I found one outstanding man who was willing to try to take Truman Talley's position—Edward T. Chase.

Ned Chase, a man of tremendous intellectual vigor, a frequent reviewer of books on public policy, planning and economics, was vice-president (public relations) of a first-class advertising agency where he had pioneered in eliciting the finest thought and expression of American business, philanthropy and education. He had an excellent war record, had taught literature at Stanford University and worked as a *New Yorker* editor—and was willing to face any obstacle to transplant his talent into the noble profession of publishing books. He was typical of the prominent young intellectuals in Truman Talley's circle.

Since Chase was a newcomer to book publishing, I devoted a great deal of time to orienting him on his responsibilities, and at the same time carried a great deal of the burden of editorial responsibility by myself, still looking for a hardcover editor. By election day I had found at least a stop-gap hardcover editorial vice-president, Timothy Seldes of Doubleday. Despite a great deal of nagging to find a successor for myself, I met with little success. At the time I felt honor bound not to divulge any of the circumstances that impelled me to create such a vacancy.

It had been impossible to take my wife on a recuperative holiday even for a weekend break, and when she settled for a choice of her own, she elected to visit Hong Kong as soon as possible. In order to make certain that her back injury had healed sufficiently to travel, I took her with me on a trip to London for one week, leaving the day after Christmas. Despite a blizzard, we had a jolly time and spent New Year's Eve with Graham Hutton, Sir John Rodgers, Sir John Wolfenden, head of the University Grants Committee, and other eminent scholars, politicians and artists. Since the trip had no ill effects, I immediately made plans to take my wife to Hong Kong in February for a sojourn by way of Hawaii and Tokyo, returning by way of Lisbon for a brief stop, all within three weeks. I fixed the date for our trip to commence the fifth of February, 1965, and made plans—although the trip was entirely at my own expense—to see authors, publishers, educators and book distributors at each stop.

The date had to be rigidly fixed to permit me to hold the chair at the February 2 NAL board meeting at which John P. R. Budlong was to be elected president, succeeding Enoch, who earlier had moved to the Times Mirror offices at 280 Park Avenue. Before John Budlong could be elected president of NAL, I relinquished my contractual claim to the chief executive job in January, in a session with Albert V. Casey, then executive vice-president, and Robert Erburu, general counsel. I also completed the relinquishment of the position of editor-in-chief, but agreed, when pressed, to continue to serve as chairman of the board from June 2 of that year.

During this period in January Rudolf Littauer asked for an appointment at my office, stating that he wanted to inquire whether I was interested in disposing of any of my Times Mirror shares, of which I held something over 200,000. I replied adamantly in the negative. I asked him why the question should arise at this time. He replied that Enoch would like to sell enough shares to finance his new apartment and its decoration and that he, himself, would like to diversify his investments and sell some of his shares.

I gave the question of selling shares no further thought until, on the opposite side of the world, I received a cable from Littauer stating that Enoch planned to sell 100,000 Times Mirror shares—half of his holdings—in a secondary offering and that Littauer decided to go along and sell practically all of his modest holdings. My decision was requested within two weeks, as the Times Mirror board was meeting on Tuesday, March 4 to approve such a secondary offering. Under contract we were jointly to deal with SEC registration and any secondary offering. I replied that I was not interested without a chance to consult my financial and legal advisors, an almost hopeless undertaking from a place such as Hong Kong where the telephone and cable services were not quick or readily available at all hours around the clock. Since I did not want to spoil the special holiday on which I had taken my wife, I told her as little as possible, although it was obviously very frustrating to have to spend most of our time completely isolated in the Mandarin Hotel trying to place telephone calls and receive cables.

I sent a cable to Norman Chandler in Los Angeles saying that I was practically fed up and would like to sell no shares at all if my Times Mirror board situation would be continued, otherwise I might sell all of my holdings. I cabled to numerous financial friends in New York and fixed a series of conference dates for Saturday, February 27, and Sunday, February 28. On Monday, March 1, just before the Times Mirror meeting, I fixed a date to meet with my attorneys, White and Case, and with financial advisors. Al Casey had had the courtesy to telephone me in Hong Kong, but I never received a reply to my cable from Norman Chandler. Instead, when we went downstairs in the hotel, I met the Chandlers just arriving on a Pan American Board Flight, and he introduced me to his Pan American colleagues as the "chief of Times Mirror's book operations." I asked if I could see him the next day when he was less occupied with Pan American matters, and wrote him a note with a copy of my cable and personally put it in his mailbox—but to this day there has been no reply.

When we reached Lisbon, where telephone service was simpler, I made a number of telephone calls to New York and Los Angeles and finally had an extensive but inconclusive telephone talk with Al Casey. Immediately after our return to New York on February 27, I had a conversation with one of my most trusted financial friends who warned me that if Enoch, at the age of seventy and reported not to be a well man, was selling 100,000 shares, half of his holdings, in Times Mirror, his action as an insider had great significance—that he would have to pay an enormous capital gains tax, close to 30 percent, to be followed, in the case of death, with a considerable estate tax. On Sunday, February 28, my wife and I met with Donald N. McDonnell of Blyth & Company. The final outcome of our conversation was that since I was withdrawing from my role as editor-in-chief, and was frequently uninformed of Times Mirror and NAL developments, we might as well diversify and join in the secondary offering. Times Mirror shares had closed on February 26 at 44½. We agreed that I would sell 140,000 of my more than 200,000 shares, and my wife would sell 8,000 of the 12,000 shares which I had presented to her. The next morning I went to White and Case, to fix the legal arrangements.

When I went to California for the Times Mirror board meeting in early May it was understood that I would not give up the editor-in-chief position until July 1—instead of June 1—because of the International Publishers Congress in Washington in May and June followed by the American Booksellers Association which, surrounded by special opportunities for trade gossip, might lead to misconstruction of my actions, detrimental to NAL and Times Mirror.

On June 28 I first called in all of NAL's editorial staff, then all of NAL's officers and, finally, all of NAL's junior executives, and read them a statement which had been cleared with Times Mirror in California and personally approved on each page with Mrs. Norman Chandler's initials.

Simultaneously with my relinquishment of the function and responsibility of editor-in-chief, The New American Library of World Literature, Inc., shortened its name to The New American Library, Inc., and moved to the J. C. Penney Building on the West Side. Enoch was ensconced like a spider in a vast web in a spacious, but stark, office in the headquarters which Times Mirror had established in the Bankers Trust Building at 280 Park Avenue. The arrangement for

NAL to move had been conducted until the last moment amid an atmosphere of mystery by John Budlong aided by George McCorkle and Richard Perkins, all of whom believed that their status was enhanced by expensive new offices in Communications Row up the street from the Time and Life Building, across the Avenue of the Americas from CBS, ABC, MGM, etc.—and across 53rd Street from the New York Hilton Hotel. The top management offices on the twenty-eighth floor faced west beyond the rear end of the Americana Hotel to the Hudson River.

From the moment that I set foot in the NAL offices in the J. C. Penney Building at 1301 Avenue of the Americas, after the NAL move over the weekend of June 28, 1965, I repented my decision to remain as chairman of the company. The decor had been contrived in California and resembled nothing so much as a flashy motel on the Strip of Sunset Boulevard. At the precise point where management ended and operation commenced, the nasty brown rugs ended. Editors pounded their way down the corridor on some sort of acoustically dreadful synthetic vinyl. The furniture was of the latest fashion with metal legs, desks so low there was no space for a center drawer, and ashtrays, coffee tables and other appurtanences were standardized. Memoranda began to buzz about —no live plants, no eating in offices except at the standard coffee-break time, as well as specific instructions as to who could and who could not use the executive washroom and windowless conference-dining room. My own furniture, which deviated from the Sunset Strip pattern, did not arrive for months. I camped out in a corner office wondering what new directive would next appear.

By arrangement with NAL I flew to London on Friday, August 13, with my wife, planning at my own expense to do as much as possible to reinforce on behalf of NAL the liaison which I had established with the principal publishers, agents and authors in the United Kingdom. The London mission involved a very busy schedule, including only one outing in the country with Fleur Cowles at her farm near East Grinstead. There was a crisis at NEL requiring several board meetings to survey the variance from its financial course, resulting in a continued substantial deficit. The managing director, Gareth Powell, assured me that he knew nothing of arithmetic. Although he was in principle supposed to understand rudimentary profit and loss figures, he talked more about his Rolls Royce than about the business. I had telephoned Budlong several times in the course of these frightening financial developments at NEL. He arranged to come to London with George McCorkle. At great effort I secured them accommodations at the Dorchester and gave them breakfast every morning at a conference in my suite. This was not entirely convenient. I had arranged for Amory and Helen Haskell to join us in London and had secured a room for them adjoining our drawing room in the hotel. Budlong was so constantly on the telephone to Enoch that he could scarcely remain in the room even to meet Beryl Griffie-Williams of Glidrose, the corporation which had purchased a substantial portion of Ian Fleming's publishing rights prior to his death. I talked with the Glidrose directors and a number of major agents and publishers on behalf of NAL, and returned to the office on September 13. I recite this sequence as it has a considerable bearing on my decision that it would be impossible, under the circumstances that were established, to be of constructive use to NAL unless the influence of my advice would get to the responsible editors and executives dealing with projects which I had originated, but who were in total isolation from my office.

The pedestrian bureaucracy that had been established along with the architecture of the move to the Avenue of the

Americas had obviously been calculated to change radically the quality and goals of the company.

In a fashion I was being used in the manner of a constitutional monarch to front for overall activities, whether I was unaware of them, or if aware, disapproved of them or not. As a sort of crown in microcosm, my sympathy grew for the Queen of England who is obligated to sanction activities and utter statements with which obviously she must often be out of sympathy. I was swamped with budgets and figures but detached from any non-board matters such as dealing with the further development of a publishing program.

Early in the year, during our Christmas holiday in London, I had begun to gather information and check my memory of my four wartime years at the American Embassy in London. In order to check material in the files, I secured an irrevocable right to examine the NAL editorial files which had been presented to New York University. In the autumn of 1965 I spent a week organizing better NAL publishing relationships with The Johns Hopkins University and Press in Baltimore. In January 1966, I spent another week as a specially invited guest at the University of Chicago.

The accumulating decline in earnings—actually, deficits —of the New English Library were now totally the responsibility of New American Library in New York since the Godfrey Phillips interests had been purchased. Moreover, the decline in earnings of New American Library were, as I had predicted, becoming frighteningly real.

Then, in order to give my wife her promised visit to Hong Kong without the interruptions which had occurred the previous year, I took her to Hong Kong again, leaving on March 5, 1966 and returning on April 2. In London on my way back from the around-the-world journey, I consulted various friends and advisors of my wartime years and spent some time visiting with Herbert Agar, Sir William Emrys Williams, George Weidenfeld and, by good chance because of my early interest in Penguin Books, Morris Ernst whom I encountered at my hotel.

I visited NEL and had an unproductive session on the morning of the British Election Day. That night Gareth Powell, accompanied by a gay group of companions, parked his Rolls Royce conspicuously in front of Annabel's, the night-club in Berkeley Square, which occurred to him as a splendid way to celebrate a socialist victory as managing director of a company that was far from over its deficits. It was a typical exhibit of "swinging London," celebrating a socialist victory on the fantastic largesse of Uncle Sam via NAL and The Times Mirror Company—a young man in a Liberty-print shirt, with a Rolls Royce, who had openly described himself as overpaid, but with no company bank account except for deposits from New York and California to cover deficits and keep the enterprise alive. His notion of progress was to publish more and more Playboy trivia and Girodias pornography—with a bit of warmed up egghead stuff from NAL in the U.S.A.

At the bar at Annabel's my wife said, "Oh!" I echoed "Oh!" That night I told my wife that within a month I doubted if I would have to worry about such repulsive real-life nightmares in sequence to my lifelong dreams. I saw no evidence of adherence to my literary or financial goals in New York or in London. It was as if the barbarians had taken over. The back list, which I had built up over nearly a generation, was the spoils. By the time the 1965 Times Mirror annual report was published, there was no mention of the subsidiary officers, just a recital of the top staff. NAL had been pulverized and I was lost among the rubble, while a strange new structure was being erected in the fine print.

It was obvious that the abrupt decline in NAL earnings—

at least $600,000 before taxes at the end of April, 1966—was the subject that most concerned Enoch and Budlong. I decided then and there that the time had come to disavow any connection with circumstances beyond my control.

I prepared my final letter of resignation which I presented directly to Norman Chandler in Los Angeles on May 9. I had flown out on the Sunday afternoon TWA flight with John Budlong. But I decided it was now my prerogative to be secretive and told him nothing of the letter which I intended to produce at the Times Mirror meeting on Monday morning completely disassociating myself from NAL and its new policies.

I immediately telephoned Miss Joyce Hester, my personal secretary, in New York to put out a release of my resignation. But over the telephone I edited an earlier draft so as not to penalize myself in my effort at securing a release from the restrictive covenant with liquidated damages which I had signed in June 1960. I could have commented on the declining profits of NAL under the new management and the staggering loss of character and reputation of the company in the year following my relinquishment of the editor-in-chieftainship. The note on my resignation was printed in *Publisher's Weekly* that very week and precipitated even more of a deluge of melancholy correspondence than the notice of my giving up the post of editor-in-chief.

I made it very clear in my conversations in California that I was well along in this memoir and that under no circumstances would I modify my manuscript or give NAL or Times Mirror any opportunity to scan it in advance of publication. This troubled Norman Chandler very much, but he assured me that he respected my right to freedom of expression and, when pressed, stated positively that up to that moment he had always considered me honorable, honest and diligent in the interest of the parent company and all of its subsidiaries.

The final document modifying my restrictive covenant was executed on October 10, 1966, and was of no use to me on my expensive and carefully arranged literary reconnaissance in England in the summer of 1966.

The recitation of my experience may seem over-detailed for the general reader. I have made my account as comprehensive as possible for the benefit of the literary profession and the publishing industry, as well as for the students of management who may want to understand the pitfalls of over-organizing a sensitive enterprise into a device for killing the spirit and threatening the profits.

It should be apparent to any man of sense that the totalitarian combination of a mechanistic parent company with an insensitive business type in a publishing house subsidiary spells the doom of creativity, of increasing profits and of the spirit which attracts the finest authors and scholars.

Chapter XIII

CREDO AND FULFILLMENT

———————◆◇◆———————

The Toad beneath the harrow knows
Exactly where each tooth-point goes . . .
—Rudyard Kipling

IN THE YEAR and a quarter after I began to withdraw from
the completely transformed Times Mirror-New American
Library complex (emerging a comparatively free man October 13, 1966) some of my professional acquaintances in
publishing, finance and public affairs assumed that I would
be happy to be "out to grass" before the age of sixty-three.
My family and, above all, my close literary and publishing
friends knew better. They realized, from the beginning of
my ordeal of escape, that I was bent on freedom not only for
its own sake, but for a purpose—to resume publishing under
my own flag, using my own criteria, harnessing my own
ideals and not being subservient to the base and often devious misuse of the essential bureaucracy of the Faceless Age
of Business that has dimmed the quality of publishing at
NAL.

During the period when I was rendered professionally
impotent by contracts and covenants—now fortunately mit-
igated sufficiently to resume my publishing career in a
modest fashion, but which unhappily keeps me out of the
field of wide dissemination of good inexpensive books—I en-

gaged in a number of pleasantly satisfying digressions. I had become, as it were, an ex-revolutionist in quality publishing. First of all I wrote this book. I reestablished more firmly than ever before my dedication to my native countryside, Carroll County, Maryland. I became a partner in the Museum of Famous People in New York City—a high level historical waxworks, the finest such enterprise in the United States, but without a "chamber of horrors" of the sort which distorts history through melodramatic shock at Madame Tussaud's in London. As previously mentioned, I visited London four times, circumnavigated the globe twice and leisurely strengthened association with a number of authors, critics, agents, publishers, scholars and members of the seven arts at home and abroad.

The most satisfying pursuit of all was closer identification with Carroll County. In 1966 I became an investor in and a director of *The Carroll County Times,* based in Westminster, the county seat, and endeavoring to provide an independent newspaper, printing the news impartially, supporting what it believes to be right and opposing what it believes to be wrong, without regard to party politics.

My associates, in actual control of *The Carroll County Times,* are Dr. and Mrs. Edgar F. Berman. Dr. Berman, still young and certainly not retired, is presently attached to the office of Vice-President Hubert H. Humphrey and has accompanied Mr. Humphrey on all of his major journeys throughout the Far East and the United States. After a brilliant medical and surgical career in Baltimore and elsewhere, Edgar felt the urge to become a sort of deluxe Schweitzer and worked for several years with the late Dr. Thomas A. Dooley in Asia. Then he and Phoebe, his charming, intelligent and dynamic wife, settled on a large estate near Lutherville in the Valley outside of Baltimore. There they spend very little of their time enjoying their thorough-

bred horses, farm, swimming pool and other indulgences
which they have magnificently organized as part of their setting. They bought *The Carroll County Times,* made Phoebe
Rhea Berman its president, surrounded themselves with a
bright young staff and eventually asked me to participate. It
is not a romantic or nostalgic escape from reality, but something of a demonstration, in microscosm, of the influence of
high ideals and professional articulation on modern society.

Carroll County, which had been purely rural in my childhood and youth, has attracted a galaxy of new and carefully
selected industries. For example, Black and Decker's plant
at Hampstead in Carroll County has tripled its growth since
it was established there in 1951, and now employs 3,500 people. Random House has built a large book distribution center at Westminster, with space for expansion for other of
their publishing activities. Bennett Cerf first beheld the
beauties and the extraordinary tranquility of the Carroll
County countryside and the intelligence of its people when
he visited the late Whittaker Chambers, whose publisher he
was, at his working farm and retreat in the Bachman Valley
outside of Westminster. Genesco, the large textile and ap-
parel manufacturing and distributing concern, is completing
a modern factory, offices and processing center, across the
road from Random House at Westminster. Down the Reis-
terstown Road, near Finksburg, Rowan Controller, of which
my son-in-law, Amory L. Haskell, Jr., is a director and senior
officer, has a thriving modern establishment, comparable to
their new headquarters and plant in Monmouth Industrial
Park in New Jersey. Westinghouse is building a tremendous
heat research and arc-welding plant at Sykesville. Dozens of
other enterprises, such as the Cambridge Rubber Company
at Taneytown—originally located in Massachusetts—and the
Congoleum Company have grown in the county. One of the
older and least typical heavy industries, the Lehigh Port-

land Cement Company, continues to exploit its quarries at Union Bridge.

Despite the growth of manufacturing, data processing, research and quarrying enterprises, the country remains fundamentally devoted to the preservation of its fair fields and rippling streams, protecting the area from becoming a suburban backyard to the metropolitan backwash of Baltimore, an hour away, and of Washington, an hour and a half away from the county seat. Only recently, Carroll County opened the Carroll County Farm Museum at Westminster, Maryland's first such museum, a permanent 140-acre agrarian demonstration which was originally the brainchild of the late Landon C. Burns and his extraordinary circle of friends. It contains thousands of exhibits, including a library set up in Landon Burns's memory. By late 1966 nearly all of the fifteen thousand enrolled pupils in the public schools of the county had already viewed it as well as tens of thousands of visitors, many from other states. Although it features the agricultural history of the region, it is not merely a bucolic antiquarian's paradise but a living symbol of the heritage of an area endowed by heaven with fertile soil, a well-educated and hardy population, and still distinguished, despite industrial growth, by beautiful modern agriculture adorned with eighteenth-century domestic architecture. Well-tended fields and green and well-watered meadows give an enchanting relief from stark modern life. There are no old fields lying empty or given over to brush, but beautifully contoured hillsides, splendid small forests and, toward the west, the eternal Blue Ridge, providing an azure curtain as if the Mediterranean had been turned on edge to provide a spectacular background.

The Historical Society of Carroll County, under the leadership of James M. Shriver, has become a Mecca for those interested in the tradition of a countryside that, as I said in the concluding pages of my biography of Francis Scott Key, is "a land of culture rather than brilliance, of averages rather than extremes, less ambitious than the West, less industrious than the North, less indolent than the old baronial South." The county villages and hamlets remain for the most part beautifully unspoiled, and some of the older small farms have been taken over by men and women of outstanding intellectual and artistic talent. The greatest scholar in the county is Charles S. Singleton at New Windsor. He is chairman of the Humanities Center and of the Romance Language Department at The Johns Hopkins University. Next to his dwelling, he maintains another house as a priceless library of his Renaissance Italian collection of books and pictures. In addition, he operates a registered vineyard and winery. Charles and Eula Singleton make frequent trips to Italy. He was honored in 1965, the Dante Septcentennial, for organizing Dante's papers and writings under a grant from the Bollingen Foundation for the Dante repositories in Florence. In the course of these labors, Charles found time to undertake the first scholarly modern translation of Boccaccio, Dante's contemporary, for me at New American Library, with a deluxe edition to be brought out by Harcourt, Brace and World.

At Westminster, which is undergoing the process of happily delayed and well-timed entry into regional planning, Western Maryland College provides a unique cultural center, with considerable emphasis on music and the theater.

It has been very heartening for me to be identified, even from afar, with the inspiring development of Carroll County —to see it becoming one of the most ideally civilized communities in the world, with a remarkable and gracious future growing out of its beautiful but somewhat sleepy past.

There are times in all men's lives when it is fruitful—as exemplified by the Founding Fathers—to devote some precious time to thought, to philosophical discourse and to consideration of one's family and the amenities of life, unharassed by the urgent demands of business or profession. The hiatus of my publishing career has been spiritually and financially productive. My new incarnation, as of the present, has given me a great deal of perspective on the fundamentals of modern life. With the assistance of an able and loyal researcher-secretary, Miss Joyce Hester from the University of North Carolina, I have not only finished this memoir but reorganized and beautified our spacious apartment in Carlyle House, New York. It has meant a great deal to me to have this task handled by Marian K. Morgan of McMillen, Inc., who, without destroying the hospitable atmosphere, has transformed with grace and style the entire premises, especially the drawing room, the dining room, the main hall, the library and my private study. Thomas Jefferson at Monticello cannot have been more dedicated to the beautification of his mansion and gardens than I have been to the fresh and unobtrusive arrangement of new and old books, pictures and furniture. I have not felt selfish in this indulgence. Throughout the process I have not been niggardly to good causes, to family or to friends. I have taken time to reread some of the books which I treasure most, and to read carefully rather than skim some of the periodicals which I had previously perused for purely professional purposes.

I have, however, spent a great deal of time observing trends in publishing, especially book publishing, and in education, philosophy, theology, sociology, medicine and law. I have been dismayed more than once by the attention given by critics to the second-rate and to the belittlement of disciplined straightforward aesthetics in art, drama and literature. I have never been shocked by the new, the experimental or the sensational in literature, pictures or music—but I have been distressed by the disdain of disciplined values in some of the flagrant decadence which characterizes our age. Some of this frantic and often juvenile tendency is readily ascribable to the frustrations of depersonalized life. I have a sense of deep sympathy with the disadvantaged minorities whose voices can only, apparently, be heard if attended by violence and tumult. I sympathize with, even when I deplore, the explosion of human anguish due to inadequacy or the absence of a chance for wholeness and fulfillment on the campuses or in the slums. But, as I reflect on some of the books I currently read and on some of the art and drama which I presently behold, I feel that they often reveal self-conscious ignorance and ugly barbarism rather than true creativity and striving for beauty and truth.

The untutored who respect computers more than morality are in danger of creating the age of mediocrity. I have recently been reminded, in an article by Charles B. Ketcham in the *Christian Century,* of the insight of the late Martin Buber who realized that " 'the necessary world of *It* (Structure) can never fulfill the function of the intimate world of *Thou* (personal relation), which is self-informing and self-affirming. Without *It* man cannot live. But he who lives with *It* alone is not a man.' The world of *It* becomes evil only when it presumes to have being and seeks total mastery over life."

This is the sort of reflection that few men except scholars on the campus have the leisure to dwell upon in these times; and it is very healthy for me, I think, that I have had a voluntary sabbatical to ponder some of the verities of human experience that are applicable not only to artists and writers but to successful businessmen in a free society. What does it avail the United States to have fifty-six million students—from kindergarten to university—in school if writers and book publishers become panderers to superficial literacy rather than dedicated advocates of that which is best?

M

No one can question the benefits of automation, electronics, synthetics and new approaches to enriching the true content of life. No one can approve of drudgery, or of preserving established methods of doing things, if they make no genuine contribution to aesthetic, cultural or economic progress. For example, in publishing, many twentieth-century advances in technology have rivaled the significance of Gutenberg's movable type. Electronic typesetting, which eliminates the composing room by the use of electronic tape, can eventually eliminate much of the chore of proofreading and consequent compounding of errors, and enable various editions and formats of a book to employ at less cost the most suitable type font for each special purpose. High-speed printing and binding certainly do not impinge on the tradition of fine book production. The use of computers to rationalize accounting and quick data processing—which includes speedy processing of costs, inventories, royalties and overheads—is essential to the modern publisher. Likewise, the most modern techniques in warehousing, dispatching and the handling of unsold copies.

However, if the computer process is utilized to give crass marketing men the whiphand over creative publishers and editors I demur, and I have boldly taken my stand. A computer cannot go to a play, a poetry reading, a church, a nightclub or a literary salon and detect presently unsung genius or near-genius of the future. On the other hand, a computer can evaluate scholastic performance through a quick analysis of examinations or classroom records and give speedy information on elements to stress in the educational life of individual students. It is no accident that the mammoth computer and electronic companies are endeavoring to acquire or affiliate themselves with juvenile and general publishers who have nurtured poets, storytellers, novelists and scholars through the intimate process of human appreciation and understanding.

Computers might be likened to priests who have instantly mastered the ritual; but in my opinion good writers and good publishers are more likely to resemble prophets rather than priests.

Eloquence and oratory may change, style of presentation may change, but the dream of the creative person, although disciplined, cannot successfully be mechanized.

I believe in good publishers and good literary agents. I consider agents as well as editors as nourishing bodies for good writers. I exclude from this dedicated company the opportunist merchandisers and the hyena tax lawyers and shark wheeler-dealer agents who are not interested in developing talent, or in salvaging it when a writer strikes an unproductive period or a block between his major projects.

Let me illustrate the advantage, and disadvantage, of blind speed and mechanization with a general example which has profound personal implications. Recently in London, I had the tailors who have made my clothes for many decades—Anderson & Sheppard of Savile Row—create a splendid new personal wardrobe for all seasons, patiently fitted after I had lost considerable weight. The result was perfect. Everything was completed from the appropriate materials and fitted through many sessions with close observation. Then we agreed to dispatch the bespoke—or custom tailored—result by Pan American Air Freight to arrive the day after my return to New York. I, personally, went to the Pan American Air Freight office in Piccadilly to be reassured of safe transport and delivery to New York. My tailors delivered the packages to Pan American—and now, more than two months later, after daily inquiries, Pan American cannot account for the shipment. They didn't seem to know, or care, what happened. They are covered by the minimum trans-Atlantic insurance and are unconcerned by their responsibility for the actual transport. I mention this episode for two reasons: first, Norman Chandler is a director of Pan Am, who knows not what his flying minions do or fail to do; second, because Pan Am is a symbol of what I consider the depersonalization of attention to things that are intensely personal.

On the day that I conclude this personal narrative, I have endured another, although minor, example of the depersonalization of experience. A day ago I took my automobile to the Cadillac Motor Division of General Motors at York Avenue and 60th Street for routine autumn servicing before driving to Maryland to visit my aged parents. When I inquired by telephone whether the job had been completed, I was confronted with a telephonic recording that the man responsible was not presently available and would return my call at his convenience, which happened not to have occurred until hours later. So I went to the garage and waited for nearly an hour for the delivery of my car—an operation that would have been efficient, instantaneous and interested in Westminster, Maryland. The front seat of the car was smeared with grease which was immediately transferred to the only flimsy topcoat which I own due to the nondelivery of the coats which I had ordered from London, and nobody cared or was present to care. The point of this personal complaint or plaint, is that the mechanization which attempts to depersonalize the simplest relationships in modern life is totally frustrating and totally ignored by pompous board members, who continue to exploit the development of enterprises which only presume to cater to the helpless individual.

I cite these costly and uncomfortable disappointments as typical of the everyday dehumanization of life, which I can never adopt in relation to the people with whom I deal—authors and poets, booksellers and readers who expect some human attention to individual and personal affairs by those charged with responsibility for them. I believe that, as a publisher, I am personally responsible for prompt attention to the welfare of my authors, of the book trade and of readers; and I will never condone the Mishaps of the Machine on Matters which are supremely important to the Individual. Pan Am and General Motors, like the Pennsylvania Railroad, on which I traveled from New York to Maryland for many years, are not visibly dedicated to personal satisfaction of the persons dependent upon their advertised services. At the point where the computer goes haywire, or reports incredible mistakes, the publisher must step in to atone for the failure of the machine. In a way, this is the moral of this book and my outlook on life.

"The toad beneath the harrow knows . . ."

I am happy to be a plowboy aware of the responsibility of the man who drives the harrow . . . Like a farmer, I must be loyal not only to past and present, but to the morrow. To people who depend upon me, whether or not they know me. And whether or not they ever read this book.

Footnote: Although my covenant with Times Mirror does not permit me to engage in the publishing and widest possible distribution of inexpensive softcover books of the sort which characterized the prime of my life in the 20th Century Book Revolution, I am—despite restrictions—again a book publisher. With Truman Macdonald Talley, I am starting from scratch as a sort of "artisan publisher," and our new firm, Weybright and Talley, Inc., is attracting talent from all over the world for our general hardcover and ultimate softcover educational program. Every morning we are at 3 East 54th Street soon after eight, surrounded by a small but able staff, dedicated to the ideals and business principles of high quality book publishing. We have recently been elected to the American Book Publishers Council, and have arranged selling, warehousing and distribution with E. P. Dutton & Company. And, thanks to these arrangements, and the efficiency of Mary M. Metcalf, secretary of the company, we are now able to concentrate upon the development of a publishing house in which vision is harnessed to practical management, rather than submerged by heartless, soulless and depersonalized, or misguided, remote control.

Footnote 2: In order to draw to the fullest extent possible upon the literary and scholarly talent of the British Isles—and of the Continent of Europe—we have established Weybright and Talley Ltd., in London. Hugh Corbett, an English writer, critic and editor, educated at Wimbledon College and at New College, Oxford, who has enjoyed twenty years of New York publishing experience, serves as managing director, aided by a distinguished board consisting of Sylvester Gates, scholar of New College, Oxford, and banker; Herbert Agar, Pulitzer prize winning American author-publisher-diplomat, now resident in England; and Lord Birdwood, a brilliant young publicist and advertising man, educated at Cambridge.

It is a rare experience to enjoy the friendship and civilized outlook of such a group—and an extraordinary privilege to work with them on transatlantic matters that also strengthen Old England, her language, her literature and, in a modest way, her Exchequer. By acting as advisors, suppliers and scouts for our New York publishing activities, they add the quality of perspective to our publishing decisions in America.

INDEX

Ministry of Agriculture (Great Britain), 133-134, 149, 157

Ministry of Information (Great Britain), 118-119, 121-133, 136, 139

Ministry of Supply Paper Control (Great Britain), 128, 154

Minor, Clark, 116

Minor, Mrs. Clark, 116

Mission to Moscow (Davies), 164

Modern American Poets (Williams), 238-239

Modley, Rudolph, 89

Monroe, Harriet, 49

Moonraker (Fleming), 281

Moore, Joseph, 62, 64

Moravia, 202, 236

Morehead, Albert, 283

Morgan, Clay, 70

Morgan, H. A., 86

Morgan, Marian K., 328

Morgenthau, Henry, 112

Morison, Stanley, 183

Morley, Christopher, 121

Morley, Louise, 121

Morris, Wright, 232

Morris House (Philadelphia), 26

Morrison, Herbert, 127

Morrison and Gibb, Ltd., 129

Moses, Robert, 309, 310-311

Moss, Howard, 232, 239

Motley, Willard, 231

Mount Vernon (Washington's home), 2

Mountbatten, Lord Louis, 282

Mountbatten, Lady Louis, 151-153

Moxon, James, 274

Muller, Frederick, Ltd., 249, 254

"Murder for the Millions" (Rolo), 212

Murphy, Frank, 86

Murray, Diana, 290

Murray, Jock, 290

Murrow, Mrs. Edward R., 151

Museum of Famous People (New York City), 324

Museum of Modern Art (New York City), 135

Mussolini, Benito, 51, 80

"My British Buddy" (Berlin), 152

Myrdal, Gunnar, 92

Mythology (Hamilton), 206

Naked and the Dead, The (Mailer), 230, 233

Nast, Condé, 64

National Association for the Advancement of Colored People (NAACP), 124, 220

National Book Awards Committee, 271-272

National Council of Social Service, 136-137

National Council of Teachers of English, 236-237

National Organization for Decency in Literature (NODL), 238

Navajo Indians, 103

Nearing, Scott, 27

Negro in American Culture, The (Locke), 94

Negroes, 20, 23, 66-67, 77, 92-